Digital Library Applications

CBIR, Education, Social Networks, eScience/Simulation, and GIS

Synthesis Lectures on Information Concepts, Retrieval, and Services

Editor
Gary Marchionini, *University of North Carolina, Chapel Hill*

Digital Library Technologies: Complex Objects, Annotation, Ontologies, Classiffcation, Extraction, and Security
Edward A. Fox, Ricardo da Silva Torres
2014

Digital Library Applications: CBIR, Education, Social Networks, eScience/Simulation, and GIS
Edward A. Fox, Jonathan P. Leidig
2014

Information and Human Values
Kenneth R. Fleischmann
November 2013

Multiculturalism and Information and Communication Technology
Pnina Fichman and Madelyn R. Sanfilippo
October 2013

The Future of Personal Information Management, Part II: Transforming Technologies to Manage Our Information
William Jones
September 2013

Information Retrieval Models: Foundations and Relationships
Thomas Roelleke
July 2013

Key Issues Regarding Digital Libraries: Evaluation and Integration
Rao Shen, Marcos Andre Goncalves, Edward A. Fox
February 2013

Visual Information Retrieval using Java and LIRE
Mathias Lux, Oge Marques
January 2013

On the Efficient Determination of Most Near Neighbors: Horseshoes, Hand Grenades, Web Search and Other Situations When Close is Close Enough
Mark S. Manasse
November 2012

The Answer Machine
Susan E. Feldman
September 2012

Theoretical Foundations for Digital Libraries: The 5S (Societies, Scenarios, Spaces, Structures, Streams) Approach
Edward A. Fox, Marcos André Gonçalves, Rao Shen
July 2012

The Future of Personal Information Management, Part I: Our Information, Always and Forever
William Jones
March 2012

Search User Interface Design
Max L. Wilson
November 2011

Information Retrieval Evaluation
Donna Harman
May 2011

Knowledge Management (KM) Processes in Organizations: Theoretical Foundations and Practice
Claire R. McInerney, Michael E. D. Koenig
January 2011

Search-Based Applications: At the Confluence of Search and Database Technologies
Gregory Grefenstette, Laura Wilber
2010

Information Concepts: From Books to Cyberspace Identities
Gary Marchionini
2010

Estimating the Query Difficulty for Information Retrieval
David Carmel, Elad Yom-Tov
2010

iRODS Primer: Integrated Rule-Oriented Data System
Arcot Rajasekar, Reagan Moore, Chien-Yi Hou, Christopher A. Lee, Richard Marciano, Antoine de Torcy, Michael Wan, Wayne Schroeder, Sheau-Yen Chen, Lucas Gilbert, Paul Tooby, Bing Zhu
2010

Collaborative Web Search: Who, What, Where, When, and Why
Meredith Ringel Morris, Jaime Teevan
2009

Multimedia Information Retrieval
Stefan Rüger
2009

Online Multiplayer Games
William Sims Bainbridge
2009

Information Architecture: The Design and Integration of Information Spaces
Wei Ding, Xia Lin
2009

Reading and Writing the Electronic Book
Catherine C. Marshall
2009

Hypermedia Genes: An Evolutionary Perspective on Concepts, Models, and Architectures
Nuno M. Guimarães, Luís M. Carrico
2009

Understanding User-Web Interactions via Web Analytics
Bernard J. (Jim) Jansen
2009

XML Retrieval
Mounia Lalmas
2009

Faceted Search
Daniel Tunkelang
2009

Introduction to Webometrics: Quantitative Web Research for the Social Sciences
Michael Thelwall
2009

Exploratory Search: Beyond the Query-Response Paradigm
Ryen W. White, Resa A. Roth
2009

New Concepts in Digital Reference
R. David Lankes
2009

Automated Metadata in Multimedia Information Systems: Creation, Refinement, Use in Surrogates, and Evaluation
Michael G. Christel
2009

Digital Library Applications: CBIR, Education, Social Networks, eScience/Simulation, and GIS
Edward A. Fox and Jonathan P. Leidig

ISBN: 978-3-031-01156-6 print
ISBN: 978-3-031-02284-5 ebook

DOI: 10.1007/978-3-031-02284-5

A Publication in the with "Springer series
SYNTHESIS LECTURES ON INFORMATION CONCEPTS, RETRIEVAL, AND SERVICES
Series ISSN: 1947-945X print 1947-9468 ebook

Lecture #32
Series Editor: Gary Marchionini, University of North Carolina, Chapel Hill

First Edition
10 9 8 7 6 5 4 3 2 1

Digital Library Applications

CBIR, Education, Social Networks, eScience/Simulation, and GIS

Edward A. Fox
Virginia Tech, Dept. of Computer Science, Blacksburg, VA 24061, USA

Jonathan P. Leidig
Grand Valley State University, School of Computing and Information Systems,
Allendale, MI 49401, USA

Chapter Authors:
Monika Akbar, Yinlin Chen, Alexandre X. Falcão, Eric Fouh, Nádia P. Kozievitch, Spencer Lee, Jonathan P. Leidig, Lin Tzy Li, Uma Murthy, Sung Hee Park, Clifford A. Shaffer, and Ricardo da Silva Torres

SYNTHESIS LECTURES ON INFORMATION CONCEPTS, RETRIEVAL, AND SERVICES #32

ABSTRACT

Digital libraries (DLs) have evolved since their launch in 1991 into an important type of information system, with widespread *application*. This volume advances that trend further by describing new research and development in the DL field that builds upon the 5S (Societies, Scenarios, Spaces, Structures, Streams) framework, which is discussed in three other DL volumes in this series. While the 5S framework may be used to describe many types of information systems, and is likely to have even broader utility and appeal, we focus here on digital libraries.

Drawing upon six (Akbar, Kozievitch, Leidig, Li, Murthy, Park) completed and two (Chen, Fouh) in-process dissertations, as well as the efforts of collaborating researchers, and scores of related publications, presentations, tutorials, and reports, this book demonstrates the applicability of 5S in five digital library application areas, that also have importance in the context of the WWW, Web 2.0, and innovative information systems. By integrating surveys of the state-of-the-art, new research, connections with formalization, case studies, and exercises/projects, this book can serve as a textbook for those interested in computing, information, and/or library science.

Chapter 1 focuses on images, explaining how they connect with information retrieval, in the context of CBIR systems. Chapter 2 gives two case studies of DLs used in education, which is one of the most common applications of digital libraries. Chapter 3 covers social networks, which are at the heart of work on Web 2.0, explaining the construction and use of deduced graphs, that can enhance retrieval and recommendation. Chapter 4 demonstrates the value of DLs in eScience, focusing, in particular, on cyber-infrastructure for simulation. Chapter 5 surveys geospatial information in DLs, with a case study on geocoding.

Given this rich content, we trust that any interested in digital libraries, or in related systems, will find this volume to be motivating, intellectually satisfying, and useful. We hope it will help move digital libraries forward into a science as well as a practice. We hope it will help build community that will address the needs of the next generation of DLs.

KEYWORDS

5S framework, AlgoViz, content-based image retrieval (CBIR), Crisis/Tragedy/Recovery network (CTRnet), digital libraries (DLs), e-science, education, Ensemble, epidemiology, fingerprints, formalization, images, geocoding, geospatial information, portals, SimDL, simulation, social networks

This book is dedicated to all those who have worked in, or collaborated with, Virginia Tech's Digital Library Research Laboratory.

Contents

List of Figures

List of Tables

Preface

Because of the importance of digital libraries, we integrated, organized, and condensed our related findings and publications into a single volume version of this DL book series, ultimately over 600 pages in length, that was successfully used in a semester-long class in 2011, as well as field tested at different universities. To make it easier for others to address their need for a digital library textbook, we have re-organized the original book into four parts, to cover: introduction and theoretical foundations, key issues, technologies/extensions, and applications. We are confident that this final book, and the earlier ones in the series, address digital library related needs in many computer science, information science, and library science (e.g., LIS) courses, as well as the requirements of researchers, developers, and practitioners.

The main reason is that our *S* (Societies, Scenarios, Spaces, Structures, Streams) framework has broad descriptive power. This is proved in part by the recent expansion of interest related to each of the five Ss, e.g., Social networks, Scenario-based design, geoSpatial databases, Structure-based approaches (e.g., databases, metadata, ontologies, XML), and data Stream management systems.

The first book, *Theoretical Foundations for Digital Libraries,* the essential opening to the four book series, has three main parts. Chapter 1 is the key to 5S, providing a theoretical foundation for the field of digital libraries in a gentle, intuitive, and easy-to-apply manner. Chapter 2 explains how 5S can be applied to digital libraries, in two ways. First, it covers the most important services of digital libraries: browsing, searching, discovery, and visualization. Second, it demonstrates how 5S helps with the design, implementation, and evaluation of an integrated digital library (ETANA-DL, for archaeology). The third part of book 1, made up of five appendices, demonstrates how 5S enables a formal treatment of digital libraries. It is freely accessible online at https://sites.google.com/a/morganclaypool.com/dlibrary/.

Book 1, Appendix A gives a small set of definitions that cover the mathematical preliminaries underlying our work. Appendix B builds on that set to define each of the five Ss, and then uses them to define what we consider a minimal digital library. Thus, we allow people asking "Is X a digital library?" to answer that question definitively. Appendix C moves from a minimalist perspective to show how 5S can be used in a real, interesting, and complex application domain: archaeology. Appendix D builds upon all the definitions in Appendices A–C to describe some key results of using 5S. This includes lemmas, proofs, and 5SSuite (software based on 5S). Finally, Appendix E, the Glossary, explains key terminology. Concluding book 1 is an extensive bibliography, and a helpful index.

The second book in the series, *Key Issues Regarding Digital Libraries: Evaluation and Integration,* covers the Information Life Cycle, metrics, and software to help evaluate digital libraries. It uses both archaeology and electronic theses and dissertations, to provide additional context, since addressing quality in highly distributed digital libraries is particularly challenging.

The following two books of this series are further elaborations of the 5S framework, as well as a comprehensive overview of related work on digital libraries.

Book 3, *Digital Library Technologies: Complex Objects, Annotation, Ontologies, Classification, Extraction, and Security,* describes six case studies of extensions beyond a minimal digital library. *Regarding Complex Objects:* While many digital libraries focus on digital objects and/or metadata objects, with support for complex objects, they could easily be extended to handle aggregation and packaging. Fingerprint matching provides a useful context, since there are complex interrelationships among crime scenes, latent fingerprints, individuals, hands, fingers, fingerprints, and images. *Regarding Annotation:* This builds upon work on superimposed information, closely related to hypertext, hypermedia, and annotation. Case studies cover fish images and Flickr. *Regarding Ontologies:* We address this key area of knowledge management, also integral to the Semantic Web. As a context, we consider our Crisis, Tragedy, and Recovery Network (CTRnet). That is quite broad, and involves interesting ontology development problems. *Regarding Classification:* We cover this core area of information retrieval and machine learning, as well as Library and Information Science (LIS). The context is electronic theses and dissertations (ETDs), since many of these works have no categories that can be found in their catalog or metadata records, and since none are categorized at the level of chapters. *Regarding Extraction:* Our coverage also is in the context of ETDs, where the high level structure should be identified, and where the valuable and voluminous sets of references can be isolated and shifted to canonical representations. *Regarding Security:* While many digital libraries support open access, it has been clear since the early 1990s that industrial acceptance of digital library systems and technologies depends on their being trusted, requiring an integrated approach to security.

This final book, fourth in the series, focuses on digital library applications, from a 5S perspective. Its chapters cover how to handle: Images, Education, Social Networks, e-Science (including bioinformatics and simulations), and Geospatial Information. *Regarding Images:* We move into the multimedia field, focusing on Content-based Image Retrieval (CBIR)—making use, for context, of the previously discussed work on fish images and CTRnet. *Regarding Education:* We describe systems for collecting, sharing, and providing access to educational resources, namely the AlgoViz and Ensemble systems. This is important since there has been considerable investment in digital libraries to help in education, all based on the fact that devising high quality educational resources is expensive, making sharing and reuse highly beneficial. *Regarding Social Networks:* We address very popular current issues, on the Societies side, namely Social Networks and Personalization. *Regarding e-Science:* There has only been a limited adaptation and extension of digital libraries to this important domain. Simulation aids many disciplines to test models and predictions on computers, addressing questions not feasible through other approaches to experimentation. More broadly, in keeping with progress toward e-Science, where data sets and shared information support much broader theories and investigations, we cover (using the SimDL and CINET projects as context) storing and archiving, as well as access and visualization, dealing not only with metadata, but also with specifications of experiments, experimental results, and derivative versions: summaries, findings, reports, and publications. *Regarding Geospatial Information:* Many GIS-related technologies are now readily available in cell phones, cameras, and GPS systems. Our coverage (that uses the CTRnet project as context) connects that with metadata, images, and maps.

How can computer scientists connect with all this? Although some of the early curricular guidelines for computing advocated coverage of information, and current guidelines refer to the area of Information Management, generally courses in this area have focused instead either on data or knowledge. Fortunately, Virginia Tech has had graduate courses on information retrieval since the early 1970s and a senior course on "Multimedia, Hypertext, and Information Access" since the early 1990s. Now, there are offerings at many universities on multimedia, or with titles including keywords like "Web" or "search". Perhaps parts of this book series will provide a way for computing programs to address all areas of Information Management, building on a firm, formal, integrated approach. Further, computing professionals should feel comfortable with particular Ss, especially Structures (as in data structures) and Spaces (as in vector spaces), and to lesser extents Streams (related to multimedia) and Scenarios (related to human-computer interaction). Today, especially, there is growing interest in Societies (as in social networks).

How can information scientists connect with all this? Clearly, they are at home with "information" as a key construct. Streams (e.g., sequences of characters or bitstreams) provide a first basis for all types of information. Coupled with Structures, they lead to all types of structured streams, as in documents and multimedia. Spaces may be less clear, but GIS systems are becoming ubiquitous, connecting with GPS, cell phone, Twitter, and other technologies. Scenarios, especially in the form of Services, are at the heart of most information systems. Societies, including users, groups, organizations, and a wide variety of social networks, are central, especially with human-centered design. Thus, information science can easily connect with 5S, and digital libraries are among the most important types of information systems. Accordingly, this book series may be fit nicely into capstone courses in information science or information systems. Further, our handling of "information" goes well beyond the narrow view associated with electrical engineering or even computer science; we connect content representations with context and application, across a range of human endeavors, and with semantics, pragmatics, and knowledge.

How can library scientists connect with all this? One might argue that many of the librarians of the future must be trained as digital librarians. Thus, all four books should fit nicely into library science programs. While they could fit into theory or capstone courses, they also might serve well in introductory courses, if the more formal parts are skipped. On the other hand, they could be distributed across the program. Thus, the first book might work well early in a library school program, the second book could fit midway in the program, and the last two books might be covered in specialized courses that connect with technologies or applications. Further, those studying archival science might find the entire series to be of interest, though some topics like preservation are not covered in detail.

How can researchers connect with all this? We hope that those interested in formal approaches will help us expand the coverage of concepts reported herein. A wonderful goal would be to have an elegant formal basis, and useful framework, for all types of information systems. We also hope that the theses and dissertations related to this volume, all online (thanks to Virginia Tech's ETD initiative), will provide an even more in-depth coverage of the key topics covered herein. We hope you can build on this foundation to aid in your own research, as you advance the field further.

How can developers connect with all this? We hope that concepts, ideas, methods, techniques, systems, and approaches described herein will guide you to develop, implement, and deploy even better digital libraries. There should be less time "reinventing the wheel." Perhaps this will stimulate the emergence of a vibrant software and services industry as more and more digital libraries emerge. Further, if there is agreement on key concepts, then there should be improvements in: interoperability, integration, and understanding. Accordingly, we hope you can leverage this work to advance practices as well as provide better systems and services.

Even if you, the reader, do not fit clearly into the groups discussed above, we hope you nevertheless will find this book series interesting. Given the rich content, we trust that those interested in digital libraries, or in related systems, will find this book to be intellectually satisfying, illuminating, and helpful. We hope the full series will help move digital libraries forward into a science as well as a practice. We hope too that this four book series will broadly address the needs of the next generation of digital librarians. Please share with us and others what ways you found these books to be useful and helpful!

Edward A. Fox, Editor
Blacksburg, Virginia
February 2014

Acknowledgments

As lead in this effort, my belief is that our greatest thanks go to our families. Accordingly, I thank my wife, Carol, and our sons, Jeffrey, Gregory, Michael, and Paul, along with their families, as well as my father and many other relatives. Similarly, on behalf of my co-editor and each of the chapter co-authors, I thank all of their families.

Since this book is the fourth in a series of four books, and draws some definitions and other elements from content that was presented in the earlier books, it is important to acknowledge the contributions of all of the other co-authors from the full series: Monika Akbar, Pranav Angara, Yinlin Chen, Lois M. Delcambre, Noha Elsherbiny, Alexandre X. Falcão, Eric Fouh, Nádia P. Kozievitch, Spencer Lee, Jonathan Leidig, Lin Tzy Li, Mohamed Magdy Gharib Farag, Uma Murthy, Sung Hee Park, Venkat Srinivasan, Ricardo da Silva Torres, and Seungwon Yang. Special thanks go to Uma Murthy for helping with the bibliography and to Monika Akbar, Pranav Angara, and Shashwat Dave for assistance with technical aspects of book production. Further, Shashwat Dave assisted with the glossary, found in the first book of the series as well as online; it is useful in this book, too.

Teachers and mentors deserve a special note of thanks. My interest in research was stimulated and guided by J.C.R. Licklider, my undergraduate advisor, author of *Libraries of the Future,*[1] who, when at ARPA, funded the start of the Internet. Michael Kessler, who introduced the concept of bibliographic coupling, was my B.S. thesis advisor; he also directed MIT's Project TIP (technical information project). Gerard Salton was my graduate advisor (1978–1983); he is sometimes called the "Father of Information Retrieval."

Likewise, we thank our many students, friends, collaborators, co-authors, and colleagues. In particular, we thank students who have collaborated in these matters, including: Scott Britell, Pavel Calado, Yuxin Chen, Kiran Chitturi, Fernando Das Neves, Shahrooz Feizabadi, Robert France, S.M.Shamimul Hasan, Nithiwat Kampanya, Rohit Kelapure, S.H. Kim, Neill Kipp, Aaron Krowne, Sunshin Lee, Bing Liu, Ming Luo, Paul Mather, Sai Tulasi Neppali, Unni. Ravindranathan, W. Ryan Richardson, Nathan Short, Ohm Sornil, Hussein Suleman, Wensi Xi, Baoping Zhang, and Qinwei Zhu.

1. In this 1965 work, Licklider called for an integrative theory to support future automated libraries, one of the inspirations for this book.

Further, we thank faculty and staff, at a variety of universities and other institutions, who have collaborated, including: A. Lynn Abbott, Felipe Andrade, Robert Beck, Keith Bisset, Paul Bogen II, Peter Brusilovsky, Lillian Cassel, Donatella Castelli, Vinod Chachra, Hsinchun Chen, Debra Dudley, Roger Ehrich, Hicham Elmongui, Joanne Eustis, Tiago Falcão, Weiguo Fan, James Flanagan, James French, Richard Furuta, Dan Garcia, C. Lee Giles, Martin Halbert, Kevin Hall, Eric Hallerman, Riham Hassan, Eberhard Hilf, Gregory Hislop, Michael Hsiao, Haowei Hsieh, John Impagliazzo, Filip Jagodzinski, Andrea Kavanaugh, Douglas Knight, Deborah Knox, Alberto Laender, Carl Lagoze, Madhav Marathe, Gary Marchionini, Susan Marion, Gail McMillan, Claudia Medeiros, Barbara Moreira, Henning Mortveit, Sanghee Oh, Donald Orth, Jeffrey Pomerantz, Manuel Perez Quinones, Naren Ramakrishnan, Evandro Ramos, Mohammed Samaka, Steven Sheetz, Frank Shipman, Donald Shoemaker, Layne Watson, and Barbara Wildemuth.

Clearly, however, with regard to this volume, my special thanks go to my co-author. He has played a key role in the unfolding of the theory, practice, systems, and usability of what is described herein. Regarding earlier work on 5S, Marcos André Gonçalves helped launch our formal framework, and Rao Shen extended that effort, as can be seen in the first two books of the series.

At Virginia Tech there are many in the Department of Computer Science and in Information Systems that have assisted, providing very nice facilities and a creative and supportive environment. The College of Engineering, and before that, of Arts and Sciences, provided an administrative home and intellectual context.

In addition, we acknowledge the support of the many sponsors of the research described in this volume. Our fingerprint work was supported by Award No. 2009-DN-BX-K229 from the National Institute of Justice, Office of Justice Programs, U.S. Department of Justice. The opinions, findings, and conclusions or recommendations expressed in this publication are those of the authors and do not necessarily reflect those of the Department of Justice.

Some of this material is based upon work supported by the National Science Foundation (NSF) under Grant Nos. CCF-0722259, DUE-9752190, DUE-9752408, DUE-0121679, DUE-0121741, DUE-0136690, DUE-0333531, DUE-0333601, DUE-0435059, DUE-0532825, DUE-0840719, DUE-1141209, IIS-9905026, IIS-9986089, IIS-0002935, IIS-0080748, IIS-0086227, IIS-0090153, IIS-0122201, IIS-0307867, IIS-0325579, IIS-0535057, IIS-0736055, IIS-0910183, IIS-0916733, IIS-1319578, ITR-0325579, OCI-0904844, OCI-1032677, and SES-0729441. Any opinions, findings, and conclusions or recommendations expressed in this material are those of the authors and do not necessarily reflect the views of the National Science Foundation.

This work has been partially supported by NIH MIDAS project 2U01GM070694-7, DTRA CNIMS Grant HDTRA1-07-C-0113, and R&D Grant HDTRA1-0901-0017. Students in our VT-MENA program in Egypt have been supported through that program.

We thank corporate and institutional sponsors, including Adobe, AOL, CNI, Google, IBM, Microsoft, NASA, NCR, OCLC, SOLINET, SUN, SURA, UNESCO, US Dept. Ed. (FIPSE), and VTLS. A variety of institutions have supported tutorials or courses, including AUGM, CETREDE, CLEI, IFLA-LAC, and UFC.

Visitors and collaborators from Brazil, including from FUA, UFMG, and UNICAMP, have been supported by CAPES (4479-09-2), FAPESP, and CNPq. Our collaboration in Mexico had support from CONACyT, while that in Germany was supported by DFG.

Finally, we acknowledge the support of the Qatar National Research Fund for Project No. NPRP 4-029-1-007, running 2012-2015.

CHAPTER 1

Content-Based Image Retrieval

Ricardo da Silva Torres, Nádia P. Kozievitch, Uma Murthy, and Alexandre X. Falcão

Abstract

Technology advancements towards image acquisition, storage, and dissemination have fostered the creation of large image collections. There is a strong requirement to apply effective and efficient digital libraries to manage those materials. One common strategy relies on the use of image visual information to support the creation of different digital library services. In particular, image content has been used to build image search systems, known as Content-Based Image Retrieval (CBIR) systems. These systems perform queries based on image visual properties such as color, texture, and shape information. The content of collection images is characterized by descriptors that encode image visual properties into feature vectors. Later, these features are compared with features extracted from a query pattern (e.g., query image) by means of a distance function. Collection images are ranked according to their distance to the query pattern.

In this chapter we exploit the 5S Framework to propose a formal description for Content-Based Image Retrieval, defining the fundamental concepts and relationships from a digital library (DL) perspective.

1.1 INTRODUCTION

Technological improvements in image acquisition and the decreasing cost of storage devices have supported the dissemination of large image collections, supported by efficient retrieval services. One of the most common approaches involves so-called *Content-Based Image Retrieval (CBIR)* [64, 82, 158, 187], yielding images similar to a user-defined specification or pattern (e.g., shape sketch, image example). The goal is to support image retrieval based on *content* properties (e.g., shape, color, or texture), usually encoded into *feature vectors*. One of the main advantages of CBIR is the possibility of an automatic retrieval process, avoiding the work of assigning keywords, which usually requires very laborious and time-consuming prior annotation of images.

Various digital libraries (DLs) support services based on image content [25, 60, 61, 90, 111, 114, 155, 261, 262, 270]. However, these systems are often designed and implemented without taking advantage of formal methods and frameworks. This chapter aims to extend the 5S (Streams, Structures, Spaces, Scenarios, and Societies) digital library formal framework [100] with services based on image content. The main contribution of this chapter is the proposal of several constructs that can aid understanding of content-based image retrieval concepts as they apply to DLs. They also can guide the design and implementation of new DL services based on image content.

We illustrate the proposed formalism by describing the use of an image searching service in the context of the The Crisis, Tragedy, and Recovery Network (CTRnet) project [137, 265].

This chapter describes the typical architecture of a CBIR system in Section 1.2. Related work and the basic concepts of the CBIR domain are presented in Section 1.3. The proposed extension to the 5S model is presented in Section 1.4. Next, the content-based image searching service is illustrated in a case study in Section 1.5. Some research challenges of the CBIR domain are introduced in Section 1.6.

1.2 CONTENT-BASED IMAGE RETRIEVAL

A typical *CBIR* solution requires the construction of **image descriptors**, which are characterized by: (i) an *extraction algorithm* to encode image features into *feature vectors*; and (ii) a *similarity measure* to compare two images based on the distance between their corresponding feature vectors. The similarity measure is a *matching function*, which gives the degree of similarity for a given pair of images represented by their feature vectors, often defined as a function of the distance (e.g., Euclidean), that is, the larger the distance value, the less similar the images.

Figure 1.1 shows an overview of a content-based image retrieval system. The interface allows a user to specify a query by means of a query pattern (e.g., a query image) and to view the retrieved

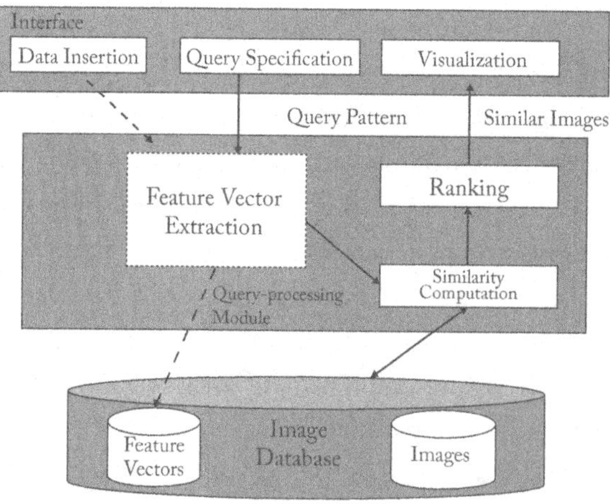

FIGURE 1.1: Typical CBIR system.

similar images. The query-processing module extracts a feature vector from a query pattern and applies a distance function (e.g., Euclidean distance) to evaluate the similarity between the query image and stored images. Next, it ranks the images according to similarity and forwards the most similar images to the interface module. Note that images often are indexed according to their feature vectors using structures to speed up retrieval and distance computations.

1.3 RELATED WORK

This section presents related work, discussing the main concepts of the CBIR domain.

1.3.1 IMAGE DESCRIPTORS

An image descriptor is a pair, *feature vector extraction function* and *distance function*, used for image indexing by similarity. The extracted feature vector subsumes the image properties and the distance function measures the dissimilarity between two images with respect to their properties. This section presents a brief overview of existing image descriptors.

Shape Descriptors

In pattern recognition and related areas, shape is an important characteristic to identify and distinguish objects [159, 267].

Shape descriptors are classified into *boundary-based (or contour-based)* and *region-based* methods [267]. This classification takes into account whether shape features are extracted from the contour only or from the whole shape region. These two classes, in turn, can be divided into *structural (local)* and *global* descriptors. This subdivision is based on whether the shape is represented as a whole or represented by segments/sections. Another possible classification categorizes shape description methods into *spatial* and *transform* domain techniques, depending on whether direct measurements of the shape are used or a transformation is applied [219].[1]

Next, we present a brief overview of some shape descriptors. More details about existing shape representation techniques can be found in [58, 159, 176, 267].

Moment Invariants. For Moment Invariants, each object is represented by a 14-dimensional feature vector, including 2 sets of normalized Moment Invariants [71, 116], one from the object contour and another from its solid object silhouette. The Euclidean distance is used to measure the similarity between different shapes as represented by their Moment Invariants.

Curvature Scale Space (CSS) [1, 180]. The CSS descriptor is used in the MPEG-7 standard [31] and represents a multiscale organization of the curvature zero-crossing points

1. Taxonomies of shape description techniques can be found in [58, 219, 267].

of a planar curve. In this sense, the dimension of its feature vectors varies for different contours, thus a special matching algorithm is necessary to compare two CSS descriptors (e.g., [245]).

Beam Angle Statistics (BAS) [12]. The BAS descriptor is based on the *beams* originated from a contour pixel. A beam is defined as the set of lines connecting a contour pixel to the rest of the pixels along the contour. At each contour pixel, the angle between a pair of lines is calculated, and the shape descriptor is defined by using the third-order statistics of all the beam angles in a set of neighborhoods. The similarity between two BAS moment functions is measured by an optimal correspondent subsequence (OCS) algorithm, as shown in [12].

Tensor Scale Descriptor (TSD) [179]. TSD is a shape descriptor based on the tensor scale concept [220]—a morphometric parameter yielding a unified representation of local structure thickness, orientation, and anisotropy. That is, at any image point, its tensor scale is represented by the largest ellipse (2D) centered at that point and within the same homogeneous region. TSD is obtained by extracting the tensor scale parameters for the original image and then computing the ellipse orientation histogram. TSDs are compared by using a correlation-based distance function.

Contour Saliences (CS) [244]. The CS computation uses the Image Foresting Transform [78] to compute the salience values of contour pixels and to locate salience points along the contour by exploiting the relation between a contour and its internal and external skeletons [149]. The contour salience descriptor consists of the salience values of salient pixels and their location along the contour, and a heuristic matching algorithm as distance function.

Segment Saliences (SS) [244]. The segment salience descriptor is a variation of the contour salience descriptor, which incorporates two improvements: the *salience values* of contour segments, in the place of salience values of isolated points, and another matching algorithm that replaces the heuristic matching by an optimum approach. The salience values along the contour are computed and the contour is divided into a predefined number s of segments of the same size. The internal and external influence areas of each segment are computed by summing up the influence areas of their corresponding pixels. In [244], SS is shown to have a better effectiveness than several other shape descriptors.

Color Descriptors

Color is one of the most widely used visual features in content-based image retrieval (CBIR) systems. Research in this field can be grouped into three main subareas: (a) definition of an adequate color space for a given target application, (b) proposal of appropriate extraction algorithms, and (c) study/evaluation of similarity measures.

Color information is represented as points in three-dimensional color spaces (such as RGB, HSV, YIQ, $L^*u^*v^*$, $L^*a^*b^*$ [70]). They allow discrimination between color stimuli and permit similarity judgment and identification [70]. Some of them are hardware-oriented (e.g., RGB and CMY color space), as they were defined by taking into account properties of the devices used to reproduce colors. Others are user-inspired (e.g., $L^*u^*v^*$, $L^*a^*b^*$) as they were defined to quantify color differences as perceived by humans.

Several color description techniques have been proposed [118, 171, 196, 235, 237]. They can be grouped into two classes based on whether or not they encode information related to the color spatial distribution.

Examples of descriptors that do not include spatial color distribution include Color Histogram and Color Moments. **Color Histogram** [237] is the most commonly used descriptor in image retrieval. The color histogram extraction algorithm can be divided into three steps: partition of the color space into cells, association of each cell to a histogram bin, and recording a count of the number of image pixels of each cell in the corresponding histogram bin. This descriptor is invariant to translation and rotation. The similarity between two color histograms can be performed by computing the L_1, L_2, or weighted Euclidean distances, as well as by computing their intersection [237]. For a more detailed discussion on appropriate distance functions, we refer the reader to [70].

Another example of a descriptor that does not consider color spatial distribution is **Color Moments** [235]. Usually, the *mean* (first order), *variance* (second), and *skewness* (third) are used to form the feature vector. These moments are defined, respectively, as $E_i = (1/N)\sum_{j=1}^{N} p_{ij}$, $\sigma_i = \sqrt[2]{(1/N)\sum_{j=1}^{N}(p_{ij} - E_i)^2}$, and $s_i = \sqrt[3]{(1/N)\sum_{j=1}^{N}(p_{ij} - E_i)^3}$, where p_{ij} is the value of the i-th color component of the image pixel j, and N is the number of pixels in the image.

Examples of color descriptors that incorporate the color spatial distribution include **Color Coherence Vector** (CCV) [196], **Border/Interior Pixel Classification** (BIC) [234], and **Color Correlogram** [118]. CCVs are created by computing, for each color, the total number of coherent (α_i) and incoherent pixels (β_i). A pixel is considered coherent if it belongs to a largely uniformly colored region. The CCV is defined as $V_c =< (\alpha_1, \beta_1), (\alpha_2, \beta_2), \ldots, (\alpha_N, \beta_N) >$, where N is the number of colors. The color correlogram, in turn, encodes the spatial correlation of colors. It can be seen as a table γ indexed by color pairs. Given any pixel of color c_i in the image, $\gamma_{c_i,c_j}^{(k)}$ gives the probability that a pixel at distance k away from the given pixel is of color c_j. The color correlogram is a table indexed by color pair, where the k-th entry for $< i, j >$ specifies the probability of finding a pixel of color j at a distance k from a pixel of color i in the image. In the BIC approach, each image pixel is classified as a border or interior pixel, based on whether it is at the border of the image itself or if at least one of its four neighbors has a different color. In the following, two histograms are computed: one considering only border pixels and the other for only interior pixels.

The MPEG-7 initiative [218], formally known as Multimedia Content Description Interface, focuses on the description of multimedia content, including content of various modalities like image, video, speech, graphics, and their combinations. One of the most important components of the MPEG-7 framework is the proposal of image descriptors. For the color property, MPEG-7 has defined a number of histogram descriptors, a dominant color descriptor, and a color layout descriptor [171].

Texture Descriptors

There is no widely accepted definition of texture. However, this image property can be characterized by the existence of basic primitives, whose spatial distribution creates some visual patterns defined in terms of granularity, directionality, and repetitiveness. There exist different approaches to extract and represent textures. They can be classified into *space-based*, *frequency-based* models, and *texture signatures* [70]. Next, some of these approaches are described.

A co-occurrence matrix [107] is one of the most traditional techniques for encoding texture information. It describes spatial relationships among grey-levels in an image. A cell defined by the position (i, j) in this matrix registers the probability that two pixels of gray levels i and j occur in two relative positions. A set of co-occurrence probabilities (such as energy, entropy, and contrast) has been proposed to characterize textured regions. Another example of a space-based method includes the use of Auto-Regressive Models [107].

Frequency-based texture descriptors include, for instance, the Garbor wavelet coefficients [170]. An example of texture signatures can be found in the proposal of Tamura et al. [238]. This descriptor aims to characterize texture information in terms of contrast, coarseness, and directionality. The MPEG-7 initiative proposed three texture descriptors: texture browsing descriptor, homogeneous texture descriptor, and local edge histogram descriptor [171].

A more in-depth analysis of other approaches for characterizing color and texture information can be found in [202].

1.3.2 CBIR SYSTEMS

Several CBIR systems have been proposed. Even though a few of them became commercial products [82], many CBIR systems were proposed as research prototypes, being developed in universities and research laboratories.

Chabot, QBIC (*Query by Image Content*) [82], *Netra*, Photobook [203]—developed by the Massachusetts Institute of Technology (MIT)—and VisualSEEK [231] allow query by image content.

Chabot [187] integrates image content retrieval based on color information with text-based queries. Its interface allows users to search and update the image database. This system does not include texture and shape descriptors.

The QBIC system was developed by IBM [82]. It uses color, shape, and texture to retrieve from image databases. Query specification follows the *query-by-example* paradigm. A user can sketch a shape, select colors, indicate color distributions, or pick pre-defined textures.

Ma et al. [164] describe a toolbox for browsing large database collections called *Netra*. This prototype uses color, texture, shape, and spatial location of image segmented regions to retrieve similar images from a database.

More recently, Cox et al. [206] present the PicHunter system. In this system, a Bayesian framework is used to model user needs during query formulation. With a different approach, Vu et al. [259] describes an image retrieval system based on regions of interest, that is, regions that contain relevant objects of a given image. Another region-based image retrieval system is the Blobworld [50]. In this system, pixels are clustered according to their color and texture properties. These clusters are supposed to represent the image content.

A more complete description of existing CBIR systems can be found in Veltkamp and Tanase [255].

1.3.3 INDEXING STRUCTURES

Not only does the effectiveness but also the efficiency (measured in terms of retrieval time) need to be taken into account during the design of CBIR systems. Usually, fast searching strategies rely on the use of effective indexing schemes. However, as pointed out earlier, images usually are represented as points in high dimensional spaces. In this scenario, traditional indexing schemes (such as the approaches based on the *R-trees* [105]), which perform reasonably well for a small number of dimensions, exhibit a poor performance. This phenomena is linked to the "curse of dimensionality." One of the approaches used to address this problem is applying dimension reduction techniques, such as Principal Component Analysis (PCA), and then using a traditional multidimensional indexing structure.

Another important research area includes the investigation of **Metric Access Methods** (MAMs). MAM is a class of access method (AM) that is used to manage large volumes of metric data allowing insertions, deletions and searches [249]. The definition of these indexing approaches relies on the use of a metric space. A metric space is a pair (O, d), where O denotes the domain of a set of objects $O = (O_1, O_2, \ldots, O_n)$, and d is a metric distance with the following properties: (i) symmetry ($d(O_1, O_2) = d(O_2, O_1)$), (ii) positiveness ($0 < d(O_1, O_2) < \infty$, $O_1 \neq O_2$, and $d(O_1, O_2) = 0$), and (iii) triangle inequality ($d(O_1, O_3) \leq d(O_1, O_2) + d(O_2, O_3)$). Examples of MAMs include, among others, the M-tree [55] and the Slim-tree [249]. Another research branch refers to the proposal of approximate methods to trade-off efficiency and effectiveness [8, 166, 239]. In these approaches, some incorrect results are returned in order to speed up running time.

Further details about multidimensional indexing structures can be found in [32, 93].

1.3.4 EFFECTIVENESS MEASURES

Image descriptors vary with the application domain and expert requirements. Thus, in order to identify appropriate image descriptors (used in extraction and distance computation algorithms), experts must perform a set of experiments to evaluate them in terms of effectiveness for a given collection of images. Effectiveness evaluation is a very complex task, involving questions related to the definition of a collection of images, a set of query images, a set of relevant images for each query image, and adequate retrieval effectiveness measures.

The evaluation of image descriptors and CBIR systems usually adopts the *query-by-example* (QBE) [13] paradigm. This paradigm, in the image retrieval context, is based on providing an image as input, extracting its visual features (e.g., contour saliences), measuring the distance between the query image and the images stored in the image database and, finally, ranking the images in increasing order of their distance from the query image (similarity).

Since each descriptor represents an image as a "point" in the corresponding metric space, its effectiveness will be higher when the clusters of relevant images are more separate in the metric space. Further, the more compact the clusters are in the metric space, the higher will be the robustness of the image descriptor with respect to an increase in the number of classes. Therefore, a "good" effectiveness measure should capture the concept of *separability*, and perhaps the concept of *compact-ability*, for the sake of robustness. More formally, the compact-ability of a descriptor indicates its invariance to the object characteristics that belong to a same class, while the separability indicates its discriminatory ability among objects that belong to distinct classes [245]. While these concepts are commonly used to define validity measures in cluster analysis [65, 73], they seem to not have recieved much attention in the literature of CBIR systems, where the most used effectiveness measures is *precision and recall* [16].

The Precision vs. Recall ($P \times R$) curve is the commonest evaluation measure used in the CBIR domain. Precision is defined as the fraction of retrieved images that are relevant to a query. In contrast, recall measures the fraction of the relevant images which have been retrieved. Recall is a non-decreasing function of rank, while precision can be regarded as a function of recall rather than rank. In general, the curve closest to the top of the chart indicates the best performance. The effectiveness in image retrieval was discussed with respect to the Precision×Recall measure in [244], where the multiscale separability [245] was proposed as a more appropriate effectiveness measure. Examples of other effectiveness measures include the $\theta \times$ recall curve [234], average precision [16], and average normalized modified retrieval rank (ANMRR) [171].

1.3.5 USER INTERACTION IN CBIR SYSTEMS

From the user's perspective, CBIR systems offer more flexibility in specifying queries than those based on metadata. On the other hand, they present new challenges. The first is how to help users in the *query specification* process. Another problem is *information overload*—how to present the result to the user in a meaningful way. A third issue is that of providing users with tools to *interact* with the system in order to refine their query. This section presents a brief overview of existing approaches that address these problems.

Query Specification

Several querying mechanisms have been created to help users define their information need. Aslado-gan et al. [13] presented a list of possible query strategies that can be employed in CBIR systems. This list includes, for example, *simple visual feature query*, *feature combination query*, *localized feature query*, *query by example*, *user-defined attribute query*, *object relationship query*, and *concept queries*. For instance, in the case of a feature combination query, a user could ask the system to "Retrieve images with blue color and stripped texture, where both properties have the same weight".

Another distinction is made based on whether the user is looking for a class of similar items to a given query pattern ("category search") or is looking for a particular target item ("target search") [269].

Result Visualization

The most common result presentation technique is based on showing a 2D (two-dimensional) grid of thumbnail (miniature) image versions [82, 187]. The grid is organized according to the similarity of each returned image with the query pattern (e.g., from left to right, from top to bottom). It is a $n \times m$ matrix, where position (1, 1) is occupied by a thumbnail of the query pattern, position (1, 2) by the one most similar to it, and so on. This helps browsing, allowing users to simply scan the grid image set as if they were reading a text [215]. This approach, however, displays retrieved images of different similarity degrees at the same physical distance from the image query, e.g., images (1, 2) and (2, 1) are displayed at the same physical distance from the query pattern, but the former is more similar to it than the latter. Bederson [23] tries to improve this visual structure by studying zoom properties to enhance image browsing. Rodden et al. [215], in turn, investigate whether it benefits users to have sets of thumbnails arranged according to their similarity, so images that are alike are placed together. They describe experiments to examine whether similarity-based arrangements of the candidate images help in picture selection.

Other display approaches try to consider relative similarity not only between the query pattern and each retrieved image, but also among all retrieved images themselves [222, 233]. These initiatives have the drawback that visually similar images which are placed next to each other can sometimes appear to merge or overlap, making them less eye-catching than if they were separated [215].

Stan et al. [233] describe an exploration system for an image database, which deals with a tool for visualization of the database at different levels of detail based on a multi-dimensional scaling technique. This visualization technique groups together perceptually similar images in a hierarchy of image clusters. Retrieved images can overlap. The overlap problem is also found in an El Niño image database [222]. In this context, Tian et al. [240] propose a PCA (Principal Component Analysis) based image browser which looks into an optimization strategy to adjust the position and size of images in order to minimize overlap (maximize visibility) while maintaining fidelity to the original positions which are indicative of mutual similarities.

Torres et al. [247] present two visualization techniques based on Spiral and Concentric Rings to explore query results (see Figure 1.8). These visual structures are centered on helping users focus on the query image and on the most similar retrieved images. These strategies improve traditional 2D grid presentation and avoid image overlaps, commonly found in CBIR systems.

Relevance Feedback

Relevance feedback (RF) is a commonly accepted method to improve the effectiveness of retrieval systems interactively [165]. Basically, it is composed of three steps: (a) an initial search is made by the system for a user-supplied query pattern, returning a small number of images; (b) the user then indicates which of the retrieved images are useful (relevant); and (c) finally, the system automatically reformulates the original query based upon the user's relevance judgments. This process can continue to iterate until the user is satisfied. RF strategies help to alleviate the semantic gap problem, since it allows the CBIR system to learn a user's image perceptions. RF strategies usually deal with small training samples (typically less than 20 per round of interaction), asymmetry in the training sample (a few negative examples are usually fed back to the system), and real-time requirements (RF algorithms should be fast enough to support real-time user interaction) [269]. Another important issue is concerned with the design and implementation of learning mechanisms. The commonest strategies use *weight-based learning approaches* [217], *genetic algorithms* [160], *genetic programming* [45, 81], *Bayesian probabilistic methods* [206], *Support Vector Machines* [241], and *graph-based approaches* [62, 63].

1.3.6 APPLICATIONS

CBIR technology has been used in several applications such as fingerprint identification, biodiversity information systems, digital libraries, crime prevention, medicine, and historical research. Some of these applications are presented in this section.

Medical Applications

The use of CBIR can result in powerful services that can benefit biomedical information systems. Three large domains can instantly take advantage of CBIR techniques: teaching, research, and diagnostics [183]. From the teaching perspective, searching tools can be used to find important cases to present to students. Research also can be enhanced by using services combining image content information with different kinds of data. For example, scientists can use mining tools to discover unusual patterns among textual (e.g., treatments reports, and patient records) and image content information. Similarity queries based on image content descriptors can aid the diagnostic process. Clinicians usually use similar cases for case-based reasoning in their clinical decision-making process. In this sense, while textual data can be used to find images of interest, visual features can be used to retrieve relevant information for a clinical case (e.g., comments, related literature, and HTML pages).

Biodiversity Information Systems

Biologists gather many kinds of data for biodiversity studies, including spatial data, and images of living beings. Ideally, Biodiversity Information Systems (BIS) should help researchers to enhance or complete their knowledge and understanding about species and their habitats by combining textual, image content-based, and geographical queries. An example of such a query might start by providing an image as input (e.g., a photo of a fish) and then asking the system to "Retrieve all database images containing fish whose fins are shaped like those of the fish in this photo". A combination of this query with textual and spatial predicates would consist of "Show the drainages where the fish species with 'large eyes' coexists with fish whose fins are shaped like those of the fish in the photo". Examples of initiatives in this area include [114, 246].

Digital Libraries

There are several digital libraries that support services based on image content [25, 90, 114, 261, 262, 270]. One example is the digital museum of butterflies [114], aimed at building a digital collection of Taiwanese butterflies. This digital library includes a module responsible for content-based image retrieval based on color, texture, and patterns. In a different image context, Zhu et al. [270] present a content-based image retrieval digital library that supports geographical image retrieval. The system manages air photos which can be retrieved through texture descriptors. Place names associated with retrieved images can be displayed by cross-referencing with a Geographical Name Information System (GNIS) gazetter. In this same domain, Bergman et al. [25] describe an architecture for storage and retrieval of satellite images and video data from a collection of heterogeneous archives.

Several researchers have worked to formalize content-based image retrieval systems [15, 248]. However, these formalisms typically describe these kinds of services from the database perspective (in general, based on the relational or object-relational models). To the best of our knowledge this chapter constitutes the first formal attempt to describe content-based image retrieval services by using digital library concepts. One benefit is that the 5S framework is generic enough to formalize these services without relying on implementation decisions.

Another important initiative for the digital library domain is related to the proposal of the Content-Based Image Search Component (CBISC) [246]. CBISC is a component that provides an easy-to-install content-based image search engine. It can be readily tailored for a particular collection by a domain expert, who carries out a clearly defined set of pilot experiments. It supports the use of different types of vector-based image descriptors (metric and non-metric; color, texture, and shape descriptors; with different data structures to represent feature vectors), which can be chosen based on the pilot experiments, and then easily combined to yield improved effectiveness. CBISC is an OAI-like search component which aims at supporting queries on image content. As in the OAI protocol [186], queries are submitted via HTTP requests. Two special requests ("verbs") are supported by this image search component: **ListDescriptors**, used to retrieve the list of image descriptors supported by CBISC, and **GetImages**, used to retrieve a set of images by taking into account their contents.

1.4 FORMALIZATION

Figure 1.2 presents the proposed concepts based on the 5S framework to handle image content descriptions and related digital library services. Some of these concepts were introduced in [243]. We extend them by taking into account digital library aspects. These concepts are precisely defined below.

Definition 1.1 An **image stream** (or simply **image**) $\hat{I}$ is a pair $(D_I, \vec{I})$, where:

- D_I is a finite set of *pixels* (points in $\mathbb{N}^2$, that is, $D_I \subset \mathbb{N}^2$), and
- $\vec{I} : D_I \rightarrow \mathsf{D}'$ is a function that assigns each pixel p in D_I to a vector $\vec{I}(p)$ of values in some arbitrary space D' (for example, $\mathsf{D}' = \mathbb{R}^3$ when a color in the RGB system is assigned to a pixel).

Definition 1.2 A **feature vector** $\vec{fv}_{\hat{I}}$ of an image $\hat{I}$ is a point in $\mathbb{R}^n$ space: $\vec{fv}_{\hat{I}} = (fv_1, fv_2, \ldots, fv_n)$, where n is the dimension of the vector.

Examples of possible feature vectors are a color histogram [237], a multiscale fractal curve [245], and a set of Fourier coefficients [204]. They encode image properties, such as color, shape, and texture. Note that different types of feature vectors may require different similarity functions.

Definition 1.3 Given a structure $(G, L, \mathcal{F})$, $G = (V, E)$ and a feature vector $\vec{fv}_{\hat{I}}$, a **StructuredFeatureVector** is a function $V \rightarrow \mathbb{R}^n$ that associates each node $v_k \in V$ with $fv_i \in \vec{fv}_{\hat{I}}$.

Figure 1.3 presents an example of the use of a **StructuredFeatureVector** function. In this case, an XML structure (structural metadata specification) is mapped to a feature vector obtained by applying the image descriptor *Beam Angle Statistics* (BAS) [12] to the image stream defined by the file "goldfish.pgm".

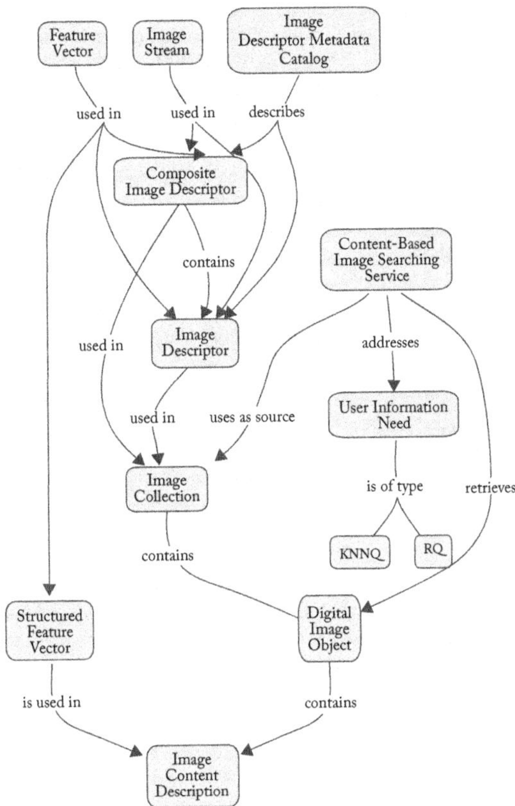

FIGURE 1.2: 5S extensions to support content-based image description and related services.

Definition 1.4 A **simple image content descriptor** (briefly, **image descriptor**) D is defined as a tuple $(h_{desc}, \epsilon_D, \delta_D)$, where:

- $h_{desc} \in H$, where H is a set of universally unique handles (labels);
- $\epsilon_D : \{\hat{I}\} \to \mathbb{R}^n$ is a function, which extracts a *feature vector* $\vec{fv}_{\hat{I}}$ from an *image* $\hat{I}$; and
- $\delta_D : \mathbb{R}^n \times \mathbb{R}^n \to \mathbb{R}$ is a *similarity function* (e.g., based on a distance metric) that computes the similarity between two images as a function of the distance between their corresponding *feature vectors*.

Figure 1.4(b) illustrates the use of a simple descriptor D to compute the similarity between two images $\hat{I}_A$ and $\hat{I}_B$. First, the extraction algorithm ϵ_D is used to compute the feature vectors $\vec{fv}_{\hat{I}_A}$ and $\vec{fv}_{\hat{I}_B}$ associated with the images. Next, the similarity function δ_D is used to determine the similarity value d between the images.

```
<?xml version="1.0" encoding="UTF-8"?>
<feature_vector:Feature_Vector xmlns:feature_vector="http://feathers.dlib.vt.edu/~rtorres" xmlns:xsi="http://www.w3.org/2001/XMLSchema-instance" xsi:schemaLocation="http://feathers.dlib.vt.edu/~rtorres/ http://feathers.dlib.vt.edu/~rtorres/feature_vector.xsd">
<feature_vector:ImageName>goldfish.pgm</feature_vector:ImageName>
<feature_vector:DescriptorName>BAS</feature_vector:DescriptorName>
<feature_vector:Type>1</feature_vector:Type>
<Curve><feature_vector:Nelements>180</feature_vector:Nelements>
<feature_vector:Curve1D>
<feature_vector:X>
<feature_vector:value>40.0</feature_vector:value>
<feature_vector:value>48.0</feature_vector:value>
<feature_vector:value>55.0</feature_vector:value>
<feature_vector:value>69.0</feature_vector:value>
<feature_vector:value>72.0</feature_vector:value>
<feature_vector:value>61.0</feature_vector:value>
<feature_vector:value>56.0</feature_vector:value>
<feature_vector:value>49.0</feature_vector:value>
<feature_vector:value>69.0</feature_vector:value>
<feature_vector:value>88.0</feature_vector:value>
<feature_vector:value>108.0</feature_vector:value>
<feature_vector:value>130.0</feature_vector:value>
<feature_vector:value>127.0</feature_vector:value>

(...)

<feature_vector:value>41.0</feature_vector:value>
<feature_vector:value>57.0</feature_vector:value>
<feature_vector:value>63.0</feature_vector:value>
<feature_vector:value>62.0</feature_vector:value>
<feature_vector:value>62.0</feature_vector:value>
<feature_vector:value>61.0</feature_vector:value>
<feature_vector:value>61.0</feature_vector:value>
<feature_vector:value>68.0</feature_vector:value>
<feature_vector:value>67.0</feature_vector:value>
<feature_vector:value>59.0</feature_vector:value>
<feature_vector:value>48.0</feature_vector:value>
<feature_vector:value>49.0</feature_vector:value>
<feature_vector:value>54.0</feature_vector:value>
<feature_vector:value>60.0</feature_vector:value>
<feature_vector:value>63.0</feature_vector:value>
<feature_vector:value>64.0</feature_vector:value>
<feature_vector:value>70.0</feature_vector:value>
<feature_vector:value>69.0</feature_vector:value>
<feature_vector:value>76.0</feature_vector:value>
<feature_vector:value>75.0</feature_vector:value>
<feature_vector:value>69.0</feature_vector:value>
<feature_vector:value>62.0</feature_vector:value>
<feature_vector:value>50.0</feature_vector:value>
<feature_vector:value>43.0</feature_vector:value>
</feature_vector:X>
</feature_vector:Curve1D>
</Curve>
</feature_vector:Feature_Vector>
```


FIGURE 1.3: Example of a structured feature vector.

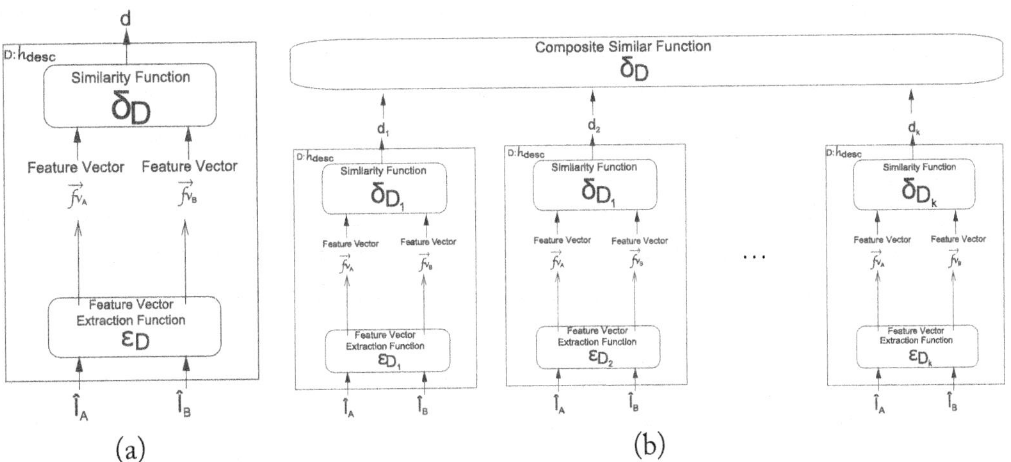

FIGURE 1.4: (a) The use of a simple descriptor D for computing the similarity between images. (b) Composite image descriptor.

Definition 1.5 A **composite image descriptor** $\hat{D}$ is a tuple $(h_{desc}, \mathcal{D}, \delta_{\mathcal{D}})$ (see Figure 1.4(b)), where:

- $h_{desc} \in H$, where H is a set of universally unique handles (labels);
- $\mathcal{D} = \{D_1, D_2, \ldots, D_k\}$ is a set of k pre-defined simple image descriptors; and
- $\delta_{\mathcal{D}}$ is a similarity function which combines the similarity values obtained from each descriptor $D_i \in \mathcal{D}, i = 1, 2, \ldots, k$.

Definition 1.6 An **image content description** (ICD) is a tuple $(FV, ST_{FVs}, Structured_{FVs})$, where:

1. $FV = \{\vec{fv}_1, \vec{fv}_2, \ldots, \vec{fv}_k\}$ is a set of feature vectors;
2. $ST_{FVs} = \{stfv_1, stfv_2, \ldots, stfv_m\}$ is a set of structural metadata specifications; and
3. $Structured_{FVs} = \{strfv_1, strfv_2, \ldots, strfv_m\}$ is a set of StructuredFeatureVector functions defined from the *feature vectors* in the FV set (the first component) of the image content description and from the structures in the ST_{FVs} set (the second component).

Definition 1.7 An **image digital object** (ido) is a digital object with the following extensions and constraints.

- ido is a *digital object* $= (h, SM, ST, StrStreams, ICD, StrICDStreams)$, where:
  1. $h \in H$, where H is a set of universally unique handles (labels);
  2. $SM_{sd} = \{sm_{sd}[i, j]\} \in SM$, where $sm_{sd}[i, j] = \langle a_i, \ldots, a_j \rangle, 0 \leq i \leq j \leq n. sm_{sd}[i, j]$ refers to substreams (regions) of an image stream;

3. $ST = \{st_1, st_2, \ldots, st_m\}$ is a set of structural metadata specifications;
4. $StrStreams = \{stD_1, stD_2, \ldots, stD_m\}$ is a set of StructuredStream functions defined from the image substreams in the SM set (the second component) of the digital object and from the structures in the ST set (the third component);
5. ICD is an *image content description*; and
6. $StrICDStreams = \{stimgD_1, stimgD_2, \ldots, stimgD_m\}$ is a set of StructuredStream functions defined from the *image stream* in the SM set (the second component) of the image digital object and from the structures in the $ST_{FVs} \in ICD(2)$ set.

Figure 1.5 illustrates the relations among the concepts used to define an image digital object.

The definition of $StrICDStreams$ allows associating feature vectors to parts (objects, regions) of image streams.

Definition 1.8 An **image collection** (ImgC) is a tuple $(C, S_{imgdesc}, FV_{imgdesc})$, where C is a collection, $S_{imgdesc}$ is a set of image descriptors, and FV_{desc} is a function $FV_{desc} : \{C \times S_{imgdesc}\} \rightarrow ICD(1)$, where ICD is $ido(5)$ and $ido \in C$.

Function $FV_{imgdesc}$ defines how a feature vector was obtained, given an image digital object $ido \in C$ and an image descriptor $\hat{D} \in S_{imgdesc}$. That is illustrated in Figure 1.6.

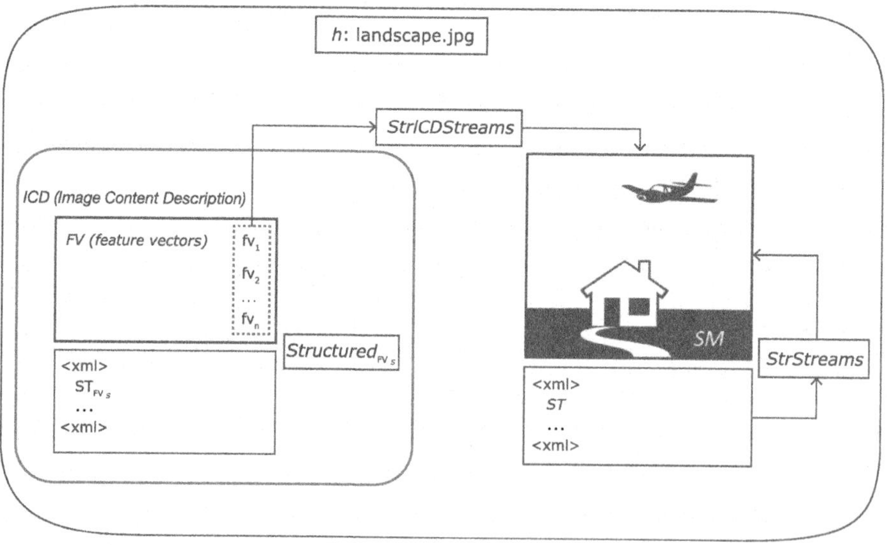

FIGURE 1.5: Image digital object elements.

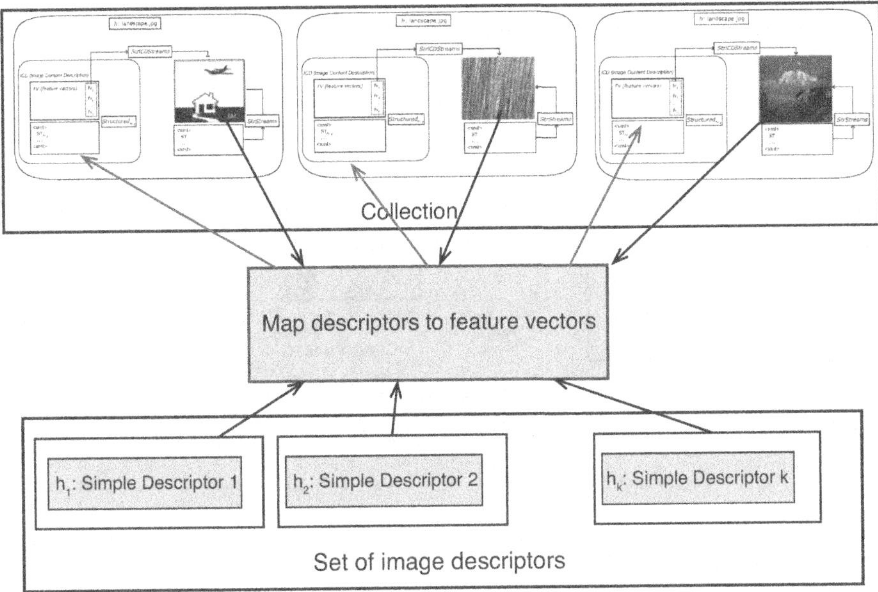

FIGURE 1.6: Use of a descriptor to extract feature vectors.

Definition 1.9 Let $S_{imgdesc}$ be a set of image descriptors with k handles in H. An **image descriptor metadata catalog** $DM_{S_{imgdesc}}$ for $S_{imgdesc}$ is a set of pairs $\{(h, \{dmdesc_1, \ldots, dmdesc_{k_h}\})\}$, where $h \in H$ and the $dmdesc_i$ are descriptive metadata specifications for image descriptors.

Descriptive metadata specifications of descriptors could include, for example, data about the author (who implemented the extraction and similarity functions), implementation date, and related publication(s).

Recall that, in general, a metadata catalog is used to assign descriptive metadata specifications to image digital objects.

Definition 1.10 A conceptual representation for user information need is materialized into a query specification. A **query specification** Q is a tuple $Q = \{(H_q, Contents_q, P_q)\}$, where $H_q = ((V_q, E_q), L_q, \mathcal{F}_q)$ is a structure (i.e., a directed graph with vertices V_q and edges E_q, along with labels L_q and labeling function $\mathcal{F}_q$ on the graph), $Contents_q$ includes digital objects and all of their streams, and P_q is a mapping function $P_q : V_q \rightarrow Contents_q$.

An example of a query specification is: $q = (H_q, Contents_q, P_q) \in Q$. For example: q is an image, which contains five spatially related sub-images (objects). A user wants to find some images similar to an existing one as shown in Figure 1.7(a). Thus, $q = ((V_q, E_q), L_q, F_q), Contents_q, P_q)$,

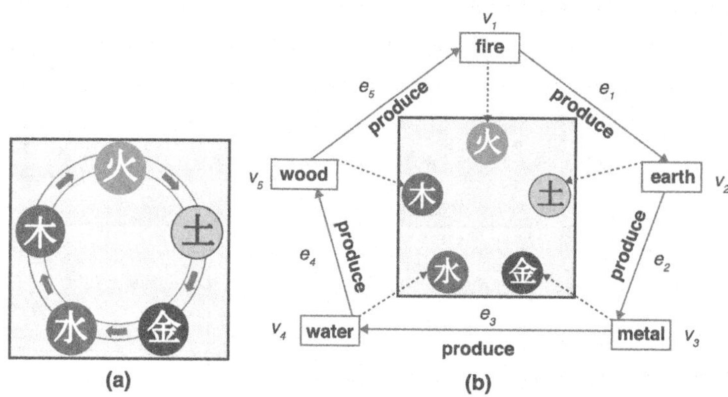

FIGURE 1.7: q is an image of five spatially related sub-images, adapted from [228].

where $V_q = v_1, v_2, v_3, v_4, v_5$; $E_q = e_1, e_2, e_3, e_4, e_5$; $L_q = 'fire', 'earth', 'metal', 'water', 'wood', 'produce'$; $F_q : V_q \cup E_q \rightarrow L_q$, $Contents_q$ is the stream of the five spatially related sub-images with their location information; and $P_q : V_q \rightarrow Contents_q$ (see Figure 1.7(b)).

Usually, two kinds of queries are supported by CBIR systems [55]. In a *K-nearest neighbor query (KNNQ)*, the user specifies the number k of images to be retrieved that are closest to the query pattern. In a *range query (RQ)*, the user defines a search radius r and wants to retrieve all database images whose distance to the query pattern is less than r. In this case, both the specification of k in the KNNQ and the specification of r needs to be incorporated into Q.

Definition 1.11 A query specification $q \in Q$ is a **K-nearest neighbor query** (KNNQ) **information need** if there exists $v \in V_q$, a real number $k \in Contents_q$, and $P_q(v) = k$.

Definition 1.12 A query specification $q \in Q$ is a **range query** (RQ) **information need** if there exists $v \in V_q$, a real number $r \in Contents_q$, and $P_q(v) = r$.

Definition 1.13 Let V_{Spa} be a vector space and $Base$ be a set of basis vectors in V_{Spa}. Let $\{VisualM\}$ be a set of visual marks (e.g., points, lines, areas, volumes, and glyphs) and $\{VisualMP\}$ be a set of visual properties (e.g., position, size, length, angle, slope, color, gray scale, texture, shape, animation, blink, and motion) of visual marks.

A **visualization operation** OP_{viz} is a set of functions $OP_{viz} = \{VisualMap_1, VisualMap_2, VisualMap_3\}$, where $VisualMap_1 : 2^C \rightarrow V_{Spa}$ associates a set of digital objects with a set of vectors; $VisualMap_2 : 2^C \rightarrow VisualM$ associates a set of digital objects with a type of visual mark;

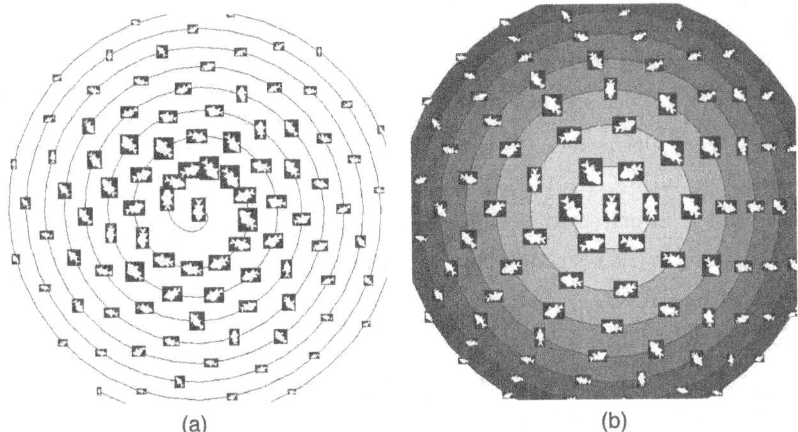

FIGURE 1.8: (a) Spiral approach. (b) Concentric rings approach.

and $VisualMap_3 : Base \rightarrow VisualMP$ associates a basis vector with a visual property of a visual mark.

Figure 1.8 shows two examples of the use of OP_{viz} to visualize results in a shape-based image retrieval system [247]. Each of the returned images is mapped to a vector in a vector space $VSpa$ by function $VisualMap_1$. $VisualMap_2$ maps returned images to thumbprints. In Figure 1.8(a), a function $VisualMap_3'$ is used to present the most similar images. This function places the query image in the center, and fills a spiral line with the retrieved images at regular distances, according to their similarity to the query image [247]. In Figure 1.8(b), a function $VisualMap_3''$ is used to present the most similar images in concentric rings. In this case, the rings are filled from the innermost ring to the outermost one, according to the image ranking [247].

Definition 1.14 A **content-based image searching service** is a set of searching scenarios $\{sc_1, sc_2, \ldots, sc_t\}$, where each scenario sc_i is a sequence of events, and each event e_i is associated with the OP_s function defined as follows:

$OP_s : (Q \times C) \times Sim_s \rightarrow 2^{Contents}$, where $Sim_s = OP_q(q, ido)|q \in Q, ido \in C$, and where $OP_q : Q \times C \rightarrow \mathbb{R}$ is a matching function that associates a real number with $q \in Q$ and a digital object $ido \in C$. The computation of OP_q relies on the use of appropriate image descriptors (e.g., their extraction and distance computation algorithms) defined in the image collection $ImgC$.

The range of function OP_s is the $Contents$ associated with collection $ImgC$. We consider the retrieved results as (a subset of) the $Contents$.

1.5 CASE STUDY

In this section, we show how the 5S extensions for content-based image retrieval can be used to define an image search service in the context of the CTRnet project. The Crisis, Tragedy, and Recovery Network (CTRnet) [137, 265] objectives include to develop better approaches toward making technology useful for archiving information about such events, and to support analysis of rescue, relief, and recovery, from a digital library perspective. CTRnet has several modules, including crawling, filtering, a Facebook application, visualization, metadata search, and Content-Based Image Retrieval (CBIR).

The CBIR module builds upon the EVA tool for evaluating image descriptors for content-based image retrieval [199]. Eva integrates the most common stages of an image retrieval process and provides functionalities to facilitate the comparison of image descriptors in the context of content-based image retrieval.

In this case study, we consider the scenario in which a user is interested in finding images in the CTRnet collection that are similar to a particular photo provided as example. The objective is to identify images that could be used in a report on damages caused by an earthquake. In this example, the query specification q would be a tuple $q = (H_q, Contents_q, P_q)$, where q is an image (see Figure 1.9). Thus, $q = ((V_q, E_q), L_q, F_q), Contents_q, P_q)$, where $V_q = v_1$; $E_q = \emptyset$; $L_q =$ '$Cathedral\_P\_A\_P.jpg$'; $F_q : V_q \cup E_q \rightarrow L_q$, $Contents_q$ is the stream of the query image; and $P_q : V_q \rightarrow Contents_q$.

The image search service considered in this case study is implemented using the BIC image descriptor [234], which can be defined as follows:

- the handle h_{desc} used is *"BIC"*;
- the feature extraction function ϵ_{BIC} classifies each image pixel as a border or interior pixel, depending on the difference among its color and the color of its neighbors. If all neighbors have the same color, this pixel is classified as interior. Otherwise, it is classified as a border pixel. The feature vector generated by this descriptor is formed by the concatenation of the color histograms of interior and border pixels; and

FIGURE 1.9: Query specification by providing an image named *Cathedral_P_A_P.jpg* as input.

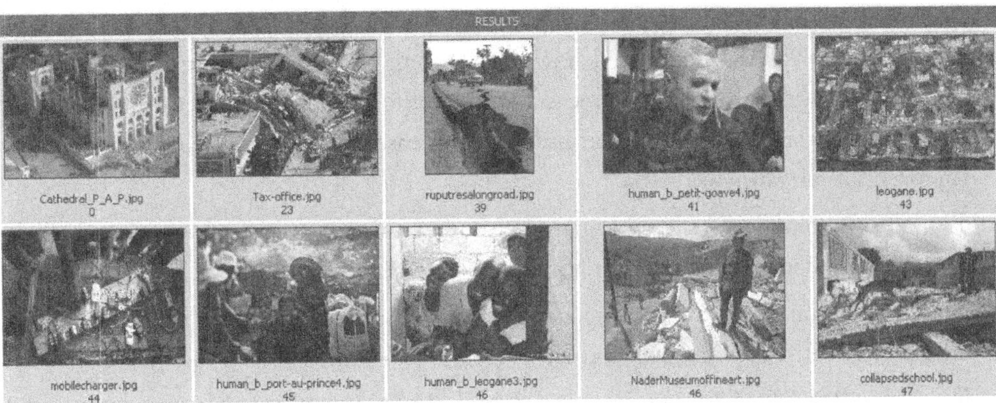

FIGURE 1.10: CBIR results containing a ranked list of image digital objects of the CTRnet collection using the BIC descriptor.

- the similarity function δ_{BIC} can be computed as the inverse of the dlog distance function [234].

In this particular case study, we are assuming that the BIC descriptor was used to extract feature vectors from all images of the *CTRnet image collection* (CTRnetImgC), i.e., CTRnetImgC $= (C, S_{imgdesc}, FV_{imgdesc})$, where C is a collection, $S_{imgdesc} = \{BIC\}$ is a set containing the BIC descriptor, and $FV_{imgdesc}$ is a function that extracts feature vectors $(ICD(1))$ that compose $(ido(5))$ each image digital object ido in C.

The **content-based image searching service** considered will be a set of searching scenarios $\{sc_1, sc_2, \ldots, sc_t\}$, where each scenario sc_i is a sequence of events, and each event e_i is associated with the OP_s function defined as follows: $OP_s : (Q \times C) \times Sim_s \rightarrow 2^{Contents}$, where $Sim_s = OP_q(q, ido)|q \in Q, ido \in C$, and OP_q is implemented, in our case, using δ_{BIC}. Figure 1.10 shows a ranked list of CTRnet images according to their similarity to the query image *Cathedral_P_A_P.jpg*, using the BIC descriptor [234].

1.6 RESEARCH CHALLENGES

The implementation of CBIR systems raises several research challenges such as the following.

- Formalisms are needed not only to describe image content descriptions but also advanced services (e.g., multi-modal search, content-based image annotation). These formalisms can guide the design and implementation of new applications based on image content.
- Not many techniques are available to deal with the semantic gap presented in images and their textual descriptions. New tools for marking/annotating images (and their regions) need to be developed. Better semantically enriched descriptions can be created by taking advantage of ontologies [2, 89]. Another possible investigation area would be to incorporate classification strategies into the image retrieval process. The idea is to apply image retrieval and then classify the resulting images to change their order. In this case, the classifier works as an automatic approach for relevance feedback.
- Tools that automatically extract semantic features from images, i.e., that extract high-level concepts contained in multimedia data, still need to be developed.
- New data fusion algorithms to support text-based and content-based retrieval combining information with heterogeneous formats.
- Novel algorithms for finding new connections and mining multimodal patterns also need to be developed. Text mining techniques might be combined with visual-based descriptions.
- Novel user interfaces for annotating, browsing, and searching based on image content need to be investigated. Research in this area will require usability studies with practitioners.

1.7 SUMMARY

In this chapter we provide formal definitions and descriptions for content-based image retrieval. The proposed extensions for digital library functionality take advantage of formalization to elucidate clearly and unambiguously the characteristics, structure, and behavior of the main concepts related to image content.

Later these definitions are explored in a case study, to exemplify how the CO and CBIR concepts apply to complex image objects. Our contribution relies on (i) the formalization of content-based image retrieval and (ii) the discussion of how to combine CO and CBIR to handle complex image objects in applications. The set of definitions also may impact future development efforts of a wide range of digital library experts since it can guide the design and implementation of new digital library services based on image content.

A straightforward benefit of this work would be the use of these definitions to create applications, like those proposed in [99, 140, 271], or the formalization of more complex services that can be created by using the proposed constructs.

1.8 EXERCISES AND PROJECTS

1.1 How might CBIR be applied so teachers with a computer and connected camera can be reminded of the names of students in their class?

1.2 Consider the two colorful images (Image A and Image B) shown below, represented in the RGB color space. Suppose that the intensity values of each pixel in all bands (R, G, and B) are the same. Furthermore, each (R, G, B) triplet is represented by a single intensity value. For example, the triplet $(R, G, B) = (2, 2, 2)$ is represented by the intensity value 2.

Suppose also that the color space was quantized in five colors with intensity values 0, 1, 2, 3, and 4.

0	0	1	2	4
0	0	3	2	4
3	3	1	0	1
3	1	4	2	1
3	4	4	2	2

Image A

4	4	2	0	1
4	4	2	0	1
4	3	3	1	1
3	3	3	0	1
2	2	2	0	0

Image B

(a) Compute the L_1 distance between the *Color Histograms* (5 bins) of the images. The L_1 distance between color histograms H_A and H_B is computed as follows: $L_1(H_A, H_B) = \sum_{i=1}^{K} |H_A[i] - H_B[i]|$, where K is the size of both histograms (5, in this case).

(b) By considering both the feature vector extraction function and the distance function defined for the descriptor *Color Coherence Vector—CCV* [196], compute the distance $\delta_{CCV}(A, B)$ between the two images.

1.3 Consider the existence of two classes (*class 1* and *class 2*) composed of five images each. Consider the existence of three different descriptors (*descriptor 1*, *descriptor 2*, and *descriptor 3*), whose feature vector extraction functions extract vectors belonging to the $\mathbb{R}^2$ space. Table 1.1 shows the coordinates of each image of each class, considering the three descriptors.

TABLE 1.1: Coordinates of each image of classes 1 and 2 for three different descriptors

Classes	Descriptor 1
class 1	{(1.50, 2.50), (1.50, 2.00), (2.00, 2.00), (1.00, 2.00), (1.50, 1.50)}
class 2	{(1.00, 1.00), (1.00, 2.00), (1.00, 3.00), (1.00, 4.00), (1.00, 5.00)}
Classes	**Descriptor 2**
class 1	{(2.00, 1.00), (2.00, 2.00), (2.00, 3.00), (2.00, 4.00), (2.00, 5.00)}
class 2	{(1.40, 1.40), (1.60, 1.40), (1.60, 1.20), (1.40, 1.20), (1.50, 1.30)}
Classes	**Descriptor 3**
class 1	{(1.50, 2.50), (1.50, 2.00), (1.75, 2.25), (1.25, 2.00), (1.50, 1.50)}
class 2	{(1.50, 5.50), (1.25, 5.00), (1.50, 5.00), (1.15, 5.00), (1.50, 4.50)}

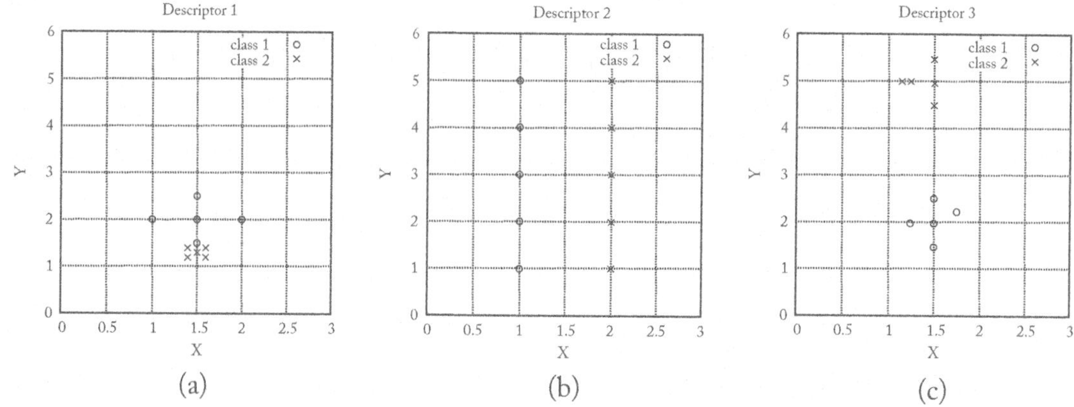

FIGURE 1.11: (a) Descriptor 1; (b) Descriptor 2; and (c) Descriptor 3.

Figures 1.11(a), 1.11(b), and 1.11(c) show classes 1 and 2 in the $\mathbb{R}^2$ space for descriptors 1, 2, and 3, respectively.

For each descriptor, compute the precision $\times$ recall curve as an average over 10 cases. Each case treats one of the 10 points specified in Table 1.1 (and Figure 1.1) as a query, ranks the other 9 points according to their distance from that query, and considers points relevant if they have the same class as the query. Based on this analysis, state which descriptor is the most effective.

1.4 Extend the 5S framework to define image search services with relevance feedback.

1.5 Consider the SuperIDR tool available at http://scholar.lib.vt.edu/theses/available/etd-04142011-175752/.

(a) Formalize the image searching services available in the SuperIDR tool, using the 5S framework.
(b) Implement a new descriptor to support image search services in the tool.
(c) Compare the performance (in terms of efficiency and effectiveness) of the implemented descriptor with the one available at the SuperIDR tool.
(d) Formalize the complex image objects available in the SuperIDR tool.

CHAPTER 2
Education

Eric Fouh and Yinlin Chen

Abstract

Education is one of the most common applications of digital libraries (DLs) and related types of information systems. The spread of e-learning has increased the importance and the presence of digital libraries in most educational processes. Educational DLs allow members of the educational community to create, evaluate, share, and preserve educational resources. Successful education DLs contain high-quality educational resources and are easy to browse, search, and access. In order to have broad impact on the communities in education and to serve the needs of teachers and students for a long period of time, digital librarians need to structure and organize the resources in a way that facilitates the dissemination and the reusability of the resources. In addition, digital librarians who collaborate with patrons have to repeatedly review, verify, and extend the resources they have collected and harvested. Thus, quality is particularly important in educational DLs. In this chapter, we use the 5S framework first to describe educational DLs, and then to review current education DL applications. Next, we discuss key concepts regarding quality in educational DLs. Lastly, two educational DLs, *AlgoViz [9]* and *Ensemble [76]*, serve as case studies.

2.1 INTRODUCTION

Libraries have been the cornerstone of education and can be viewed as a sign of great scholastic and technological achievement. With educators and students relying more on computers in most educational activities, the need for software and digital educational materials that will support those activities becomes a major challenge in e-learning. Digital educational materials need to be organized in educational digital libraries (EDLs) in order to improve the accessibility and reliability of such resources.

EDLs aim to address several needs of the educational community: how to find educational resources, how to use or integrate the resources gathered, how to share educational materials, and how to assess the quality of the resources. The 5S framework provides us with a formal model to describe and build effective digital libraries, that has been used in several DL applications [85, 87]. Accordingly, this chapter focuses on presenting a 5S perspective on educational DLs.

2.2 RELATED WORK

The United States National Science Digital Library (NSDL) is a national network of digital environments dedicated to advancing science, technology, engineering, and mathematics (STEM) teaching and learning, in both formal and informal settings. Ensemble is an NSF (United States National Science Foundation) NSDL Pathways project working to establish a national, distributed digital library for computing education. Based on their experience, and lessons learned from working with different NSDL projects, the Ensemble working group proposed eight principles for distributed portals (PDPs) [86]. They advocate for:

- articulation of EDLs across communities using ontologies;
- browsing services tailored to collections;
- a close integration across interfaces and virtual environments;
- metadata interoperability and integration;
- social graph construction using logging and metrics;
- superimposed information and annotation integrated across distributed systems;
- streamlined user access with IDs; and
- Web 2.0 multiple social network system interconnection.

Some DLs are built using open source software, such as PLoS ONE[1], which is a communication tool for peer-reviewed science and medicine. PLoS ONE is built upon the innovative technologies of Topaz, Fedora, and Mulgara, providing an open publishing platform that combines an online scientific journal with community features such as tags, annotations, discussions, and ratings.

Forced Migration Online [214] is a comprehensive website that provides access to a diverse range of relevant information resources on forced migration. It is a technically and intellectually administered resource, combining specialist subject knowledge with high standards of information management.

The ARROW [209] project's aim is to identify, test, and develop software or solutions to support best practice institutional digital repositories. While initially a research project, ARROW has now co-developed a working institutional repository solution, well suited to institutions of higher education.

1. http://www.plosone.org/home.action

The three above-mentioned systems use the Fedora Commons software[2]. On the other hand, more than 1000 DLs are built using DSpace [20]; almost all of them are academic and research center projects. DSpace is free software developed by HP and MIT to primarily help educators build open digital repositories. Its design was driven by the following goals: provide an easy way to browse, submit, and retrieve documents using a digital asset store; be economically viable; provide authentication mechanisms; create a community; etc. Since the middle of 2009, Fedora Commons and the DSpace Foundation have been working together to create the DuraSpace organization [133].

Sumner et al. presented a model composed of three concepts to build EDLs [236]. They claimed that their constructs provided a structural way to build educational digital libraries that will fully capture the interaction between humans and technology along with contextual information. They present EDLs as *cognitive tools*, meaning that they should have interfaces, tools, and services that will help the users to make sense of information from different sources and of different types (text, image, etc.). Their second construct refers to EDLs as *component repositories*, using component-based software engineering concepts in order to allow for the creation of new educational resources by reconfiguring and reusing existing materials. They argue that EDLs should be designed with the goal of improving the quality of education by enhancing the reuse of resources, sharing best practices, etc. Their last construct depicts EDLs as *knowledge networks* indicating that EDLs' services and tools should foster interactions between all users in order to support knowledge building.

The separation between the *content* of the EDL and the *context* in which the resource is going to be used is also an important principle. Further, the growth in the number, size, and diversity of digital collections makes metadata quality an increasingly important issue. All the projects presented in this section gave us some guidelines on how to build educational digital libraries. In order to build systems that will meet the above requirements and address the concerns raised when designing a DL, we need to have a formal model to analyze and describe all of the elements involved in the design and implementation processes. To the best of our knowledge the 5S framework is the most appropriate tool.

2.3 INFORMATION SEEKING IN AN EDL

EDLs have several stakeholders, each having a specific role in the educational process. EDL stakeholders include the following.

Authors. Users in this role are engaged in creating digital educational resources; this group comprises instructors, researchers, and sometimes students. Most educational DLs divide

2. http://www.fedora-commons.org/

resources into *standalone* "modules" to increase the reuse of educational resources. Each module typically talks about a specific concept.

Learners. This group typically comprises students. They consume EDL resources to learn about a subject/topic.

Educators/Instructors. They use or reuse educational resources for teaching purposes. They sometimes integrate documents retrieved from the EDL into course materials.

Educators and learners have several ways of accessing information within an EDL. Educators typically use a digital library to find educational materials that can be used during learning activities. They can just browse or search the collection. Also, based on their rights and permissions they can create, review, or edit documents. Commenting, rating, and tagging digital resources also are common scenarios that add value to digital objects.

Brusilovsky and Tasso [42] defined four techniques to access information within a DL; each technique is related to one or more scenarios. Ad-hoc information retrieval is when users issue a query to a DL or search engine and analyze the results to find the relevant documents. Information filtering (recommendation) is when the DL recommends documents to users based on users' profile information (personalization). Users browse the collection by following the links that connect documents in hypertexts. Information visualization allows the users to manipulate interactive visualizations (e.g., concept or knowledge maps) in order to find relevant documents [42].

In addition to the four techniques aforementioned, educators usually search for domain experts or peers who are users of, or contributors to, the collection [7].

Personalization aims to automatically recommend resources (at an appropriate time and in an appropriate setting) to the user by analyzing metadata information, content, and/or user behavior. **Metadata analysis** is an example of static recommendation where the system tries to find resources with metadata information matching what is in a user model, for example suggesting all of the documents about the user's topics of interest.

A **behavior model** builds on a study of user activity and generally uses machine-learning methods to find useful patterns in a log of the user's behavior [177]. In this approach, the system records items visited by the user and applies some heuristics (e.g., time spent on the resources, number of hits, etc.) to mark them as interesting or not interesting. Then machine-learning techniques are used to find items similar to "interesting" resources. Machine learning techniques include [177]:

- content-based filtering: computing resource-to-resource similarity; in the case of text documents the "cosine similarity" is frequently used to measure the similarity;

- collaborative filtering: looking at item reviews (e.g., tags, comments, and ratings) by the other members of the online community;
- heuristic-based recommendation: analyzing semantic relationships between resources; and
- composite filtering: combining some of the above approaches and assigning a weight to each.

2.4 INFORMATION ORGANIZATION IN AN EDL

In order to design an EDL that will fully support the scenarios described in Section 2.3, standards have been defined to structure resources/learning objects and their metadata.

The IEEE Learning Technology Standards Committee published the *Learning Object Metadata (LOM)* standard to "specify the syntax and semantics of Learning Object Metadata, as well as the attributes required to fully describe a Learning Object" [121]. Some of the goals followed by LOM include [121]:

- to enable learners or instructors to search, evaluate, acquire, and utilize LOs;
- to ease the sharing, exchange, and interoperability of LOs across multiple learning systems;
- to enable the development of learning objects in units that can be combined and decomposed in meaningful ways;
- to enable computer agents to automatically and dynamically compose personalized lessons for an individual learner;
- to complement the direct work on standards that are focused on enabling multiple Learning Objects to work together within a open distributed learning environment;
- to enable, where desired, the documentation and recognition of the completion of existing or new learning and performance objectives associated with Learning Objects;
- to enable a strong and growing economy for Learning Objects that supports and sustains all forms of distribution: non-profit, not-for-profit, and for profit;
- to enable education, training, and learning organizations, including government, public, and private, to express educational content and performance standards in a standardized format that is independent of the content itself;
- to provide researchers with standards that support the collection and sharing of comparable data concerning the applicability and effectiveness of Learning Objects;
- to define a standard that is simple yet extensible to multiple domains and jurisdictions so as to be most easily and broadly adopted and applied; and
- to support necessary security and authentication for the distribution and use of Learning Objects.

LOM schema are hierarchically organized and describe LOs in nine categories: General, Life Cycle, Meta-Metadata, Technical, Educational, Rights, Relation, Annotation, and Classification. LOM-based metadata schema are being used in MERLOT [168], a Web portal providing instructors with a large collection of digital learning materials along with evaluations and instructions on how to use them.

NSDL defined its own metadata schema to describe educational resources. It follows the Dublin Core (DC) standard and is called NSDL_DC. Dublin Core has two implementations: "Simple" and "Qualified" (with component refinements and encoding schemes). NSDL_DC has been built up as a variant of Qualified Dublin Core. The idea behind the design of NSDL_DC was to have a standardized and common approach to metadata among all the NSDL pathway projects. In addition, the Open Archives Initiative Protocol for Metadata Harvesting (OAI-PMH), used by NSDL to collect metadata, expects Dublin Core as a required encoding schema, though other metadata formats can be used in addition. The minimal required elements in the NSDL_DC schema include: Title, Identifier (URL/URI), Description, Subject (and/or keywords), Education Level, and Type.

2.5 A QUALITY-ENHANCED MINIMAL 5S DL

Metadata quality is a important issue in EDLs because it would be a serious problem to provide poor quality or incomplete educational materials or services to their audience. Thus, EDLs should always ensure that their collections and services are of high quality and suit their audience's need. To achieve this goal, they need to ensure continuously the quality of both the contents and services they provided. EDLs create interactive services for users to find and learn new knowledge and get users input to refine and improve their services. Therefore, a quality-enhanced minimal 5S DL can be built under this kind of EDL. This quality-enhanced minimal 5S DL would apply quality measurement into several DL components. It would gather user's feedback to improve current collections and refine existing services. Figure 2.1 shows an enhanced 5S model that includes services such as commenting, labeling, tagging, rating, and feedback for users, as well as recommendation and evaluation to improve the quality. This would allow designers to construct a quality 5S minimal DL. The quality assessment is added into the 5S minimal DL. It connects with the Societies model and the Spaces model under different EDL quality situations (Scenarios). The demonstration of EDL built on this quality-enhanced 5S minimal DL is shown in the case study of the Ensemble portal.

The overall architectural design aims to continue acquiring new high-quality metadata resources from various digital libraries and websites and to meet users' information needs. Crawlers based on interesting topics carry out focused crawling to get educational resources. Applications extract information and generate metadata to store into the EDL. Finally, users retrieve information which interests them through services provided by the EDL. An overview of the quality-enhanced

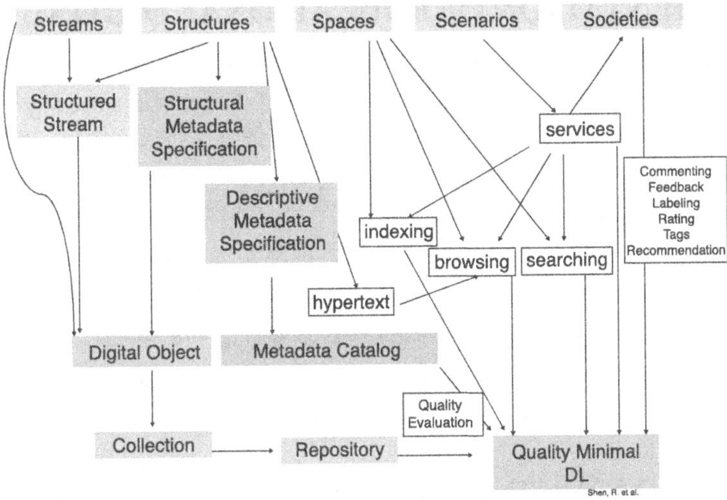

FIGURE 2.1: A quality-enhanced minimal 5S DL.

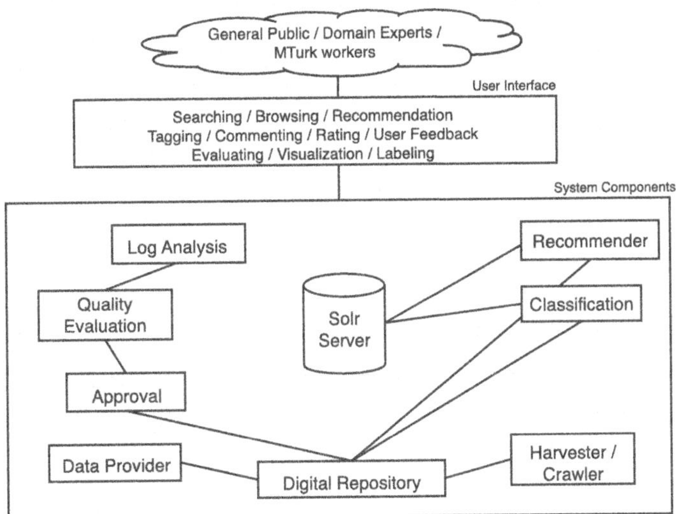

FIGURE 2.2: An overview of the quality-enhanced 5S-based architecture.

5S-based architecture is shown in Figure 2.2. The quality assessment will evaluate metadata records in the EDL repository, analyze user log activities, collect user feedback, and make decisions on newly acquired records. It further will apply quality measurement to improve EDL services for indexing, searching, and browsing. It also provides services for different users to help in evaluating and improving the quality of resources in EDLs.

2.6 IMPLEMENTATION OF EDUCATIONAL DIGITAL LIBRARIES

When creating an EDL, digital librarians have to decide on the type of EDL they want to create. One criterion that has been used to classify EDLs is the nature of the content stored by the system. That is whether the EDL stores only metadata or LOs or both [175]. EDLs are thus divided between:

- *portals:* systems that only store resources' metadata and have a link to the actual location of the resource. AlgoViz is an example of a portal system;
- *warehouse:* systems storing all (actual) content locally. Connexions [18], a digital educational ecosystem environment, is an example of a warehouse system; and
- *hybrid:* systems that are the combination of the two above systems. Ensemble [76] is an example of a hybrid system.

2.6.1 FEDERATED SEARCH AND HARVESTING OF METADATA

Federated search and harvesting are two important mechanisms in DLs, particularly portals and hybrid EDLs. They provide the users with a large amount of educational resources from different sources. Federated search allows the user to search multiple databases from a single entry point. Here any query is run against the system's database; when desired (or as a default in many cases) that also leads to processing of the query against the data from other systems. One challenge of federated search is to select a set of systems likely to provide relevant answers. Metadata harvesting consists of gathering copies of metadata from other sites and storing them locally. To ensure interoperability between systems, the harvester and the data providers have to use the same protocol, and metadata must conform to a specified schema. The NSDL uses the OAI-PMH protocol to harvest metadata and its own metadata schema to validate harvested data. All NSDL data providers have to comply with that schema.

2.6.2 EDL WITH CONTENT AUTHORING CAPABILITIES

With the democratization enabled by the personal computer, the need for more digital educational resources has increased in all fields. Before the Internet boom, most electronic resources were delivered via CD-ROM (inside a hardcopy book). The goals of early authoring tools (ATs) included to provide instructors (with limited programming skills) a platform to easily and rapidly create their class materials. Some of the most used authoring tools included HyperCard, Macromedia Authorware, Dreamweaver, Microsoft Word, and FrontPage. Brusilovsky et al. developed the InterBook system [41] using Microsoft Word as an authoring tool to create *adaptive* electronic textbooks; the documents are converted into HTML files. Authoring tools also have been widely used to make Intelligent Tutoring Systems, e.g., InterBook [41] and EDUCA [44]. In most cases, instructors use ATs to create learning materials, and to specify the relationship between these materials, while a learner or instructor consumes the information provided by the system. Some systems, on the other hand, involve the learner in the learning material creation process. For example, in EDUCA [44], all learners have a user profile (feature vector) containing data like uploaded resources, websites visited, grades, etc. When the student visits an external webpage while using the system, information from the page is added to the learner profile, and the system engages in text mining so that suitable information can enhance the content of the webpage in the learning materials.

Example of EDL with Content Authoring Capabilities

Connexions [18] is a Web-based system for authoring, storing, and sharing educational materials. Resources are organized within Connexions as small modules that can be exported (as PDF files, text files, or webpages) and integrated into existing class materials. See Figure 2.3 for module utilization within Connexions. They also can be combined to make new class materials. Connexions brings together a community of educational resource authors (faculty members, industry professionals, and students) in order for them to create new materials in a collaborative way. This online community also peer-reviews the resources, thus enhancing the overall quality of the digital content in Connexions.

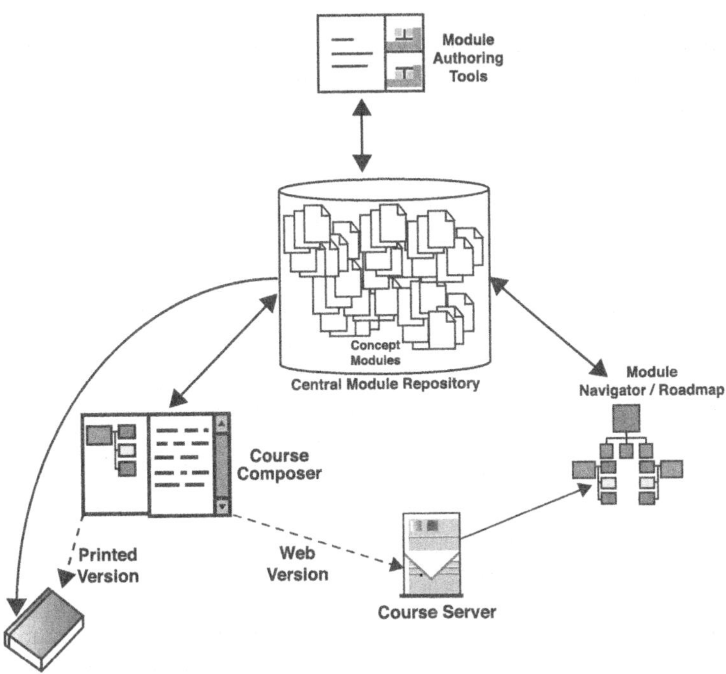

FIGURE 2.3: Connexions architecture [18].

Resources in Connexions are structured using an XML schema and are stored in a central repository. Metadata information (module title, authors, keywords or tags, and the relations with other modules) related to each module is stored in a database that enhances the search and retrieval of resources. Connexions implements the standard metadata tags from the Dublin Core Initiative.

2.6.3 METADATA INTERCHANGE

The Object Management Group (OMG) created XMI (XML Metadata Interchange), an interchange format for sharing metadata information using XML [190]. Recently, JSON (JavaScript Object Notation) has emerged as an alternative to XML for structured data in a repository [59]. JSON, similar in nature to XML, aims to structure data stored in a digital library or other information system. JSON is being used to describe data in Freebase [33], a collaborative database project with a faceted Web user interface. Unlike resource metadata that can be reused and transferred between different systems using standardized protocols, user models still lack reusability and interoperability in the majority of cases. Most DL systems represent user information and data in proprietary formats; as a consequence, they can provide limited structured (user model) answers to other systems.

Carmagnola et al. [49] listed systems that provided structured user model information: JSON and UserML (an XML-based language) are among the languages used. In addition, Google, Yahoo!, and MySpace, grouped in the OpenSocial[3] foundation, have constructed APIs to help developers to build social applications that access and share users' data from different websites.

2.7 FORMALIZATION

Education can be viewed as a form of formal training happening in an institutional setting. Education engages all stakeholders into different types of learning activities. The stakeholders include the learner(s) and the instructor(s).

Definition 2.1 An **educational digital library 2.0** is a 6-tuple, Edu-DL 2.0 = (R, U, S, RSR, RSU, USU), where:

- $Resources(R)$ in a educational DL are data or metadata objects and information that are collected, created, captured, generated, stored, and shared in the digital library;
- $Users(U)$ is the set of people in a educational DL who interact with the digital library, for example, educators, students, researchers, developers, policy makers, etc.;
- $Services(S)$ refer to the operations that allow interactions between and among resources and users;

3. http://docs.opensocial.org/display/OS/Home

- RSR represents the modeling and representation of resources within an edu-DL;
- RSU refers to the connections between users and resources indicating that there should be a number of ways to interact with the resources (e.g., comment, review, rate, tag); and
- USU refers to the connections users have with other users.

Davis et al. advocated that innovative design and delivery of services should leverage technology in order to create services that will increase self-service, automation, globalization, choice, information, and fidelity [66]. In the context of EDL, self-service means the user needs less time and minimal external help or support when interacting with the system. It should come as a result of all the (underlying) services being automated. It also is desirable to have all the system resources available anywhere (globalization). All these changes should lead to more choices for the user because of the availability and the (high) amount of accessible information. An EDL should acknowledge the contributions of the most active members of the community. Some of the most important of those contributions are new resources.

Definition 2.2 A **learning object** (lo) is a digital object which can be used, re-used, or referenced during technology supported learning [263]. It is a tuple: $lo = (h, SM, ST, StructuredStreams, c)$ where:

1. $h \in H$, where H is a set of universally unique handles (labels);
2. $SM = \{sm_1, sm_2, \ldots, sm_n\}$ is a set of streams;
3. $ST = \{st_1, st_2, \ldots, st_m\}$ is a set of structural metadata specifications;
4. $StructuredStreams = \{stsm_1, stsm_2, \ldots, stsm_p\}$ is a set of StructuredStream functions defined from the streams in the SM set (the second component) of the digital object and from the structures in the ST set (the third component); and
5. c is a tuple $c = (c_i, c_j)$ with c_i is the context within which learning takes place. Examples include: K-12, higher education, etc. To complete that, c_j is the subject context of the learning. Examples include: Computer Science, Mathematics, etc.

Digital objects can be combined together to form "compound (or complex) learning objects (clos)".

Definition 2.3 A **compound learning object** is defined as a tuple $clo = (h, SCLO, S)$ where:

1. $h \in H$, where H is a set of universally unique handles (labels);
2. $SCLO = \{LO \cup SM\}$, where $LO = \{lo_1, lo_2, \ldots, lo_n\}$, and lo_i is a learning object or another complex learning object; and $SM = \{sm_a, sm_b, \ldots, sm_z\}$ is a set of streams; and
3. S is a structure that composes the compound learning object clo from its parts.

Accordingly, Wiley divided a *clo* into two categories: *closed clo* and *open clo* [263]. A *closed compound learning object (cclo)* is a set of *los* aggregated in a logical way during the design phase by its author(s). Further, an *open compound learning object (oclo)* is a set of *los* aggregated on the fly by a software system during the retrieval phase. The logic on how to combine the *los* is stored in the digital library, in the metadata or elsewhere, as part of provenance. Compound learning objects are packaged into "learning modules".

The definition of an EDL captures all of the dimensions of the 5S framework: stakeholders (Societies) of the EDL should be clearly identified, their needs and Scenarios of use (of the educational materials) should be studied in order to design and implement Services that will satisfy their information needs. Content (collected Streams) should be organized (Structures) in a way that makes it easy to store, retrieve, and share them.

2.8 CASE STUDIES

2.8.1 ALGOVIZ

AlgoViz is a Web portal for algorithm visualization (AV). It is driven by *Drupal*,[4] a Content Management System. AlgoViz includes a catalog of more than 500 AVs, and a large bibliography of related research literature. It aims to provide instructors with information about AV availability and usage.

Societies in AlgoViz include: AV developers, instructors looking for AVs to use as class materials, and any other AV user. AlgoViz allows all the members of this online community to add qualitative information on top of that which is delivered by a simple AV catalog. This information adds more value to the content and is the result of direct interaction and collaboration between community members. AlgoViz implements several modules and tools to support such interactions, including a forum. In addition, users can comment, rate, or tag resources and also share their experiences on how to make the best use of content, through what is called a "field report."

Structures in AlgoViz are limited since it is a portal-type of EDL; thus, it does not store LOs locally. A relational database management system stores information about all the resources, the users, and all the events occurring within the portal. AlgoViz uses taxonomies to help organize AVs, with each taxonomy term coming from a controlled vocabulary. One of the many advantages of using a taxonomy is it is easier for the indexer to locate the key feature of a resource. This is materialized through "faceted search and browsing" in AlgoViz; see

4. http://drupal.org/

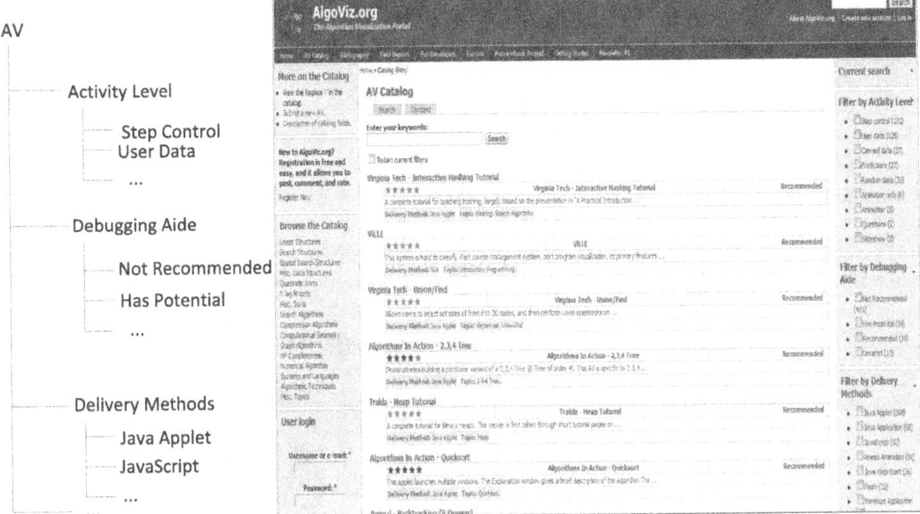

FIGURE 2.4: AlgoViz's taxonomy organization translated in faceted browsing.

Figure 2.4. Metadata are formatted following two standards: the Dublin Core (DC) Metadata Standard and the NSDL Metadata Standard. This allows AlgoViz's resources to be harvested and validated by any system following DC standards and by the NSDL or any NSDL partner (e.g., Ensemble).

Spaces relate to the 2D portrayal used in most AVs. Further, resources in AlgoViz are indexed using Solr,[5] an "open source enterprise search platform from the Apache Lucene project".[6] It uses a combination of a Boolean Model and a Vector Space Model to represent documents. The Solr index consist of documents, each document having several fields containing resources' metadata information.

Scenarios support the AlgoViz community. Users come to AlgoViz not only to find AVs, but also to provide feedback on AVs they have tested and used. AV developers can create entries in the catalog for the artifacts they have developed. In AlgoViz, users can interact directly with each other through a forum, and find related research literature.

Streams can be used to describe the forum communications. Further, catalog entries in AlgoViz provide not only textual information about AVs but also screenshots of the AVs and in some cases a short video describing the artifact, as shown in Figure 2.4.

---

5. http://lucene.apache.org/solr/

6. http://lucene.apache.org/

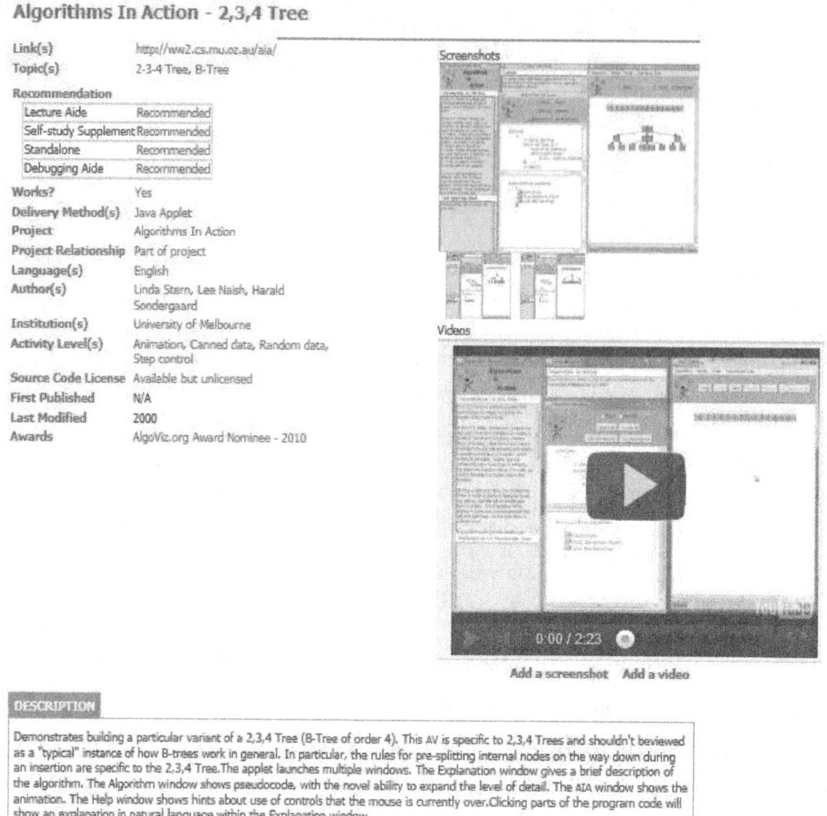

FIGURE 2.5: A catalog entry in AlgoViz.

2.8.2 ENSEMBLE

Ensemble is an NSDL Pathways project working to establish a national, distributed digital library for computing education. The project is building a distributed portal providing access to a broad range of existing educational resources for computing while preserving the collections and their associated curation processes. The developers want to encourage contribution, use, reuse, review, and evaluation of educational materials at multiple levels of granularity and seek to support the full range of computing education communities including computer science, computer engineering, software engineering, information science, information systems, and information technology, as well as other areas often called computing + X, or X informatics.

Societies. Ensemble defines different user roles to manage the operation of the Ensemble site. For example, administrators manage the site-wide configuration and service upgrade, conference managers manage user contributed content, and group managers handle the collections related to a group among the Ensemble communities.

Structures. Ensemble acts as data harvester and also data provider. All the metadata in Ensemble has two formats, one is Dublin Core metadata and the other one is NSDL DC metadata. All of the metadata harvested from other DLs is cataloged and represented in a user readable record page in Drupal, that also is accessible to the general user. Each record page contains text, links, labels, and graphs in the hierarchy's structure. All user-contributed content and educational materials collected through crawlers are transformed into these two formats and other DLs can harvest Ensemble metadata through the Ensemble data provider.

Spaces. All of the content in Ensemble is indexed using Solr. Ensemble uses the functionalities provided by Solr to provide faceted search and supports searching with browsing capabilities. Ensemble also provide several interactive services to gather user feedback, such as comments, tags, and ratings.

Scenarios. Users can find educational materials in Ensemble through browsing and searching services. They can create groups in Ensemble and invite others with similar interests to join those communities. They also can contribute their educational content and add to the Ensemble user contributions collection.

Streams. Computing educational contents in Ensemble include textual information (HTML, PDF, Word, and PowerPoint), screenshots of educational tools, and a short introductory video describing educational tools. Figure 2.6 shows an educational record in Ensemble.

2.9 SUMMARY

In alignment with many other digital library implementations, educational digital libraries are becoming more complex systems, managing an increasing amount of digital resources. They should benefit from a formal model to rely on for design and implementation. Most of the models and concepts proposed in the field of EDLs are based on lessons learned and best practices. The 5S framework is a robust and general framework, backed by a strong theoretical work, and has been used to design and build several DL applications. In this chapter we presented how EDLs extend minimal DLs in order to provide services and tools that will satisfy the educational community information needs. We studied several examples of systems and showed how the 5S framework can be used to fully describe them.

An Educational DL was defined by the UNESCO Institute for Information Technologies in Education working group as an "environment bringing together collections, services, and people to support the full cycle of creation, dissemination, discussion, collaboration, use, new authoring, and preservation of data, information, and knowledge [251]." Figure 2.7 presents a concept map based

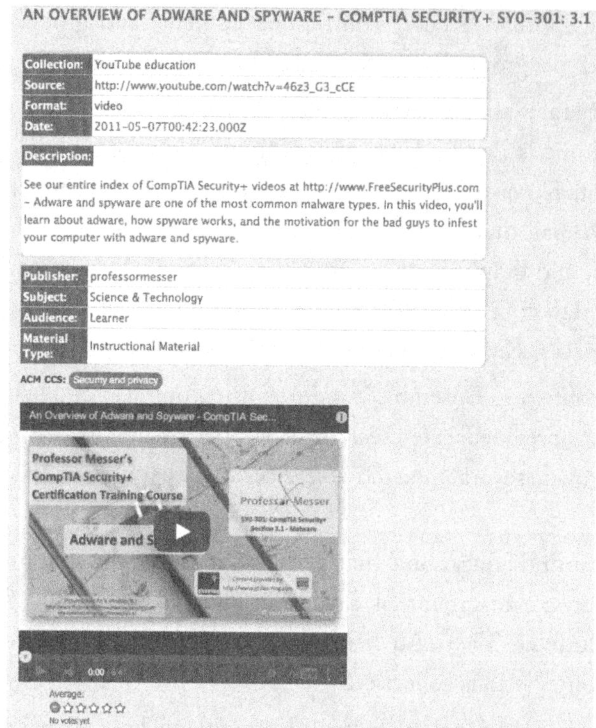

FIGURE 2.6: An educational record in Ensemble.

on this definition, allowing us to group related concepts under the umbrella of each element of the 5S framework.

2.10 EXERCISES AND PROJECTS

2.1 Besides the content, what most differentiates an educational digital library from other digital libraries? Why?

2.2 Based on the minimal DL definition, and the EDL definition, will you classify Course Management Systems (Moodle, Blackboard, etc.) as DL or EDL? Pick one, such as CMS, and summarize how its description could be made formal.

2.3 Should future versions of AlgoViz utilize CTR feedback to produce an absolute, standardized measure of content quality or instead personalize recommendations to a user's profile? Why?

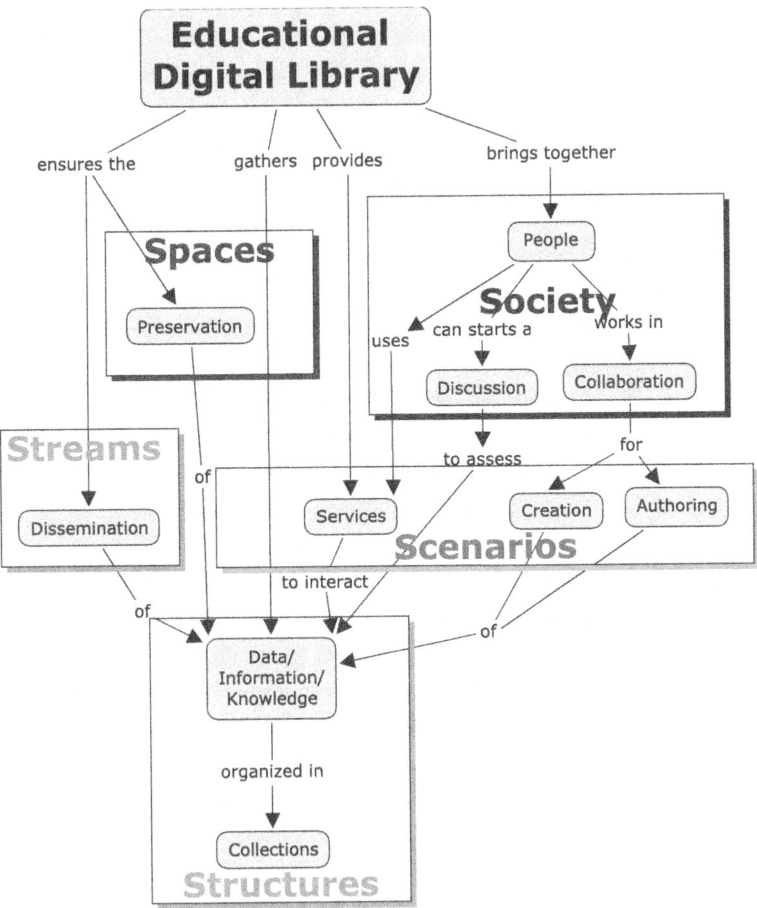

FIGURE 2.7: EDL concept map.

2.4 Are educational level and subject sufficient to define a learning context of a learning object? What additional metadata would be useful to describe learning contexts for the Ensemble case study?

2.5 How does informal learning relate to the discussion in this chapter? Compare and contrast EDLs with a DL designed for informal learning.

CHAPTER 3

Social Networks in Digital Libraries

Monika Akbar and Clifford A. Shaffer

Abstract

Online communities and social networks on the World Wide Web are growing rapidly, allowing users to connect, share, and learn in a collaborative environment. That has been aided by digital libraries which store and allow access to digital objects. Especially now, users need better searching and browsing capabilities. One way to achieve this is to take advantage of the experiences of prior users of the library with similar interests. While e-commerce sites like Amazon are well known for this, it is a challenge for digital libraries since users do not explicitly provide feedback on the resources.

In this chapter, we describe how log files can be used to build deduced social networks (DSNs) within digital libraries. These networks can allow us to automatically detect communities, interests, and trends among the users in a digital library. We present a case study for using a DSN within an educational digital library. While this chapter emphasizes educational digital libraries, the methods discussed here have the potential to be useful in other digital libraries and information systems as well.

3.1 INTRODUCTION

Just like real-world libraries, a digital library has some target audience, that is, one or more groups of users with specific interests. Individuals within the audience will have differing needs and requirements. Interactions and communications among the group can lead to an online community. Researchers have studied different aspects of establishing an online community in a digital library [36, 120, 173]. Additional research has focused on design issues [11, 104], studying and analyzing the overall architecture [68, 242], and identifying success factors [146, 157].

Success of a virtual community is largely dependent on the DL's ability to provide community support with suitable services, and on the performance of these services (e.g., fast, efficient search). Although the initial design of the WWW was targeted towards individual users, Web 2.0 supports online group-based activities and communications [191]. Online communities are now common for groups of people with similar interests who are located in different places. In many domains, such as health [6] and education [14], communities are essential for research and development.

Educational digital libraries provide access to a range of educational resources (e.g., syllabi, book reviews, collections of teaching aids), as well as a wide range of services to support the life cycle of information: collection, creation, dissemination, use, and reuse [101, 229]. Finding potentially useful resources among the collections within a DL can become difficult. An active community of users who provide feedback on the resources can help mitigate this problem. Active feedback from educators could not only generate additional information on available resources (e.g., indicating quality information for materials through ratings or reviews) but also list common practices about the use of those resources. However, while a number of educational DLs exist, instructors as a community typically are not actively engaged in most educational sites [9, 197]. Our key question is: Can we obtain helpful information without explicit participation by users in the form of ratings and reviews?

While most digital library architectures support collaborative tasks like commenting and rating, there has been less work done on successfully incorporating community behavior within a digital library. Extending the traditional DL would allow it to be more adaptive and better reflect the community it serves. The digital nature of a DL means that it can capture and present useful information about the collection to end users that cannot be done easily in a real life library. Such information includes object access rates, object usefulness based on user ratings and reviews, listings of similar objects, etc. Some of this information is generated automatically based on content similarity, some by the actions of those who use the digital object (e.g., counts of object views). But still, most users are in the dark about knowledge that exists only collectively within the community such as which resources are useful. With our proposed concept, deduced social network, it is possible to identify such knowledge and expose it to users.

In this chapter we explain how to use implicit user information to deduce a social network. Such networks can allow a DL to have tailored services based on user needs and trends, even when users are not explicitly providing their feedback.

3.2 RELATED WORK

Online communities are defined by their between-user interactions. Girgensohn et al. [95] looked at social interactions in websites. They identified three sociological design challenges for building a successful socio-technical site: encouraging user participation, fostering social interactions, and promoting visibility of people and their activities. They also mentioned two technical design issues that are important in a socio-technical site: usability and low maintenance cost. Two of their target sites, CHIplace and Portkey, used a number of services like featuring news in the front page, sending newsletters, providing extrinsic reward for various activities, and varying levels of registration to increase user participation.

Koh et al. [134] studied user participation in virtual communities in detail. They explain that participation can be of two types: passive (i.e., viewing) and active (i.e., posting). Each of these activities depend on different stimuli. They listed four major factors for an engaging virtual community: active leadership, offline interaction (e.g., offline meetings), usefulness of the content, and sound infrastructure.

User participation in online communities has been studied in depth from other perspectives. Nov et al. [185] examined the effects of different types of participation on the levels of membership in the community. Ludford et al. [162] studied the effect of showing both similarity and distinctness information about a member and the groups where s/he belongs as a means for increasing online community participation. Similar studies based on social theories were done by Beenen et al. [24]. Millen et al. [178] investigated design decisions, member selection, and facilitating stimulating discussion topics for engaging the members of an online community. Preece et al. [208] studied community members to find out reasons behind lower participation among a particular group of less active users known as *lurkers*.

Researchers have used the structural properties of the network to identify communities or groups of entities [84]. Behavioral networks[1] introduce an object-centric approach for connecting people. While social networks mostly depend on human ties, behavioral networks harness user trends to connect users who are otherwise disconnected. Esslimani et al. [77] used behavioral networks for deducing social networks among users.

Following user trends and learning from those trends allow a DL to be adaptive to its users. Often, common navigation tendencies are used to guide new users. Further, diverse areas including document recommendation [53], social network analysis [136], and Usenet news [135] rely on user trends and preferences to cope with information overload.

User trends are often used in recommendation systems. These recommendation systems can be divided into three categories: content-based, collaborative, and hybrid. In a collaborative recommendation system, similarity between users is calculated in order to find the ratings of users that most likely have similar preferences. Reviews and ratings of similar users are used to find the item that is likely to be of greatest interest. Thus topics of recommendation are not limited to similar subjects and, based on population trends, they can vary widely. One of the first examples of collaborative filtering is Tapestry [97] which allowed users to help each other perform filtering over emails or electronic documents. This system also supported content-based filtering. Online retailers like Amazon and Netflix are using collaborative filtering to provide

1. A network of users constructed based on behavioral data such as similar navigational patterns.

best matched items for a particular user taste. Hybrid recommendation systems use a combination of both content-based and collaborative recommendation systems. Fab, a Web-based recommendation system [17], uses both of these techniques to collect and rate items. Many existing recommender systems depend on user profiles to model user behavior. Many digital libraries see significant user activities from anonymous users. This group of users have limited features associated with them, making it difficult to effectively model these users. Deduced social networks solely rely on anonymous user data and can be useful to deduce user behavior trends.

3.3 FORMALIZATION

A specific user community may contain disparate networks. Discovering these networks for a digital library will allow us to get a better understanding of user interactions [39]. That knowledge can be used to provide personalized user services.

Networks can be constructed using logs and metrics. A large number of personalized services depend on Web metrics. Usage log analysis shows key pieces of information like average time spent on a certain page, bounce rate, and exit percentage for a webpage. Identifying similar users depending on their interests and providing them with possibly helpful contents to explore is another advantage of having a robust logging system. It is also possible to facilitate social navigation (e.g., show contents that are viewed together in a user session).

Generic social networks connect users with other users of the same site. Besides user-user interaction, it also is possible to derive connections between users by way of different objects, such as the pages they view [77]. Analysis of these networks and their contextual information can reveal interesting user behavior, different user roles, and communities with similar interests. While there exists a number of different types of digital libraries that serve different domains, this chapter is focused on educational DLs (see Definition 2.1).

Definition 3.1 A **Deduced Social Network** (DSN) is a graph with tuple (V, A, k), where:

- V is a set of vertices;
- A is the set of attributes of V which are used to create edges; and
- k is a constant or a function that returns the minimum number of elements of A that must be common between two V to create a connection (i.e., edge) between them.

Figure 3.1(top) shows examples of deduced social graphs. Assume, for each user visiting a DL, that we know certain log information including his topic of interest, URLs visited, comments he made, etc. The top figure shows two social graphs constructed among users based on two different types of log information: their topic of interest and the URLs they visited. While the networks

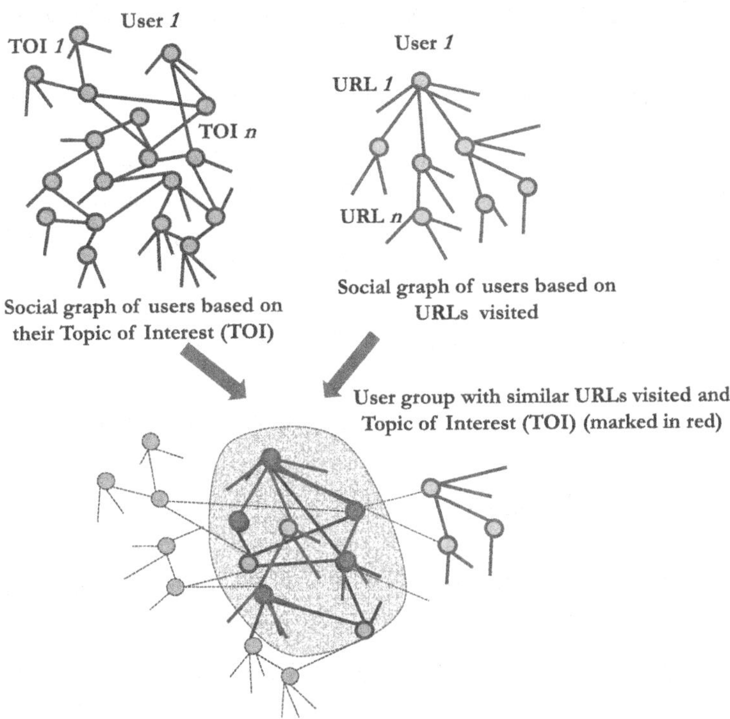

FIGURE 3.1: (top) Two social graphs between users based on their Topic of Interest (TOI) and URLs visited. (bottom) The overlapping social graph reveals groups with common topics of interest and viewing trend.

themselves can show interesting patterns, the overlap of these networks (Figure 3.1(bottom)) can further reveal complex trends such as certain groups of users who share common topics of interest and who visited the same URLs.

3.4 FINDING COMMUNITIES IN A DIGITAL LIBRARY

Building and sustaining an active online community is difficult. Although DLs serve different user groups, encouraging the users to become and stay active has proven to be a challenge. One way of engaging users in various activities in the library (e.g., view, rate, comment) could be to show what others have done. Trends or communities can be discovered by examining the DL's social networks.

Social networks can serve a number of purposes in a digital library. They can help in harnessing and spreading community knowledge. They can be used to identify common practices of users. They even can help users with a similar interest to interact with each other.

We can divide social networks into two broad categories: active social networks and passive social networks.

Active Social Networks

These networks involve websites that specifically allow users to link with other users by sending requests. Social networking sites such as LinkedIn, CiteULike, or Delicious follow this principle. Along with building the network in these sites, users provide information on their background and preferences.

Passive Social Networks

There exists another set of sites where the focus is more on providing information than on creating social networks. Many digital libraries fall in this category. These sites act as a rich source of information and provide services to facilitate information retrieval. User activity in DLs can be roughly divided into two categories: Implicit and Explicit. Implicit user activity includes, often anonymously, viewing a page or downloading an object. Explicit user activity, which occurs much less often, includes when content is contributed by the user (usually who has logged into an account) that can appear in many forms: new resources, ratings, reviews, comments, etc. This chapter presents ways to find and utilize implicit user behavior.

User logs provide useful information on implicit user activities. Just as with websites, DLs typically log user data. These data can allow us to deduce the underlying networks involving users. Such networks, which can connect one user with another based on their navigation history, can be interpreted as behavioral social networks.

Passive social networks take a more object-centric approach rather than the relationship-centric approach of active social networks. A wide range of objects can be used in a DL as a basis to create passive social networks. For example, in an educational DL, there are often groups, collections of metadata, and tools for teaching. It is possible to use these objects and user trends to form different networks. Described next are two examples of how a network can be deduced in such a DL.

1. We can connect users based on their activities in the site. For example, we can create a network of users based on their viewing of the same pages. In this network, the users will be the nodes, and an edge between two users will indicate that they have viewed a same page. The following subsection contains more details on formalizing and constructing such DSNs.
2. There are a number of different types of DSNs other than the user-user DSN. A connection between objects or activities can be similarly interesting. In a page-page DSN, two pages are connected, for example, if they were both seen in a session. An activity-activity DSN could connect two resources if they were, for example, rated in the same session.

Passive networks such as DSNs can help us understand how users behave in a DL. When used appropriately this information has the potential to improve DL services.

3.5 ANALYSIS OF PASSIVE SOCIAL NETWORKS

Network analysis can help us understand hidden trends and user preferences. Depending on the characteristics of the network, a number of analysis approaches can be employed. For example, for dense graphs, graph partitioning can help us to find smaller sub-graphs that might reveal interesting information. Similarly, it is possible to analyze pairs of passive networks to identify complex trends (e.g., people who viewed similar pages and commented on similar resources.). We describe next some approaches that might be useful for analyzing the passive networks discussed in the previous section.

3.5.1 GRAPH PARTITIONING

After constructing the DSN, the properties of the resulting graph may be studied in order to gain meaningful insight into the users' behavior. There are a number of ways in which graphs can be analyzed, graph partitioning being one of them. Graph partitioning breaks down the graph into disjoint subsets such that the number of connections within the subsets is high but the number of connections between the subsets is low. Graph partitioning has been studied in various areas including Web science [122], epidemiology [106], sensor networks [216], and parallel computing [112, 139].

Networks have been extensively studied in a variety of fields including physics, biology, and sociology to find communities [56, 193, 224]. Newman and Girvan used betweenness as a measure for removing edges and finding communities in graphs [96]. Clauset et al. [56] used hierarchical agglomeration algorithms for detecting communities in large networks. Among various clustering techniques, spectral clustering and modularity clustering, as discussed below, are gaining momentum in community detection.

Spectral Clustering

Spectral clustering depends on the eigenvectors of the similarity matrix to partition the data points into disjoint clusters such that the similarity of points within the cluster is high while that across them is low [258]. Spectral clustering transforms the objects into a set of points in space that then can be clustered using standard clustering algorithms. Fortunato [83] described a number of techniques for community detection including spectral clustering.

While spectral clustering has been used effectively in areas such as image segmentation, it can encounter difficulties in detecting different community structures within the graph. For example, a dense community may consist of nodes of similar degrees, while another community may have few central nodes with high degree but many nodes with lower degree. The Web now consists of networks of different structure, dynamics, and behaviors. Users are now connecting with other users, joining groups, or following one another. Shah and Zaman [227] used network centrality to propose the leader-follower algorithm for communities that are formed around a few central users. Their approach, when compared to spectral clustering, performed better in locating such communities. Thus, in some scenarios, spectral clustering may perform poorly at identifying groups.

Modularity Clustering

Modularity, introduced by Girvan and Newman, is a quality measure for clustering that has been successfully adopted in many areas [96, 184]. Modularity clustering is dependent on edge betweenness—a measure that assigns a weight to an edge as the number of shortest paths between pairs of vertices containing this edge. If a network contains multiple communities then the number of edges connecting the communities will be less than the number of edges within the communities, and all shortest paths between those communities will contain one of those edges that connect the communities. Thus, the edges that connect the communities will have relatively higher edge betweenness values.

3.5.2 TOPIC MODELING

Finding groups of users is not itself sufficient to understand user interests. One way to identify a group's interest is to use topic modeling on the pages viewed by the group members. Probabilistic models such as Latent Dirichlet allocation (LDA) [29] have been used extensively to detect topics for a document corpus. LDA is a generative probabilistic model that uses a fixed vocabulary and assigns a Dirichlet distributed vector to each document while detecting the topics in a document corpus. One of the shortcomings of LDA analysis is its requirement that there be a fixed number of topics. Blei et al. [28] addressed this issue with Bayesian nonparametric methods and introduced hierarchical Dirichlet processes (HDPs), which can handle arbitrary numbers of topics and can generate new topics for previously unseen documents.

LDA also has been expanded to analyze linked documents. Chang and Blei combined relational topic modeling [51] with LDA. The links between the documents are modeled as binary variables that suggest whether a pair of documents is linked or not. According to this approach, the link information is connected to the content of the documents. While most topic modeling research focuses on document corpora, Ramage et al. [213] used LDA to analyze topics appearing in micro-blogs.

3.6 CASE STUDY: THE ALGOVIZ PORTAL

Online communities can use social navigation to guide users through large collections. The distributed communities and content in an educational DL also can benefit from a system that will allow a user to see how other users have navigated through the information space. AlgoViz is an educational digital library with an international user community that hosts a comprehensive catalog of algorithm visualizations (AVs). It also has a rich bibliography related to algorithm visualization.

AlgoViz collects user history in several different tables in its database. A sample of one of these, the Accesslog table, is given in Table 3.1, showing data on the session, user ID, hostname, timestamp of when the page was visited, etc. AlgoViz content is open for public viewing, hence it is possible for users to search for content without registering. These are referred to as Anonymous users and so have a default user ID of 0. Hostnames (i.e., IP addresses) are used instead of user IDs to identify trends in the user base. For any given hostname, we are able to determine which pages were viewed in a session—identified by the *session ID* variable—and the time when the page was loaded. We used these data to deduce a behavioral social network. Additionally, the Accesslog table uses a variable named *access-id* (AID) as the primary key of the table. It also stores session information. Each page viewed in a session generates a new AID (i.e., row) in the table. On average, a month has 100,000 rows in the table. Much of the data are generated from spammers, crawlers, bots, etc. We followed a three-step process to clear the log data of such outliers.

TABLE 3.1: A sample of log data for AlgoViz

Session ID	Page Title	Internal Path/ Page URL	Hostname[a]	User ID	Timestamp
ievav83	Lifting the hood of the computer . . .	node/1413	93.x.y.z	0	1276272047
t5fuuba	biblio/export/ tagged/118/ popup	research.cs. vt.edu/algoviz /biblio	207.x.y.z	0	1276260935
ivuks8s	Has an AV helped you learn a topic in computer science?	research.cs. vt.edu/algoviz /poll/	95.x.y.z	0	1276260943

a. IPs are changed to protect user identity.

1. Filter data based on page titles: Many pages in AlgoViz are generic and less informative for understanding user behavior. At the first stage of data cleaning, we prune the rows based on the titles of the pages. Examples of pages titles that are less informative and less important include: "Welcome", "Access denied", "Page not found", etc.
2. Filter data based on the path: Sometimes the title of the page alone is not sufficient to understand content. For example, the profile page for a user contains the user name as the title. The Accesslog table stores the internal path of the page. These paths are used to prune rows that include generic internal paths such as "user/register", "user/login", etc.
3. Filter data based on the session information: In this phase, we can detect aggregate behavior such as average pageviews per session, average length of session if at least two pages were viewed, etc. With such information, we are able to identify the outliers, possibly bots, in the log data, and filter them out. The session-based pruning was done in three stages.
    1. Pages per session: Count of the number of unique pages generated in a session; prune if this value is greater than a certain threshold x.
    2. Seconds per page: On average, in a session, how much time was spent on a page; prune if this value is less than a certain threshold y.
    3. Number of sessions with one pageview: Usually a session would contain multiple pageviews. We observed a tendency of generating a large number of sessions with only one pageview, for certain hostnames (i.e., IP address). We pruned all the rows containing each such suspicious hostname.

3.6.1 DEDUCED SOCIAL NETWORKS

The filtered data are then used to connect pairs of users based on their common pageviews. These connections lead to the DSN where nodes represent users and edges indicate that pairs of users have viewed common pages. We used a *connection threshold* parameter to vary the network strength. A *connection threshold* of size k for an edge indicates that two users have viewed at least k common pages.

Figure 3.2 shows a DSN based on the log data of AlgoViz for the months of September and October 2010 with a connection threshold of 10. We used a force-directed graph layout [74] to draw these networks. Node size is proportional to the degree of each node. IPs are changed to protect user identity. The network shown in Figure 3.2 (top) has 195 nodes and 2,255 edges, while the network in Figure 3.2 (bottom) contains 130 nodes with 1180 edges.

Network Characteristics

Among various measures, node degree distribution and betweenness centrality are used frequently to understand the characteristics of large networks. Figures 3.3 and 3.4 provide these values for the respective DNSs. Provided next is a brief description of these values and their usefulness.

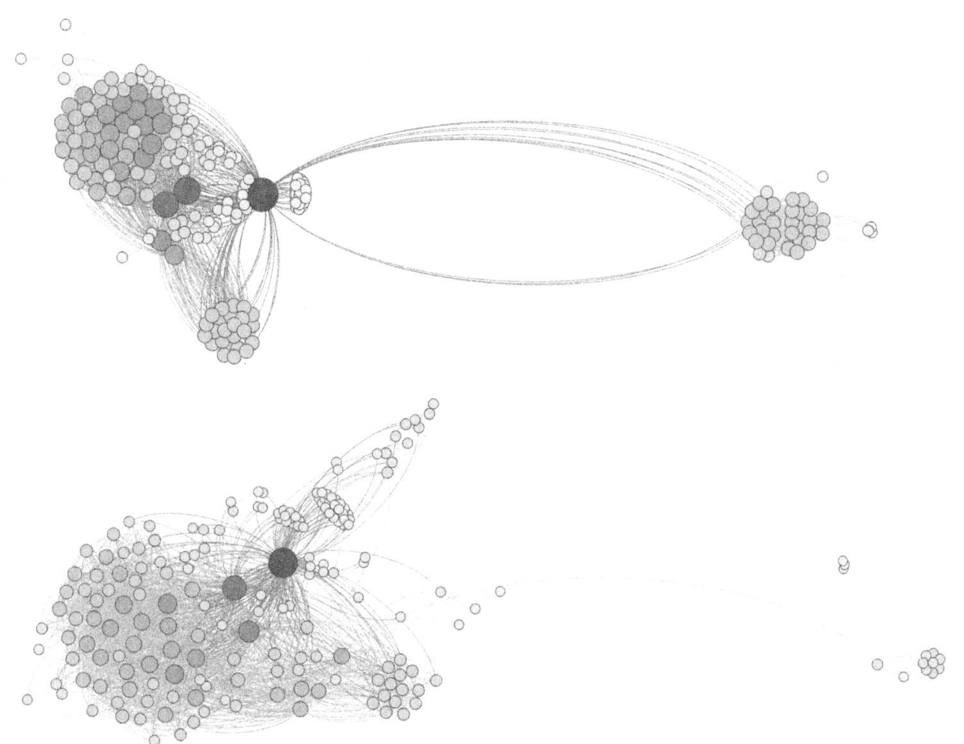

FIGURE 3.2: Using log data to find user groups with similar interest (connection threshold k=10). (top) AlgoViz September 2010 DSN; (bottom) AlgoViz October 2010 DSN.

Distribution of node degree. DSNs are undirected graphs where the node degree of a node is the number of edges connected to it. Degree distribution is an important measure for understanding whether the network is random or scale free.

Betweenness centrality. The betweenness centrality value assigns weights to a node based on how many times this node appears in the shortest path between all the other nodes. We use a normalized value so that the betweenness centrality of each node is a number between 0 and 1. If betweenness centrality is high it indicates that the node is present in many shortest paths. Removing a node with high betweenness centrality can create strongly connected components in a network, thus revealing sub-groups.

3.6.2 COMMUNITY DETECTION ON DSN

As seen from Figure 3.2, the graphs are dense, making it difficult to analyze user trends. Graph partitioning methods are used to find sub-graphs or communities within such dense graphs. We

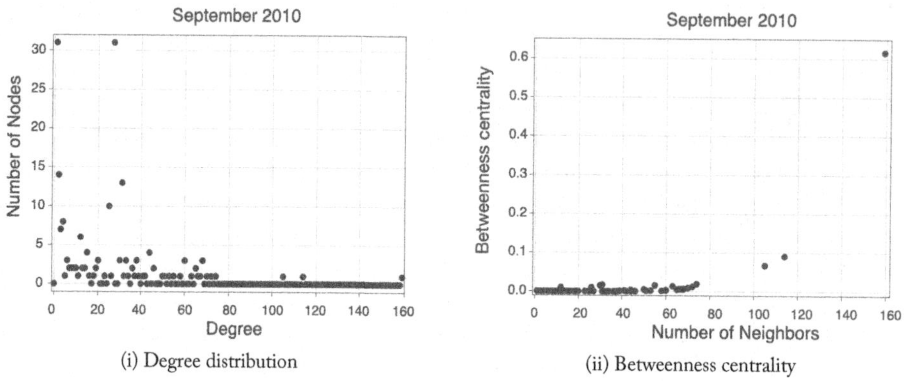

(i) Degree distribution (ii) Betweenness centrality

FIGURE 3.3: Network statistics of the DSN for September 2010 (connection threshold k=10).

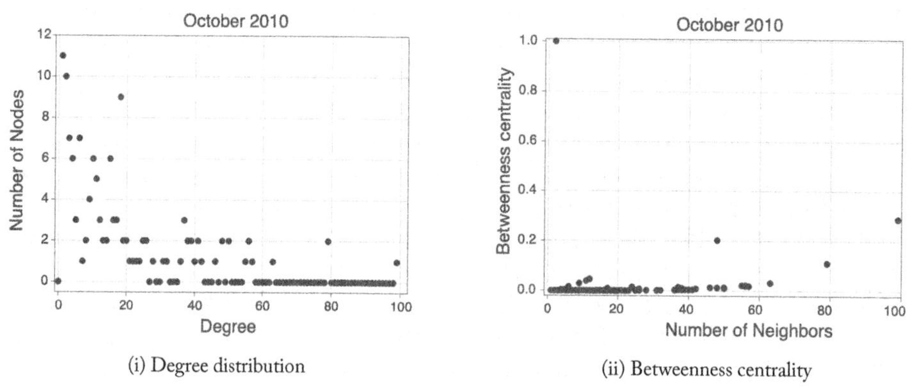

(i) Degree distribution (ii) Betweenness centrality

FIGURE 3.4: Network statistics of the DSN for October 2010 (connection threshold k=10).

used Modularity clustering [96, 184], which has been successfully used to find communities within large networks in other domains. The result of the clustering and the user distribution in the clusters are given in Figure 3.5. Figure 3.5(ii) shows that most of the clusters consist of more than 20 users. The clusters with a low numbers of users indicate possible outliers (e.g., cluster 4 in September 2010 has 2 members). Thus, the clustering result has the potential to be used for further data cleaning.

3.6.3 COMMUNITY INTERESTS

The clustering results in the previous subsection were used to identify topics within the clusters. We used the API for Mallet,[2] which uses the LDA approach to find topics appearing in the page titles

2. http://mallet.cs.umass.edu/

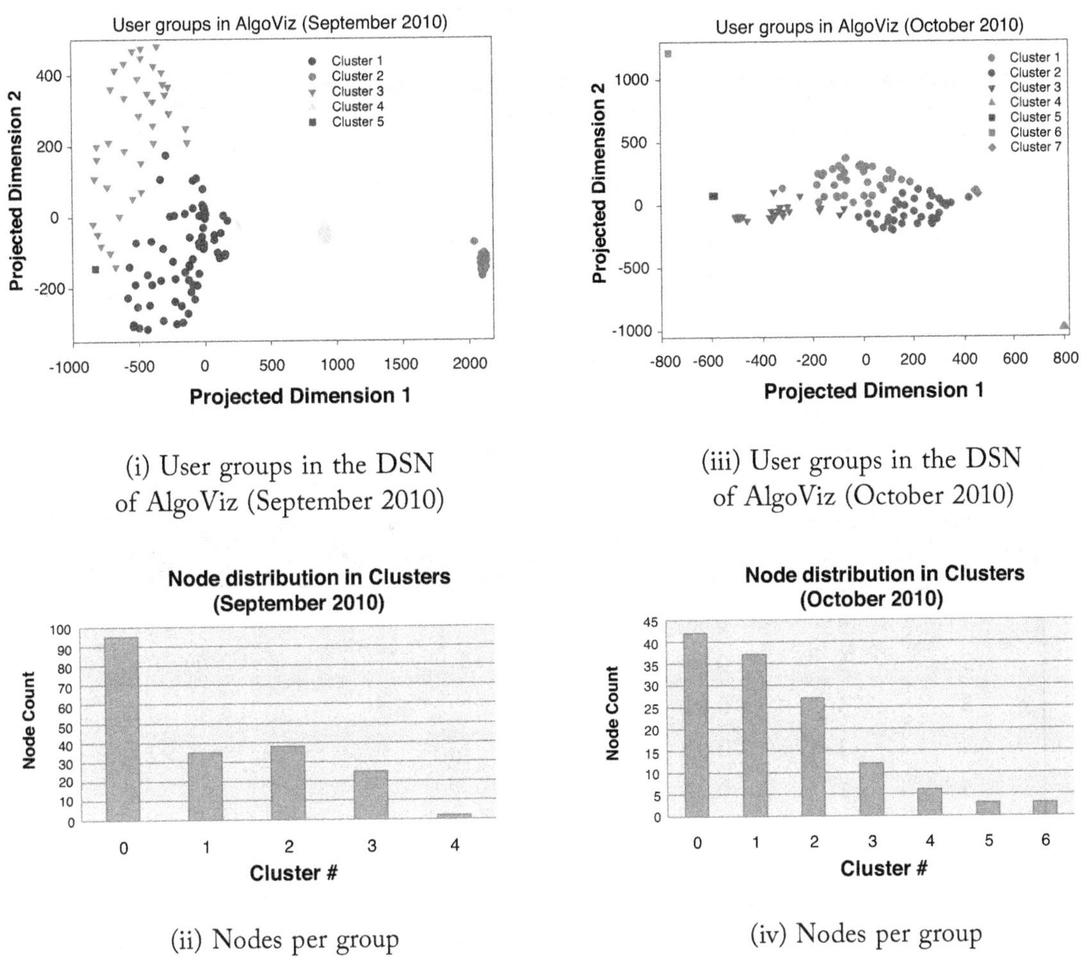

(i) User groups in the DSN of AlgoViz (September 2010)

(iii) User groups in the DSN of AlgoViz (October 2010)

(ii) Nodes per group

(iv) Nodes per group

FIGURE 3.5: Clusters found in the DSNs of Figure 3.2.

of that cluster. While building models, we set the number of topics similar to the number of clusters that were generated for each month. For example, in September 2010, there were five clusters and we opted for five topics for those clusters. Table 3.2 shows the five topics with some of the most important words in that topic. The number of sampling iterations for the topic model of each month was 200.

Three of the top-most topics in the September 2010 DSN include words related to the AlgoViz bibliography entries (i.e., biblio). One of the prominent collections of AlgoViz is the bibliography of publications related to algorithm visualizations. The collection can be sorted by

TABLE 3.2: Top five topics in the AlgoViz September 2010 DSN using LDA

Topic ID	Some words appearing in the topic
1	biblio, export, author, popup, tagged, bibtex, catalog, entries
2	biblio, author, bibtex, export, function, algorithm
3	biblio, forum, export, popup, author
4	sigcse, algoviz, awards, publication, softvis, winners, call, acm
5	biblio, tagged, export, catalog, entries, av, popup, trees

TABLE 3.3: Topic distribution using LDA for AlgoViz September 2010 DSN, T=5 topics

Cluster ID	Top Topic (1)	Contribution	Top Topic (2)	Contribution	Top Topic (3)	Contribution
1	4	0.85				
2	5	0.89				
3	3	0.86				
4	3	0.82				
5	1	0.91				

author, title, publication type, or publication year. Also, these entries can be exported in RTF, bibtex, and XML formats. The last two topics are less related to bibliography entries.

Table 3.3 shows the topic distribution within the clusters in the September 2010 DSN. The first column shows the cluster ID, while the subsequent pairs of columns show the topic ID and its proportion in the cluster. We show the top three topics for each cluster. However, each topic shown must have at least 10% topic proportion value within the cluster. For example, in Cluster 1, Topic 4 is most dominant. Clusters 3 and 4 are dominated by Topic 3.

The important words in each topic for the October 2010 DSN is shown in Table 3.4. The topic distribution for the groups of the October 2010 DSN is shown in Table 3.5. Cluster 1 consists of biblio entries (e.g., biblio, export, rtf), and other content pages (e.g., linked, functional). Topics 3, 6, and 7 are mostly related to bibliography entries and these topics are dominant in Cluster 7. Topics 1, 2, 4, and 5 are mostly related to AlgoViz catalog entries. These topics are prominent in Clusters 2, 4, and 5.

TABLE 3.4: Top seven topics in the AlgoViz October 2010 DSN using LDA

Topic ID	Some words appearing in the topic
1	forum, list, binary, education, path, biblio
2	trees, learning, automata, animations, visual, systems
3	biblio, export, rtf, linked, functional, teach
4	algorithm, visualization, animation, computer, data, java
5	author, algorithms, program, animal, software, programming
6	biblio, export, bibtex, xml, author, node
7	author, view, sort, tree, limit, structure

TABLE 3.5: Topic distribution for AlgoViz October 2010 DSN, T=7

Cluster #	Top Topic (1)	Contribution	Top Topic (2)	Contribution	Top Topic (3)	Contribution
1	3	0.987				
2	1	0.828	2	0.138		
3	6	0.421	5	0.145	3	0.12
4	1	0.815				
5	5	0.253	4	0.217	6	0.137
6	3	0.264	6	0.161	4	0.144
7	6	0.306	3	0.221	7	0.119

3.7 APPLICATIONS AND FUTURE DIRECTION

In this chapter we have addressed the problem of gathering data about community preferences of artifacts from passive user interactions. The deduced social network concept provides an approach to log data analysis that is particularly relevant to educational digital libraries. We presented a case study where we used the DSN to describe and visualize some aspects regarding usage of the AlgoViz portal. The clustering results indicate that AlgoViz users have clusters of interests when it comes to using online resources related to AVs. Some users are mainly interested in AV research, particularly bibliography entries. Other users are more interested in AV catalog entries. Of these, interest clusters around sorting or graph visualizations. Along with their interests, we are able to detect the size of each cluster. Knowing the groups, their interests, and the group size gives us leverage on better serving the target audience. The results of the analysis can be used in many different ways including recommending content, updating content ranking, highlighting recent user interests, etc.

Using the DSN, we developed an alternative catalog ranking process that provided better performance than the existing system built from the expert opinion on the appropriate configuration of AV-specific parameters. Additionally, we developed a recommendation system that uses DSN-derived information to recommend content. In the future we plan to use the page content to model topics within each group. Creating navigation networks of pages based on common viewers is another area we plan to pursue.

3.8 SUMMARY

Educational digital libraries serve groups of users with different interests. Identifying these groups and their interests can help us better serve their information needs. In this chapter we present the concept of deduced social network (DSN). In the absence of active social networks, DSNs can help us to understand user trends. The knowledge gained from DSN analyses can be used to tailor DL services.

3.9 EXERCISES AND PROJECTS

3.1 Authority control systems use distinct naming conventions for authors of resources in a library. How does an authority control system relate to developing and maintaining a digital library with an integrated social network?

3.2 Suppose that Virginia Tech's courseware management system, Scholar,[3, 4] provides researchers with user log data. What information can you find from the data that can be beneficial to the user as well as the developers of Scholar?

3.3 The case study presented in this chapter employed a user-user DSN. What are some possible ways for creating page-page DSNs? What kind of information will these DSNs reveal? Name some applications that could make use of a page-page DSN.

3.4 The case study given is about AlgoViz. This is a relatively homogeneous digital library, focused on algorithm visualization. There are other educational digital libraries, like Ensemble (http://www.computingportal.org) and the National Science Digital Library (http://www.nsdl.org),

3. https://scholar.vt.edu/

4. https://scholar.vt.edu/portal/help/main?help=sakai.iframe

both of which harvest from other digital libraries so as to have more heterogeneous content. Thus, Ensemble aims to cover everything related to computing (including AlgoViz), and NSDL aims to cover all of the science, technology, engineering, and mathematics (STEM) areas, including content from Ensemble. For each of Ensemble and NSDL, please discuss how the DSN approach might be utilized. How would it be deployed? What could be learned? What do you expect would be the results and findings? Does having heterogeneous data help or hurt? Note: Addressing these questions could be covered in a small to moderate sized project, or even a thesis.

3.5 The DSNs being constructed in the case study are based on log data. But systems like AlgoViz also have comments, ratings, tags, and other information related to content and/or users. How could such information be used in a similar manner to the log data? What problems might result from use of such data? Could those problems be addressed if DSN construction used both such information, and log data, working together? How might that be implemented? What would be the likely results?

3.6 Educators often feel that they have rather particular needs. Is this a real issue, or just a cultural artifact? After all, with the spread in popularity of MOOCs and other similar services, it appears that very large populations of learners are happy with key information that is not individualized. Given all this, might not wider sharing of educational resources be broadly accepted if they were better advertised and if more encouragement was given? Assuming that to be the case, how might the findings of this chapter be applied to help broaden the use of digital libraries for education?

3.7 In this chapter, the definition of a DSN follows on discussion of EDLs. But DSNs could be constructed for other types of digital libraries, or even, more broadly, for a range of other similar types of information systems. Please give a list of other types of information systems where DSNs might be constructed. For each, discuss how such construction might occur, and what benefits are likely to accrue. What are the limits to such construction, i.e., what is the scope of applicability of DSNs?

3.8 DSNs change over time. Please develop an incremental algorithm for DSN update. Describe its computational complexity, considering both time and space.

3.9 Graph partitioning and topic modeling are given as techniques related to DSNs. Should one partition first and then model the topics for the partitions? Are there other approaches? Would it be efficient to somehow integrate graph partitioning and topic modeling, e.g., by clustering around the key important topic titles? Could a taxonomy or ontology or category system be useful to help with all this, e.g., the ACM Category System or the Computing Ontology? How might that work?

3.10 Seonho Kim's doctoral work which utilizes implicit rating data to demonstrate the effectiveness of implicit rating data in characterizing users, user communities, and usage trends of digital libraries, relates to this chapter. How might that be extended based on the discussion in the chapter? (Seonho Kim, "Visualizing Users, User Communities, and Usage Trends in Complex Information Systems Using Implicit Rating Data," May 2008, Ph.D. dissertation, http://scholar.lib.vt.edu/theses/available/etd-04252008-122316/.)

3.11 Assuming that DSNs are shown to be helpful for AlgoViz, how might the user interface for the system be enhanced to use the resulting information?

3.12 How can DSN-type approaches scale up? Can they be used on the entire WWW, by companies like Google? What challenges would need to be addressed? What benefits might accrue?

3.13 Vannevar Bush spoke of trails, so one researcher or learner could help others with similar interests. How can the ideas of this chapter be extended if what people want is not just to learn about a single educational resource, but rather to learn about a pedagogically useful path through a set of resources? (Bush, Vannevar (July 1945). "As We May Think". *The Atlantic Monthly*, 176: 101-108. http://www.theatlantic.com/magazine/archive/1945/07/as-we-may-think/303881/)

CHAPTER 4

eScience and Simulation Digital Libraries

Jonathan P. Leidig, Spencer Lee, and Sung Hee Park

Abstract

Digital libraries have historically been used in publication, cultural heritage, and document contexts. Recent trends in scientific fields (e.g., toward eScience) have provided impetus towards the generation of scientific digital libraries. Content producers such as high energy physics instruments and high performance computing simulation systems generate continuous streams of content at a large scale. Research groups in scientific fields require management of summarized datasets, experimentation environments, and findings. Applications from bioinformatics, scientific algorithms, and modeling and simulation contexts provide a representative sample associated with these research groups. Formal definitions of content, users, user requirements, generic services, and science-specific services are produced for each context. The definitions are used to evaluate the coverage and performance of services; provide interoperability between content, systems, and services; and serve as a basis for a service registry. Three digital library implementations serve as case studies from the contexts.

4.1 INTRODUCTION

Scientists and research organizations produce enormous quantities of digital content through experimentation. Sensors and instruments produce continuous streams of data, often formatted into collections composed of thousands of files. Large-scale scientific applications executed on high-performance computing resources currently produce several petabytes of output for single experiments (e.g., climate modeling and bioinformatics). The above mentioned organizations are comprised of computer scientists, mathematicians, physicists, statisticians, and multiple domain experts. Scientific research groups rarely have expertise or collaborators in the information sciences, yet managing large quantities of scientific content is increasingly being identified as a problem by content producers. Unfortunately, current practices for many of the largest data-producing applications existing in academia and national laboratories ignore automating the management of content and metadata. In many cases, the only datasets archived are input configuration files and the only metadata tracked is related to application profiling in order to improve the scheduling and performance of computing resources (e.g., expected memory and computation resources required by an important application).

A new class of digital libraries are needed to support scientific research. Accordingly, a bioinformatics, scientific, and simulation supporting digital library (SimDL) motivates the formalization of scientific DLs. Due to the size of scientific datasets, collaborator access, and restricted ownership, actual data must be stored in a distributed fashion. A scientific DL may be used to federate multiple data storage systems using metadata in locating and retrieving individual datasets. Active, parallel efforts exist in developing linked data approaches. Federation across multiple domains, production systems, and research groups requires ontologies or domain models in order to describe content using appropriate context-specific metadata. A scientific digital library also requires connections to external components in an infrastructure. Research environments commonly include user interfaces, high-performance computing resources, instruments or simulation systems, analyses, visualizations, and data mining components. Content collections may be formed at each stage of an experimental workflow. A simulation workflow might have collections of simulation models, underlying datasets, input configurations, simulation results, result summaries, analysis results, visualizations, human-drawn conclusions, and publications.

Services for managing scientific content require high degrees of automation. The first step in this process begins with assistance in human-intensive development of metadata description sets (schemas) and description of infrastructural workflows. An ideal DL system would next automatically capture content as it is produced in each stage of the experimentation workflow. Metadata values from each object may be extracted and indexed. Traditional similarity measures are ineffective in ranking and searching scientific content due to a lack of full-text and the presence of numeric content. Curation services are needed to archive or remove content from system storage. Communication brokers are required to transfer content to and from other infrastructure components. Additional services are needed for specific functionality required by individual user roles, as described in Section 4.3.

Previous digital library efforts have been insufficient in automating typical experimentation workflows and supporting scientific content. Novel formalisms and service implementations demonstrate the opportunity to modify traditional DLs to efficiently support science. This chapter will use concrete examples motivated by computational epidemiology systems, fingerprint analysis research, and modeling and simulation of extremely large networks. These examples are representative of bioinformatics, science, and simulation applications.

4.2 RELATED WORK

Scientific data management practices have been a major focus for eScience and cyberinfrastructure research. Scientific data management is carried out in a variety of fields including earthquake simulation repositories [129], embedded sensor network DLs [37], NASA NVO,[1] community earth systems [72], D4Science II [147], mathematical-based retrieval [268], chemistry systems [156], national research data plans [131], and science portals [181].

Traditional workflow management systems are not tailored for simulation workflows. Standard workflow systems include Kepler [161], Taverna [188], Triana [167], and Pegasus [69]. Computational epidemiology workflows build upon model design and software implementation by model developers. Additional workflow stages include study design, input configuration design, simulation execution, result summarization, analysis execution, analyses gathering, publication, and policy decision making by public health researchers. This workflow may be defined in an ontology and minimal set of SimDL services. In other infrastructures, SimDL might interface with standard workflow systems instead of static, ontology described workflows.

Currently, there are few deployable digital libraries for research-based research institutions. Off-the-shelf digital libraries lack a means of communicating specifically with cyberinfrastructure components, provisioning numeric-focused services, automatically constructing metadata records, supporting simulation tasks, and allowing federation across simulation infrastructures, software models, and model versions.

4.3 FORMALIZATION

Formalisms defined in the 5S framework expose the differences in science-supporting DLs and traditional full-text or digital humanities-supporting DLs. Common services appearing in both of these classes of digital libraries have been defined in previous books in this series, and the formal definitions are reused here where possible. This class of simulation-supporting digital libraries is formalized through a compilation of additional user, content, and services definitions.

Efforts to define digital libraries have progressed towards digital library reference models [4, 101]. The early 5S framework consisted of formal descriptions of core DL functionality. It has since been extended through the addition of subsequent definitions tailored to describe aspects of digital libraries within a variety of domains. Common DL services include indexing, searching, and browsing content as well as query and annotation processes [101]. Definitions of new services or aspects to DLs may build on top of existing definitions, and producing formal descriptions of digital libraries is facilitated through reuse of the existing set of definitions.

SimDL is used here as a representative of the class of DL software that aims to support scientific research. Computational scientific domains outside of public health and bioinformatics will require variations of these content and service descriptions. Observations 1-3 below underlie

1. see www.us-vo.org

the reasoning for expending efforts in formally describing the foundation for eScience-supporting DLs [144].

Observation 1. DLs can provide interoperability through UI generation, infrastructure functionality, and managing experiments.

Observation 2. Formal descriptions of research and scientific content, services, and users can fully characterize this class of DLs.

Observation 3. Formal descriptions of DL components and functionality may be leveraged to produce and deploy DL instances and services with the stated capabilities.

The following set of 5S extending definitions describe the content, functionality, and services of a scientific experiment supporting DL instance.

4.3.1 WORKFLOWS, CONTENT, AND ONTOLOGIES DEFINITIONS

Workflow of Models

A simulation experiment workflow requires simulation models and software implementations of the model. Services support tasks including input configuration generation, model execution, result harvesting, analysis execution, analysis harvesting, human-intensive review, and publication or documentation. This workflow can be described in an ontology and modified for alternative workflows. As an example, data mining of a corpus of results will include the composition of result harvesting, analysis, and human-intensive review.

Workflow of Content

Content definitions build upon the set of previous 5S definitions (i.e., handles, streams, structures, digital objects, complex objects, and annotations) [144].

Definition 4.1 A *schema* is a digital object of tuple $sch = (h, sm, S)$, where

1. $h \in H$, where H is a set of universally unique handles (labels);
2. sm is a stream; and
3. S is a structure that composes the schema into a specific format (e.g., XSD structure of elements and attributes of restricted values).

Definition 4.2 An *input configuration* specification matching a schema is a tuple $icfg = (h, sm, ELE, ATT)$, where

1. ELE is a set of XSD elements; and
2. ATT is a set of XSD attribute values for an element ELE_i.

Definition 4.3 A *sub-configuration*, a subset of an input configuration, is a tuple $sub - icfg = (h, sm, icfg, ELE, ATT)$, where:

1. $icfg$ conforms to a schema and $icfg \supseteq sub - icfg$;
2. ELE is a set of elements where $ELE \subseteq icfg$'s ELE; and
3. ATT is a set of attribute values for an element in ELE.

Definition 4.4 *Analysis* of a set of experiments is a complex object consisting of textual or numeric documents and images (e.g., plots and graphs) and is defined as a tuple $ana = (h, SCDO = DO \cup SM, S, icfg)$, where

1. $DO = do_1, do_2, \ldots, do_n$, where do_i is a digital object;
2. $SM = sm_1, sm_2, \ldots, sm_n$ is a set of streams;
3. S is a structure that composes the complex object cdo into its parts in $SCDO$; and
4. $icfg$ is the input configuration and one-to-one mapping to a raw dataset.

Definition 4.5 An *experiment* is a complex object consisting of the full range of information and sub-documents related to a specific replication of an investigatory process within a domain and is defined as a tuple $exp = (h, SM, sch, icfg, ana, D, A)$, where:

1. $D = d_1, d_2, \ldots, d_n$ a set of additional documents, e.g., summary or publication; and
2. $A = an_1, an_2, \ldots, an_n$ a set of annotations describing the overall experiment and individual digital documents.

See Figure 4.1 for an Open Provenance Model representation overview of the preceding definitions [182]. Provenance investigations follow directly from definitions of the structured workflow

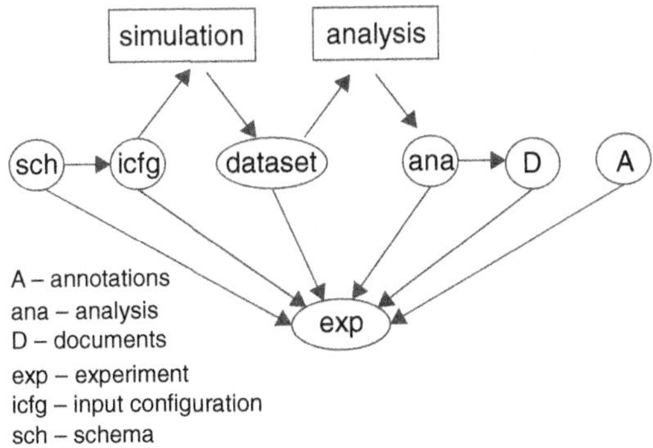

FIGURE 4.1: Context-specific simulation-based digital object provenance [144].

of scientific studies and simulation experiments. A digital library's presentation of an entire provenance stream allows claims to be supported, organizes the body of previous work, and allows data mining of simulation collections.

Linking heterogeneous collections is accomplished by leveraging the one-to-one mapping between sets of items produced by each experimentation stage. Model schemas allow digital library services to make use of contextual information, e.g., query model parameters in search functions. In epidemiology, connecting non-standardized models requires human-intensive collaboration between model builders and falls outside of SimDL's initial scope of automated services. Interoperability will eventually be useful in testing hypotheses across semantically linked systems, models, and datasets from different groups.

Domain Ontologies

eScience DLs may utilize several categories of ontologies. Simulation experimentation ontologies model a workflow of tasks. This category of ontology may be used by an infrastructure to identify and compose a sequence of the minimal set of services to support a workflow. An example workflow might consist of producing validated input configurations according to a model schema, submitting simulation requests, running a simulation model, capturing results, running standard analyses, and capturing analyses results. Model describing ontologies contain the logic used by DL services for tailoring towards specific simulation contexts. Another category of ontologies, a metaontology, could potentially use semantics to link related model describing ontologies through term harmonization and organization. While specific DLs have been constructed for arbitrary scientific domains, DL practices currently lack a methodology for customizing services at the granularity of individual simulation models. Domain ontologies in standardized formats have the potential to customize generic eScience services for specific domains.

Ontology development for a scientific domain is a significant, complex undertaking involving multiple experts. The human-intensive developmental process is eased by an ontology pre-processing generation service. An ontology generation service can assist in this process by parsing sample structured simulation content, e.g., input and output files, and suggesting potential ontology terms to a domain expert modeler. The domain expert then may revise the ontology and provide a URL namespace for each term's description. Aggregating domain ontologies from multiple simulation models is conducted through services for graphical harmonization of semantically related terms.

Domain ontologies may be used to tailor services within a model-independent framework. As presented in [145], domain ontologies may be used to expose simulation parameters in generic interfaces, organize content, and provide domain-specific metadata. SimDL offers a pre-processing ontology service to assist in the generation of domain-specific metadata description sets. These metadata schemas are used to guide the automatic production of searchable metadata records for simulation content. Input and output files are parsed with document-specific metadata extraction functions to produce metadata records as defined by document-specific model ontologies.

Inclusion of domain terms, when defined in appropriate URL namespaces, allows for customization of services while preserving the generality of service software. Generic user interfaces (UIs) to search, browse, and acquire inputs to new simulation models may make use of UI services to parse a model-specific input-file ontology. Interoperability is provided within a DL by encapsulating domain-specific information in ontologies and constructing generic DL services. User studies are needed to evaluate the performance of ontology generation tools and ontology-using generic services.

Model ontologies may be used to generate metadata schemas for digital objects related to the simulation model. Support for domain specific services, such as semantic searching between models, may be tailored through ontologies that describe individual simulation applications and ontologies aggregated to the domain level. We have developed a semi-automatic process for generating model ontologies based on the structured inputs and outputs of the simulation software. This process leverages model-ontologies for organizing storage, presenting a model-specific interface to users, and providing model-specific content discovery [145]. The ontologies, at various levels of domain and model granularity, are envisioned as ideal mechanisms to customize services, e.g., eScience model-specific search.

Scientific Images, Plots, and Graphs

Scientific digital libraries have been applied by academic institutions in fields such as geology, athletics, and biometry [194]. Fingerprint-based biometry motivates the following discussion on scientific multimedia.

The FBI's Integrated Automated Fingerprint Identification System (IAFIS) is a large fingerprint management system, supporting search capabilities against both latent and ten prints, storing electronic images, and electronically exchanging fingerprints. The Universal Latent Workstation (ULW) is the first latent workstation supporting interoperability and sharing latent identification services with local and state authorities and IAFIS, all with a single encoding. However, it does not support a series of digital library services for experiment setting, distorting, plotting, and visualizing. Previous work also supported scientific communities in a Web-based integration framework [260]. Fingerprint analysis has been challenged by various distortions such as merged prints, pressured impressions, humidity on fingertips, partial prints, or simultaneous prints. Distortions are likely to affect minutia extraction quality, ridge tracing quality, matching scores, and image quality. The Analysis, Comparison, Evaluation and Verification (ACE-V) and Scientific Working Group on Friction Ridge Analysis, Study and Technology (SWGFAST) groups (see swgfast.org) have worked on fingerprint analysis. [189] proposed a multiscale directional operator and morphological tools for reconnecting broken ridges in fingerprint images. [117] proposed singular point detection.

From the object perspective in very large digital libraries, [138] proposed a solution to integrate four different very-large fingerprint digital libraries. A proposed compound object (CO) scheme uses the 5S formal framework to model different types of objects found in those DLs, allowing uniform use in an integrated DL. Our work is focused on designing a DL framework, from a services perspective, to deliver analytical results of an experiment that integrates related services designed by different researchers. Formal definitions of scientific content and workflows provides a potential basis for service definitions in case studies.

4.3.2 USER ROLE AND TASK DEFINITIONS

User Modeling

Content, user, and task definitions for user roles informally describe the necessary services in a DL [144]. Communities form and maintain inter-community relationships through activities as described through a set of community-specific digital library scenarios.

Tool builders define a proposed DL; locate and reuse existing components; generate components; deploy instances; integrate with a simulation or digitized experimentation infrastructure.

DL administrators set data management policies; clean datasets; curate content; manage access; evaluate components.

Related systems (non-human agents within a community) submit and retrieve content with experimentation applications and high-performance computing architectures; analyze the submission and retrieval with analyst oriented software; validate inputs.

Study designers generate model schemas and transform updated versions; contribute input configurations; utilize sub-configurations; validate configurations; submit studies for execution; monitor experiments.

Analysts submit analysis requests; view automated and requested analyses.

Annotators add annotations (e.g., notes, footnotes, comments, tags) on streams of content.

Explorers search collections and experiment streams of documents.

User Collaboration and Cooperation

Simulation digital libraries support typical user communities as well as previously undefined communities (e.g., study designers, analysts, and simulation and analysis brokers).

The formal definitions for experiment-related DLs provide tool builders of proposed digital libraries a mechanism for collecting requirements, describing the desired DL, identifying sets of reusable components from a well described existing component pool, and guiding development of customized functions.

Collaborations between computational epidemiology institutes have identified the need for SimDL. SimDL aims to provide a generic digital library generating framework. The use of schemas allows SimDL to support simulation applications for domains and contexts that have structured input requirements and experiment launching brokers. Non-simulation scientific content also may be handled by SimDL instances sans the execution component (e.g., wet labs or instruments producing digital data points along with environmental input conditions).

SimDL was designed out of a need to automate the management of information produced by multiple simulation applications. Tool builders desired automated deployment of a basic DL instance and low continued maintenance effort. The management of scientific data requires policy decisions for data preservation, curation, and distribution. Shared access to a digital library hosted by an institution allows experts to collaborate, communicate, cooperate, and coordinate research efforts. The automation of conducting simulation studies is accomplished by the integration of SimDL into a simulation infrastructure. Until scientific digital libraries become mainstream in the simulation community, DLs will likely continue to be integrated into existing systems. Customization of the simulation-launching component may be required to transmit inputs to simulation software (e.g., transmitting XML input files to a waiting computation request broker). The generic user interface, shown in Figure 4.2, uses managed SimDL content to display widgets and content appropriate to a given simulation application.

Through SimDL, various types of users can interact in one place. Multiple experts are required to conduct complex simulation-based research. Similarly, multiple user roles exist for simulation-based digital libraries which support collaboration, participation, and privacy as defined in [123]. Collaboration is assisted by sharing content produced from complex tasks performed by users at different stages of the experimentation process. Although the submission of simulation results to predefined analysis may be automated, participation from users is required to launch new simulations, perform customized analyses, draw conclusions, and annotate streams of content. Practical consideration may restrict the number and allocations of users with a simulation launching role to reduce the stress on computational and data storage resources. Most user roles interact with a digital library's content and have the ability to interact with schemas and content across many simulation applications, domains, and contexts within a single, generic interface. By selecting tabs in a DL UI, users with a particular role may transition to another role (e.g., study designers switching to analysts when viewing simulation results).

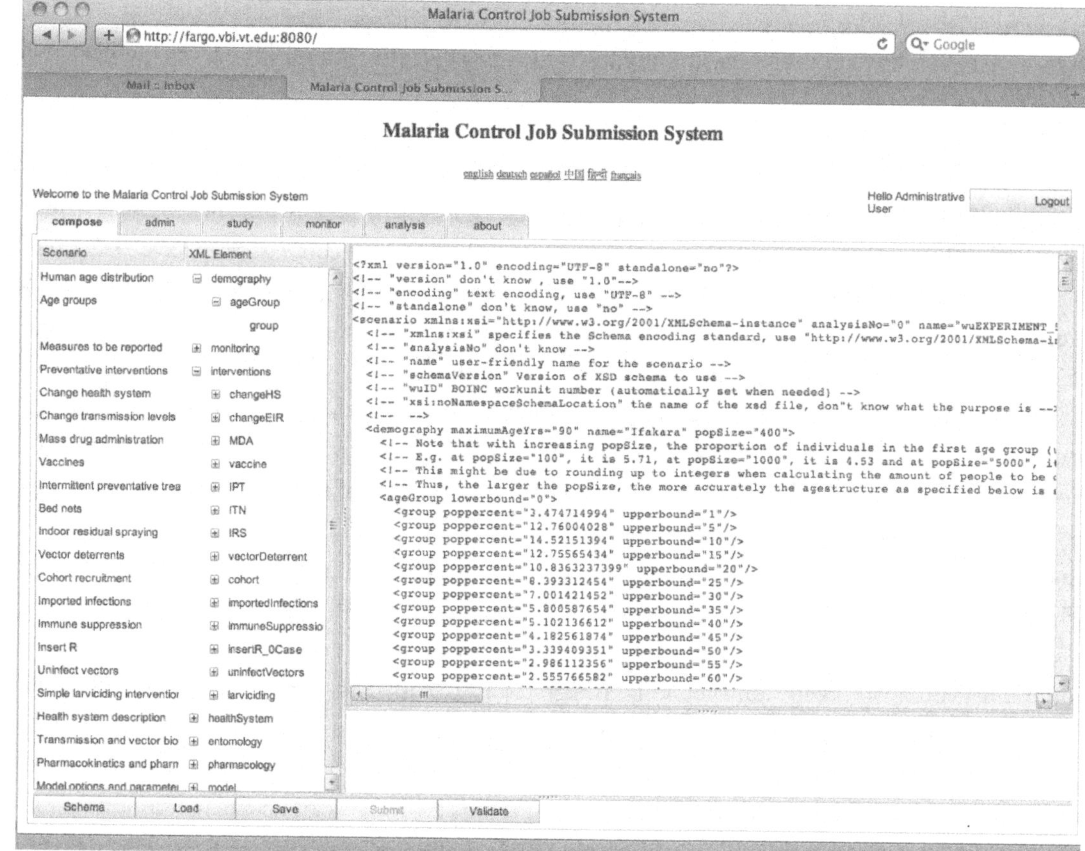

FIGURE 4.2: SimDL's automated, generic Web UI snapshot displaying a model's schema. The left pane displays an interactive schema containing the parameters to a simulation system. The right pane displays modifiable and archived input configurations.

A standardized DL generation framework, e.g., SimDL, provides automated services to support each of the following societies. Tool builders are provided with formally defined DL software. The use of schemas automates generic UI generation, database mapping, simulation launching, and collection management processes. Human involvement consists of developing schemas for a model and contributing the schemas to a schema collection. For study designers, the digital library reduces the complexity of launching and analyzing simulations. Domain experts (e.g., studying mosquito vectors or population demographics) contribute high-quality sets of input parameters to be reused by users with less knowledge of an epidemiological model. The designer may share and reuse existing sub-configurations, submit simulation requests, and use data management services. Analysts are able to retrieve datasets and summaries along with the input conditions from which the results are derived by following provenance links. Automated tasks for analysts include the generation of plots and summary statistics. Explorers may discover existing content or identify a lack of previous effort in a segment of the simulation system's multi-dimensional input space.

4.3.3 SERVICE DEFINITIONS

Digital libraries and software packages are heterogeneous in the provision of services. The DL community benefits from formal definitions of digital libraries along with their services. Formal definitions of scientific content allows the development of services for discovery, reuse, and provenance investigations. Simulation related content forms a chain of staged data produced by successive steps in the experimental process. A minimal digital library for simulation infrastructure must track provenance, manage content, organize input and output files, support commonly used HPC systems, and integrate simulation models into a workflow.

Formal definitions provide a means of explicitly specifying the requirements for simulation-based services. Formal definitions allow for services to be identified within a service registry and reused in multiple DL implementations. Requirement gathering and software development may use formal definitions to guide these efforts. Definitions make it possible to prove or disprove sufficiency and completeness of services. With formal definitions of services, we envision a future registration system for simulation-specific services described by languages such as UDDI, OWL-S, and the 5S framework. A service registry would be useful in rapidly prototyping DL service layers that support science as described in [103, 119]. The following set of services form a minimal simulation supporting digital library. See Table 4.1 for an elaboration on the lower-level terms the service definitions build upon.

TABLE 4.1: Basic terms and definitions of 5S formalization [98]

Term	Definition	Term	Definition
DO_i, DO_j	digital objects $i, j \in C$	V	Vertex
C	a collection $\in$ $Coll$	Stm_i	$\Psi_{ij}.Dom$
$Coll$	a set of collections	$\Psi_{ij}.Dom$	V $\times$ Streams
stm_j	a stream	S^3	Streams $\cup$ Structures $\cup$ Spaces
st_j	a structure	tfr	$S^3\times$ Spaces
Ψ	V $\times$ Streams $\Rightarrow$ (N $\times$ N)	sp_j	a space j
St^2	a set of functions Ψ		

Discovery and Dissemination

Browsing scientific content is similar to browsing textual documents with the added assumption that documents will be displayed in a faceted design. SimDL has implemented faceted browsing for a clustered document space based on the simulation model source and the stage of the workflow producing each type of content as described by existing ontologies. Browsing requires as input an initial simulation facet, $anchor_f$, and potential links, $Hyptxt_j$. Browsing produces as output a set of digital objects, $\{do_i : i \in I\}$. The pre-condition for browsing is that the anchor must exist in the network of hyperlinks, $anchor \in Hyptxt_j$. The post-condition restricts the resulting digital objects to existing documents in the collection valid for $Hyptxt_j$, where $\exists C \in Coll : \{do_i : i \in I\} \subseteq C$.

Existing search functions are typically tailored for textual documents and extracted metadata. Simulation content requires search over numerical metadata and summarized content. Search implementations relying on text-based approaches, such as term frequencies, thesauri, dictionaries, stemming, and term co-occurrence, break down in scientific digital libraries. However, queries may be segmented into k Boolean clauses for numerical metadata terms. In this type of querying system implemented for SimDL, a similarity score between a document and query is provided by a weighted summation over the k clauses as presented in [145]. The formalism for scientific search is identical to full-text search as a query (q), collection (C_i), and index (I_{C_i}) are required to produce a set of weighted results, $\{(do_i, w_{qk}) : k \in K\}$. A detailed formal definition of the technical aspects used to implement a search service would be required to differentiate between search mechanisms.

Discovery mechanisms are aided by model-specific ontologies for browsing and model-specific search. Content from successive simulation workflow stages are derived from preceding stages. Results from browsing and searching at one stage are linked through unique identifiers to each item's provenance stream. SimDL requires data fusion between ontology-specific collections with an attached richly defined ontology in addition to typical fusion between institutional repositories. Input configuration retrieval is specifically used to examine the search space of existing studies and to reuse portions of an input configuration when designing new simulations. Search over output results yields datasets supporting data mining and customized analysis.

The experimentation workflow and model ontologies allow for guided browsing of each collection from a specific model version. Customized analyses, publications, and related documents may involve comparisons between datasets and models. Collections in the later stages of the experimental workflow retain provenance links back to underlying datasets and have a one-to-many mapping between collection and ontologies. Current versions of SimDL services and the generic UI provide suggested documents to users based on recent work and recommended content. The browsing design forces users to first select a model and stage of the experimental workflow for a faceted view of available documents.

Dissemination of scientific content consists of *exposing* content and providing the ability to *retrieve* specific content. *Exposing* is a composition of general services for *acquiring*, *cataloging*, *indexing* to support search functions, and *classifying* to support faceted browse functions. *Retrieval* consists of requesting a document, where $\exists C \in Coll : do_i \in C$; identifying handles for the requested document, $h_i = do_i$; and provision of the document as output, $\{do_i\}$. The pre- and post-conditions for *retrieval* are $\exists do_i, C : do_i \in C \wedge h_i = do_i$ and $do_i = h_i$, respectively. Exposing and retrieval are fully supported in our implementation of SimDL.

Matching and Searching

Algorithms for *matching* and *searching* scientific content are domain-specific. In fingerprinting, one algorithm attempts to use 3-, 6-, or 9-point triangles of high-quality minutiae locations to identify matches between two images due to the susceptibility of distortions [115]. This matching algorithm stems from attempts to reduce the effects of small distortions on the identification of minutiae location points and quality.

This search process can be defined as a *binary* operation service $f(do_i, do_j) = k, \ k \in R$, where a real number k is a similarity score.

Ranking

Search in SimDL is domain specific. Simple searching allows users to filter content based on exact matches to input configuration parameters, and metadata fields. Filtering involves selecting a schema and then metadata parameters of interest on which to filter. A novice user, desiring to reuse previous study designs, may use filtering to discover and reuse sub-configurations for a given model.

Ranked searches require the development of distance or similarity metrics (sm) and a ranking system. With scientific collections, searches may be conducted to discover the content produced by the steps of an entire complex experiment based on the characteristics of data from one particular stage. The goal of a user's search may be to discover a set of experiments that best fit given ranges. The user formulates a search query, q, of multiple clauses with Boolean logic. A clause, c_i, consists of a metadata parameter, a value, and clause descriptions (e.g., contains, equals, between). The disjunctive normal form clauses, are translated into a Boolean query and compared to documents in a collection. For a document, each clause's value, v_i, is evaluated to "1" or "0". Similarity scores for a document-query pair are produced by setting the total distance over k clauses as $sm(q, d_i) = \frac{\sum_{i=0}^{k} v_i}{k}$. The query may be customized by assigning a clause weight, w_i, for each of the query dimensions with a total clause weight of k. The total distance is then calculated as $sm(q, d_i) = \frac{\sum_{i=0}^{k} v_i * w_i}{k}$. Distance functions based on textual term frequencies are not as appropriate given the numeric metadata values for scientific data.

FIGURE 4.3: 5S graph of collaboration and related services.

Collaboration

Collaboration services consist of tasks supporting multiple researchers at various stages of the simulation workflow. Scientific collaboration is a composition of generic and simulation-specific services; see Figure 4.3. Collaboration consists of tasks for annotating, locating, rating, recommending, reviewing, and submitting content. Locating includes processes for user acquisition of content by browsing, searching, and retrieving. Submitting includes processes for indexing, managing, and disseminating content within a DL. *Collaboration* reuses generic services for annotating, rating, recommending, and reviewing; *locating* invokes simulation-specific services for browse, search, and retrieval; and *submitting* invokes generic services for indexing and disseminating. Generic versions of these services for text-based documents are defined in [98].

The experimentation workflow assists in collaboration within a simulation model's user community. In designing experiments, users share, reuse, and recommend portions of input configurations. In epidemiology, high quality population datasets are shared and reused. Novice users of a SimDL infrastructure might heavily reuse sub-configuration blocks produced by model experts. Advanced users, with detailed knowledge of a model, contribute by sharing detailed input sub-configurations. This approach encourages collaboration by experts (e.g., population modelers, disease modelers, entomologists, and public health officials). The provenance links between content stages allows researchers with different interests to contribute to the experimentation process. Researchers' efforts are concentrated on retrieving staged content and performing non-automated activities, e.g., custom analyses and publication efforts. As shown in Figure 4.4, SimDL's internal services make use of the collection structure that is organized through ontologies. SimDL's use of a generic interface provides a domain-free, model-exposing system.

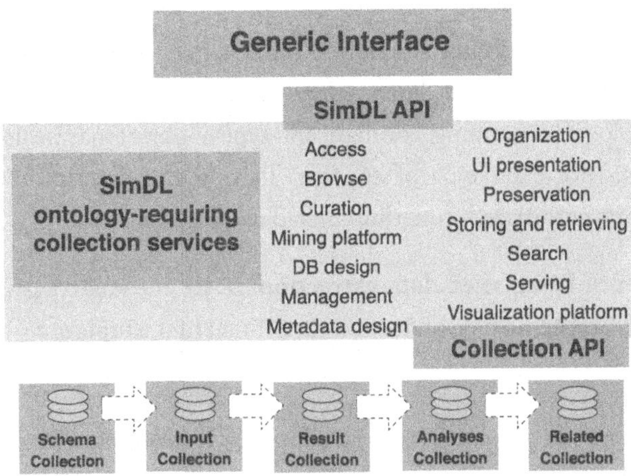

FIGURE 4.4: Ontology-requiring, model-independent services in SimDL.

Curation

Scientific content produced as output from HPC simulation systems scale to infeasible storage requirements. Large simulation result datasets may be summarized or reproduced as needed. Content curation is a means of establishing policies for content removal as well as arbitrary user-specified deletion and migration. Simulation-based $curation$ requires processes for identifying removable or reproducible documents, removing documents, and either removing the document's metadata or specifying a method of re-generating the document.

Definition 4.6 Curation is defined in eScience contexts as the process of archiving, preserving, and deleting content, representated in the tuple $cur = \{\{h_x, \ldots, h_y\}, q, C_i, I_{C_i}, c_s\}$.

As input, curation requires a set of document handles, $\{h_x, \ldots, h_y\}$; a filter or query for pre-defined curation, $\{q, C_i\}$; and a specification for the type of curation, c_s. Types of curation include archiving, preserving, transforming, migrating, soft deleting, and deleting. Specifications for documents that should remain indexed but physically removed for storage reclamation (soft deletion) additionally require input for a regeneration method consisting of a software executable, sw_i, and input configuration, $icfg$. The output of $curation$ is a modified collection, $C_i \Rightarrow C_i'$, and an altered index for the collection, $I_{C_i} \Rightarrow I_{C_i}'$. Pre-conditions for $curation$ are $\forall h_i \in \{h_x, \ldots, h_y\}$: $\exists do_i, C_i : do_i \in C_i \wedge h_i = do_i : C_i \in Coll$. Post-conditions for $curation$ are $none$ as removal criteria may exist without triggering document removal. SimDL's default policy is to maintain all information and relies on infrastructure designers to define processes for result summarization and dataset deletion.

Metadata Extraction

Content generated by the execution of simulation models must be automatically processed due to the volume of digital objects produced. Fortunately, metadata extraction need not require human-intensive efforts as ontologies describing a domain and type of object may be used to build a metadata description set (schema) for each type of content. Pairing the description set with a metadata extraction script supports automated, run-time metadata record harvesting.

Definition 4.7 eScience-based **metadata extraction** is an automated process for determining appropriate metadata for a specific type of document, defined in the tuple $me = \{ont, MD_s, ext_s, do_i, I_{do_i}\}$.

This process requires an ontology, ont; metadata description set, MD_s; extraction script, ext_s; and structured metadata harvested from a content source, do_i. The output of the extraction process is the inclusion of metadata regarding do_i in the collection index, I_{do_i}. The pre-conditions are an existing collection, $C_i \in Coll$, and script ext_s to extract content from do_i to I_{do_i} as described in MD_s. The post-condition is a modified collection index, $I \Rightarrow I'$. Metadata extraction in SimDL is handled by extraction scripts paired with a model ontology and is provided by simulation model developers. It is assumed that all input files or output files from a specific version of a simulation model may be processed by the same extraction script.

Provenance Linking

Simulation systems produce streams of content at multiple stages including model schemas, input configurations, results, analyses, documents, annotations, and publications. Preserving provenance information from findings and results is necessary for simulation researchers. Provenance is maintained by defining each type of content in a localized ontology and harvesting content collections for each stage of the experimentation process. Similar to indexing a document do_i in an index I_{do_i}, provenance information can be encapsulated in an index structure where two sets of documents, $\{do_i, \ldots, do_k\}$ and $\{do_j, \ldots, do_m\}$, are indexed in $P_{\{do_i,\ldots,do_k\},\{do_j,\ldots,do_m\}}$.

Definition 4.8 **Provenance streams** may be defined by the tuple $Prov = (h_{\{do_i,\ldots,do_k\}}, C_i, h_{\{do_j,\ldots,do_m\}}, C_j, rel)$, where:

1. $h_{\{do_i,\ldots,do_k\}}$ represents handles for a preceding set of digital objects;
2. C_i is a collection in $Coll$;
3. $h_{\{do_j,\ldots,do_m\}}$ represents handles for a successor set or type of digital objects;
4. C_j is a collection in $Coll$;
5. rel is a provenance stream classification, e.g., precedes, succeeds, yields, etc.; and
6. $\{do_i, \ldots, do_k\} \in C_i$; and $\{do_j, \ldots, do_m\} \in C_j$.

Workflows

SimDL interacts with infrastructure workflow management systems to communicate with other components within an infrastructure. This communication interface is used to archive and manage input files, output files, analyses, plots, and publications. In other infrastructures, SimDL could interface with bioinformatics workflow systems such as Kepler [161], Taverna [188], Triana [167], and Pegasus [69]. Note that these systems exist to compose multiple stages of a workflow where each stage manages inputs, executes software, and organizes results. SimDL extends traditional workflow system functionality by providing simulation-specific services. A set of model-independent APIs and brokers supports the integration of SimDL with a single computational platform (e.g., grid or cloud), local institutional infrastructure (e.g., internal platform), or large-scale coordinated cyberinfrastructure (e.g., multiple, distributed platforms).

Scientific Analysis and Experimentation

To support typical fingerprint algorithm analysis, a DL services model and instantiation were developed to combine scientific content and images with software. The workflow includes five domain-specific stages: image harvesting, distortion image generation, algorithm execution, result harvesting, and algorithm performance analysis. With this infrastructure, researchers may test how a fingerprint algorithm performs with synthetic, field-quality images. The framework allows content (i.e., fingerprint scans) to be combined with managed software (i.e., fingerprint analysis algorithms).

Image and Dataset Extraction

Image processing is a common function in scientific research due to analysis plots, graphs, and visualizations and encapsulated data, e.g., in microarray or sensor images. Informally, *distorting* and *image processing* take a digital object and produce a distorted version by changing its streams, structures, or structured streams. *Distorting/image processing* is a service defined as $f : do_i \Rightarrow do_j$, given a digital object do_i. The input and output structures for this service are do_i and do_j. The pre-condition and post-condition for this service are $\exists C \in Coll : do_i \in C$ and $\exists C \in Coll : do_j \in C$. A minutiae extraction algorithm is used to identify the locations and quality of major features, e.g., ridge bifurcation and termination. Other algorithms attempt to automatically trace the ridges in images resulting from smears, partial smudges, or high humidity. High humidity leads to an overly oily or wet print that causes ridges to run together. These feature extraction algorithms are examples of a broader service, *extracting*, that can be informally defined as "given a digital object, produce a descriptor from the object that represents the digital object". User input is required as stm_i and outputs are (st_j, Ψ_{ij}). The pre-condition and post-condition are $stm_i \in Streams$ and $st_j \in Structs; \Psi_{ij} \in St^2; stm_i \in \Psi_{ij}.Dom; st_j.V \in \Psi_{ij}.Dom$, respectively. [194] contains a description and formal definitions of algorithmic evaluation, visualization, and plotting services.

4.4 CASE STUDIES

The formally definitions, given above, for content, users, workflows, and services, have led to the design and implementation of SimDL. SimDL has been integrated within large scale cyberinfrastructure and in local institutions to manage applications including OpenMalaria [232], EpiSimdemics [19], EpiFast [26], and GaLib. SimDL is a digital library that meets the minimal requirements for the computational epidemiology simulation community [144].

4.4.1 COMPUTATIONAL EPIDEMIOLOGY

SimDL was designed to support experimentation with multiple simulation models, including [232] as presented in Figure 4.2, within a reusable model-independent design. Figure 4.2 displays the Web interface for gathering input documents to add to a SimDL instance for a set of malaria models. Simulation researchers develop simulation systems which are too complex for non-model developers to execute. The ontologies for a simulation model were found to aid in a model's UI presentation through the generic simulation study launching browser. A model-independent UI was built to expose disease models to researchers and provide access to input, result, study design, analysis, and document collections. Infrastructure brokers also were developed to support the UI in submitting input configurations, compliant with XML Schemas, to large computational systems. The SimDL services described in this chapter supported several public health institutes with content collection building, information satisfaction, and study execution workflows.

4.4.2 FINGERPRINT ALGORITHMS

A framework for fingerprint algorithm experiments was developed using SimDL with image processing services. The system consists of DL services to manage a distorted image collection, select and execute algorithms, and execute analyses. The analysis process allows a researcher to hold several parameters constant in order to parameterize algorithms by a careful selection of distortion parameters, e.g., x-axis translation, rotation, and skin plasticity.

The DL contains a collection of real-world fingerprint images. For selected images, a range of distorted images were generated along with a service for generating new distorted images, e.g., to match images likely to be found at crime scenes. An experiment was successfully designed, executed, and analyzed to determine the effects of image distortions such as humidity, x-translations, y-translations, rotations, and skin plasticity on minutia extraction. The system includes online collection images and a mechanism for selecting and composing service workflows. The Google chart API is utilized to present results of completed analysis tasks. A Web interface is used to browse the image collection, image information, distortion parameters used to generate specific images, extracted minutiae, and ridge information.

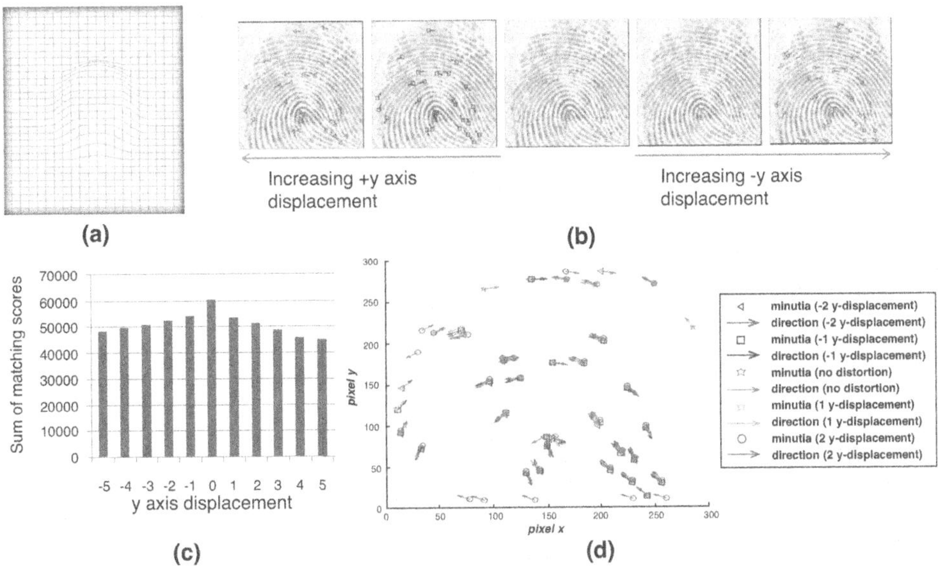

FIGURE 4.5: Example analyzing effects of y-axis displacements on matching quality: (a) skin distortion model selected; (b) distorted images; (c) histogram of y displacement vs. sum of matching scores; and (d) plotting of minutiae spatial distribution [194].

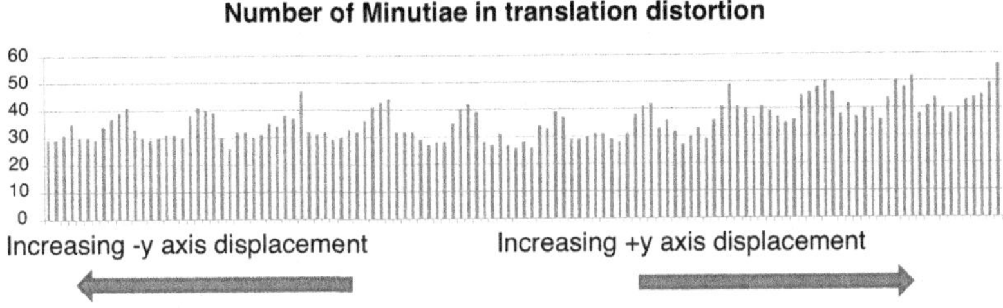

FIGURE 4.6: Number of minutiae in translation distortion [194].

The prototype system maintains a test collection of 137,785 high-resolution fingerprints, sourced from FVC2000 (3,520 images), FVC2002 (3,520 images), SD27 (516 images), self-collections (629 images), and distortion algorithms (129,600 images). An example experimental result yielded the following: (1) matching scores of minutia extraction modules MINDTCT and BOZORTH3, which were produced by the National Biometric Image Software, and the BIST matching algorithm (see Figure 4.5); (2) minutia counts of the MINDTCT algorithm (see Figure 4.6); (3) minutia reliability of MINDTCT algorithm (see Figures 4.7 and 4.8); and (4) improvement of existing schemas [138].

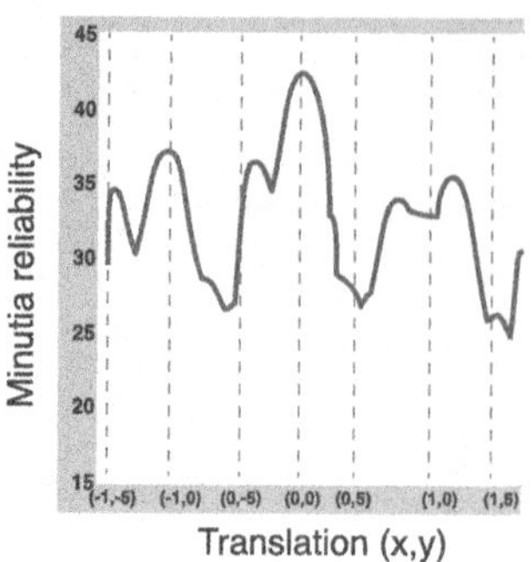

FIGURE 4.7: Average minutiae reliability: images distorted by translation [194].

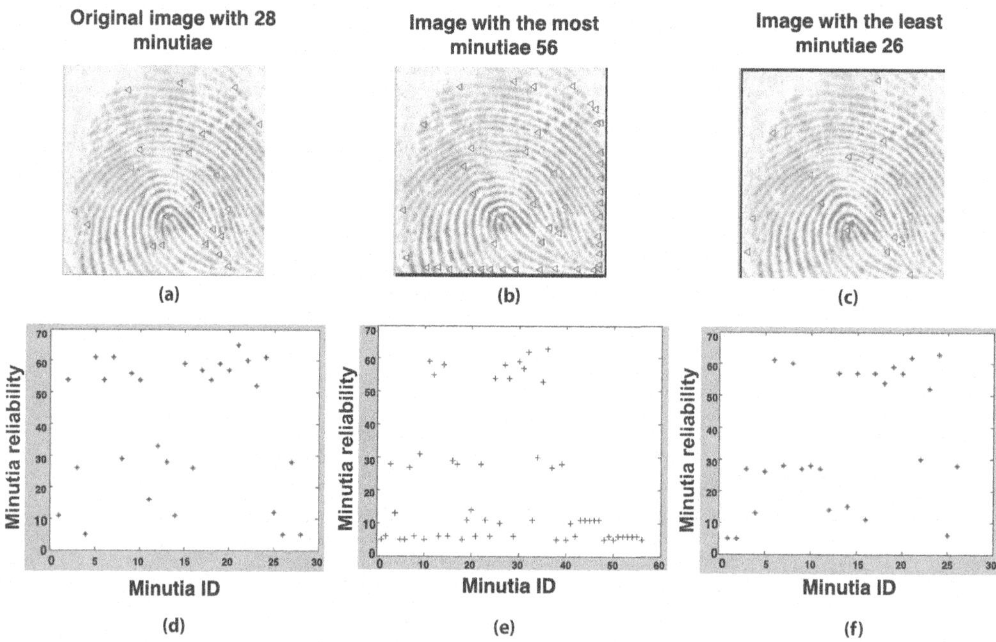

FIGURE 4.8: Spatial distributions of minutia reliability: (a) original image with 28 minutiae; images which increased (b) and decreased (c) the most in minutia points after distortion (56 and 26 minutiae, respectively); and (d)–(f) minutia reliability of each image [194].

4.4.3 LARGE-SCALE NETWORK SIMULATIONS

Network science utilizes large computational systems, scalable algorithms, and network graph datasets to study a variety of domains. The networks scale from small graphs with dozens of nodes to large social networks (e.g., city populations) with millions of nodes and billions of edges. A cyberinfrastructure for network science (CINET) was designed and developed to provide a computational platform for researchers, educators, and students to collaborate in executing network science simulations. One component of the infrastructure is a SimDL instance that maintains collections of large network graphs, software, study designs, and simulation results. These graphs are representative of a variety of domains such as co-authorship, communication, energy, social networks, and transportation. The digital library and its network science supporting services have been described in prior work [108].

4.5 SUMMARY

SimDL is a formalized representative of the broad class of eScience DLs. It serves as an example of an extensible platform for deploying digital libraries to manage scientific content. Formalisms of scientific content, users, and services assist in developing highly tailored DL software. These software toolkits would be of use in future software development reuse efforts. The formal definitions provide the minimal set of DL services required to support basic research in bioinformatics, scientific, and simulation-based domains. These services include metadata definition, schema generation, metadata extraction, collection management, workflows, and component communication. Services that exist for text collections often require modification to work effectively for scientific content. As examples, previous DL service algorithms may be adapted to annotate and recommend scientific studies; ask high level semantic search queries; query across federated instances; access and provide metadata; and provide a method for researcher communication within the DL system (e.g., message boards). Further application of eScience DLs is appropriate in other simulation domains, medical informatics, and scientific fields.

4.6 EXERCISES AND PROJECTS

4.1 Bioinformatics, scientific, and simulation applications: Summarize the digital library users, user roles, and service requirements you might expect for two of the following projects: earthquake simulation repositories [129], embedded sensor network DLs [37], community earth systems [72], mathematical-based retrieval [268], chemistry systems [156], fingerprints [169], and epidemiology [19].

4.2 Workflow applications: Install one of the following and determine the types of digital libraries it may be suited to support: Kepler [161], Taverna [188], Triana [167], and Pegasus [69].

4.3 Formalisms: Create your own formal definitions for the following digital objects: medical records, protein folding predictive simulations, and transportation modeling simulations. Include a text description that informally defines the domain-specific object.

4.4 Summarize how the curation requirements regarding documents in eScience differ from those of other domains. How suitable are the OAIS and DCC curation models for eScience digital objects?

4.5 Compare the types of services required by eScience applications and educational digital libraries.

4.6 How can the CBIR techniques discussed earlier be utilized in fingerprint-supporting services?

CHAPTER 5

Geospatial Information

Lin Tzy Li and Ricardo da Silva Torres

Abstract

Geographic information is part of our daily life. There is a huge amount of information about or related to geographic entities—documents, photos, and videos that are related to somewhere on Earth—and people are interested in locating them on maps. The use of map-based browser or geospatial search services is of great relevance in numerous digital libraries. The implementation of such services, however, demands the use of geocoded data collections. Geospatial information and the challenges to handle it have been for a long time the main concern of Geographic Information Systems (GIS). More recently, with the growth in the number of documents on the Web, the Geographic Information Retrieval (GIR) area emerged to deal with geospatial information found in documents typically handled by Information Retrieval (IR) and digital library techniques. Furthermore, Web multimedia data like images and videos have been extensively associated with geospatial information. That opened novel research opportunities related to the development of multimodal information retrieval approaches targeted to support queries based, at the same time, on textual, visual, and geospatial information.

In this chapter, we introduce the key concepts related to geospatial information, the use of geographical information retrieval techniques, and the use of multimodal retrieval approaches in geocoding tasks. We also present a case study in the context of the CTRnet digital library focused on geocoding multimedia documents aiming at the creation of map-based browsing services.

5.1 INTRODUCTION

Geographic information is characterized by the existence of an attribute which is related to a localization on Earth, for example a geographic coordinate, or a relationship to some other object whose geographic location is known. It might be a fully complete address (street name, number, and postal code) or even a single reference such as the airport name LaGuardia Airport which also indicates the name of the city where it is located (New York).

There is daily use of geographic information. Thus, it is not surprising to find a great amount of information on the Web about geographical entities and great interest in locating them on maps.

There are many devices with a GPS unit embedded, such as cellphones and cameras, that add location tags to photos and other user-published content like Twitter updates, Facebook posts, and other posts in social media. Accordingly, location information is commonly stored as metadata. On the Web, tools like Google Maps[1] and Google Earth[2] are very popular, and partially meet the needs of Web users for geospatial information. By using these tools, users can, for example, find an address on a map, look for directions from one place to another, find nearby points of interest (e.g., restaurants, coffee shops, museums), and list the nearby streets.

An example of a query that most existing *Information Retrieval* systems do not support is: "Which are the webpages of the cities which are neighbours of Blacksburg?" The reason is that spatial operators usually are supported by spatial databases, and those are not integrated with Web search systems. This kind of problem is tackled in the Geographic Information Retrieval (GIR) area, which improves upon information retrieval (IR) by adding handling of geographic information found in Web documents and queries.

In this chapter, we survey the GIR area. Some of the concepts are related to geospatial (or geographic) information. Others are related to multimodal retrieval, as it integrates with geographic information. Additional insights come from computer vision and content-based image retrieval. A key challenge is recognizing places based on image or video content [109, 130, 141, 163]. Thus, there is considerable extension beyond text analysis based only on metadata [254].

5.2 BASIC CONCEPTS

Fundamental concepts in this field are related to the world of geographic information, which is at the heart of a Geographic Information System (GIS).

A geographic entity/object (e.g., city, country, lake, etc.) can be located on Earth because of the use of a coordinate system. Given an (x, y) coordinate point, x representing a horizontal position and y a vertical position, we can distinguish from other points in the coordinate system space.

The most popular and ancient coordinate system to locate points on Earth is the geographic coordinate system; every point is at the intersection of an meridian (longitude) and a parallel (latitude). The coordinates are measured in degrees in relation to the center of the sphere that represents the Earth (Figure 5.1).

A meridian is an imaginary arc on the Earth's spherical surface that is drawn from the North Pole to the South Pole. The meridians are vertical lines of longitude. Longitude 0 degrees is called the Prime Meridian, which is usually the Greenwich Meridian, that passes through the Greenwich

1. http://maps.google.com/

2. http://www.google.com/earth/

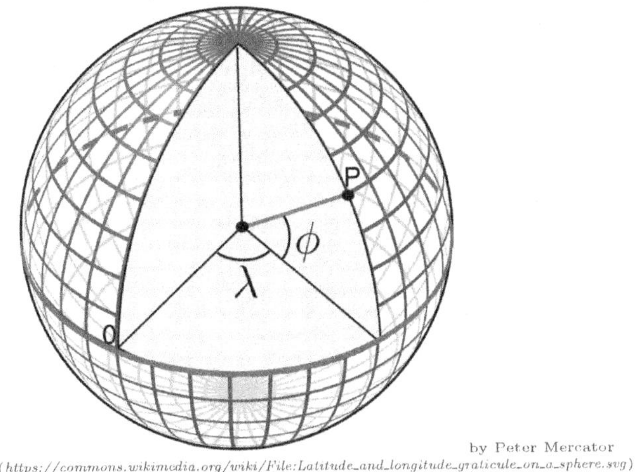

FIGURE 5.1: Cutaway view of Earth sphere: P is located at latitude $\phi°$ N and longitude $\lambda°$ E.

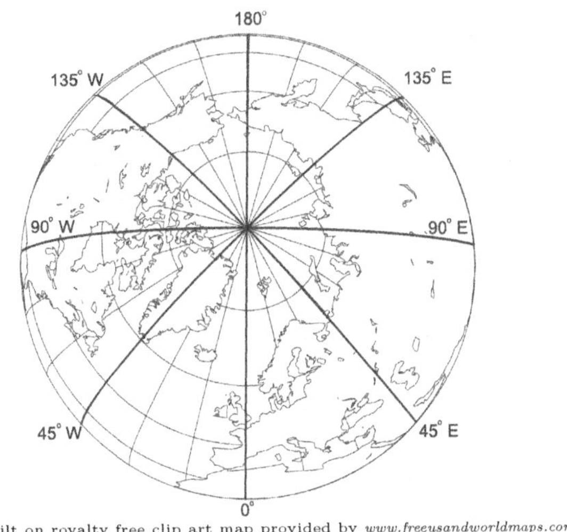

FIGURE 5.2: North Pole globe: longitude lines (radiuses) and latitude lines (concentric circles). Blue lines identify some longitude lines.

Observatory in England. To the east of the Prime Meridian there are 180° of longitude and to the west another 180°. The east and west directions can be replaced by positive and negative signs, respectively. For example, 105° W is equal to -105°. Figure 5.2 shows a schematic view from the North Pole to illustrate longitude lines and how they are drawn.

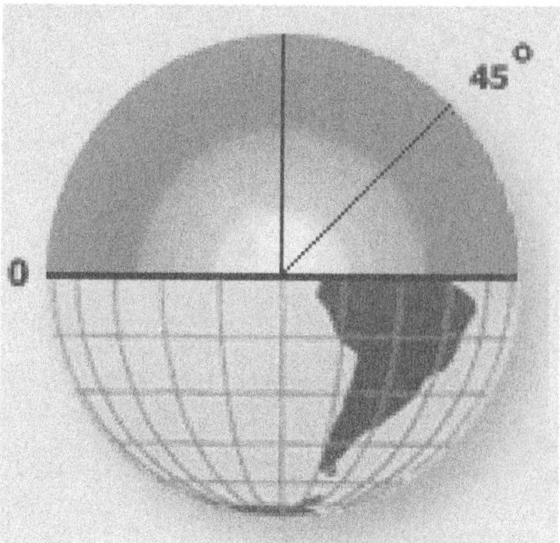

FIGURE 5.3: Cutaway view of Earth showing latitude 45° N, which is the angle measured from the center of the sphere. (nationalatlas.gov)

On the other hand, the Equator is an imaginary line around the Earth that divides it into two equal halves (north and south). It marks the 0 degree latitude line. All other latitude lines are parallel and equidistant from each other; thus the latitude lines are known as parallels. There are 90° of latitude to the north and to the south. Parallels above (north of) the Equator are represented as positive degrees and conversely those below (south) appear as negative degrees. For example, 45° N is equal to +45°. Figure 5.3 shows how latitude is measured.

5.2.1 RASTER AND VECTOR DATA

There are essentially two kinds of geographic data used in GIS.

Raster data. comes from satellite images or digital aerial photos, for example, and it is stored as a matrix of cells (or pixels) arranged in rows and columns. Each cell stores some data value which is the target information. Raster data will have an origin point that will serve as reference for other cells' relative position. Based on its raster coordinate system, a GIS is able to calculate the real-world location for every cell in a raster. This kind of data is useful for continuous data where contours or well-defined shapes are not necessary.

Vector data. represents geographic objects like rivers, city boundaries, and houses as basic geometric forms of lines, polygons, and points. As we have seen previously, geographic objects have coordinates (such as latitude and longitude) that associate them with a location on Earth. A point is defined by a coordinate, a line by two coordinates, and a polygon by three or more.

Examples of these data formats, overlaid together, are shown in Figure 5.4.

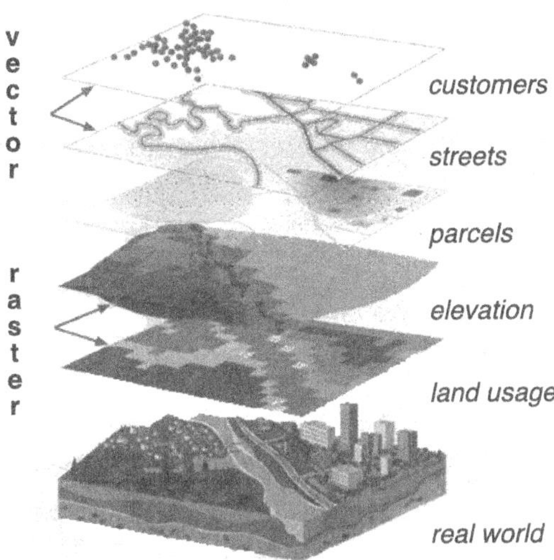

FIGURE 5.4: Overlaid vector and raster data. Source: ESRI.

Some current database management systems (DBMSs) support storing geographic vector data and provide special operators and functions to query them, e.g., MySQL and PostgreSQL (with PostGIS extension).

5.2.2 SPATIAL RELATIONSHIPS AND QUERIES

Spatial relationships refer to relative positions between objects in a space (geographically speaking, although clearly this also fits with the "Space" part of the 5S framework) and they can be classified [34] as follows.

Topological. This kind of relationship indicates connections between objects such as adjacent to, containing, or is contained, but it does not include measurement or direction. Egenhofer [75] classifies the topological relationships between two dimensional objects as: disjoint, meet, overlap, covers, contains, equal, covered by, and inside. Clementini et al. [57] summarize them as: disjoint, inside, touch, cross, and overlap (Figure 5.5).

Metric. This relationship expresses quantitative measurable attributes like area, distance, length, and perimeter.

Directional. This relationship is used to express orientation such as cardinal points (e.g., North, South, East, and West), as well as order or position like ahead, above, and under.

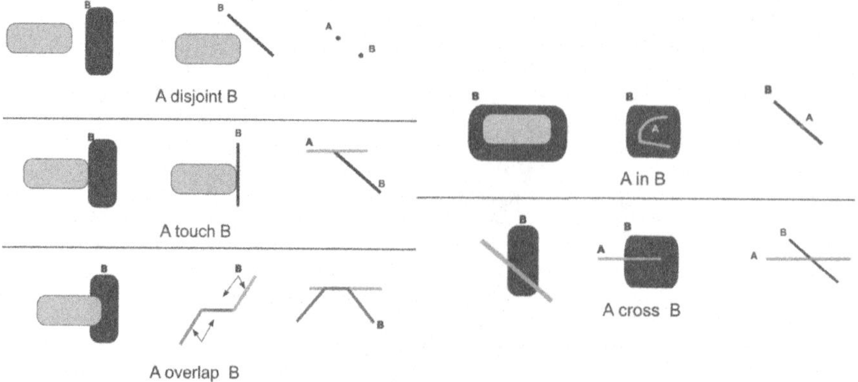

FIGURE 5.5: Examples of topographic relationship [46].

These concepts lead us to spatial queries, also known as geographic queries, which express spatial relationships between two objects in a very well defined space, either with or without geographic coordinates such as latitude and longitude. According to [142], spatial queries can be as follows.

About a given point. This uses a coordinate system, like "What can be found at the point given by the following latitude and longitude: 37.228, -80.423?"

About a region. This asks what has something inside it, e.g., "In which state or region is the Grand Canyon located?"

About distance and a buffer zone. This is illustrated by queries like "Which are the cities 50 miles from Blacksburg's boundaries?"

Path. This involves searching along a structured network comprised of connected lines, such as electric lines and networks, water or gas pipes, or transportation lines. Examples include the shortest path between two points in a network and even a more complicated query like "What is the fastest path from Blacksburg to Washington, D.C.?", which involves distinct variables such as distance, direction, and even time.

Multimedia. This is when a query requires a variety of information types (e.g., text, image, and geographic), e.g., "In which rivers can we find fishes similar to a given picture, and that are from the darter family?"

5.3 RELATED WORK

This chapter introduces related work on Geographic Information Retrieval, Multimodal Retrieval for Geographic Information, and how they are associated with initiatives concerning the creation of Digital Libraries.

5.3.1 GEOGRAPHIC INFORMATION RETRIEVAL

Geographical Information Retrieval (GIR) is an area concerned with challenges such as recognizing, querying, retrieving, and indexing geographical information. It combines research in database, human-computer interaction (HCI), geographic information systems (GIS), indexing, information retrieval (IR), and georeferenced information browsing [142], as well as visualization of information on maps. According to [127], GIR aims to improve information retrieval centered on geographic information in non-structured documents such as those found in the Web.

Two main concepts of this area are geoparsing and geocoding. Geoparsing is a process of recognizing references with locations inside documents, while ignoring false references (e.g., a place name that is also the name of an organization or person), while geocoding is a process to associate a document with some specific latitude and longitude based on locations recognized by geoparsing. Thus, geocoding consists of mapping a document to a location on Earth. For example, based on where its content refers to, we can assign a latitude and longitude to a document, so later a user can retrieve this document based on geographical queries (e.g.,"Give me all documents that refer to parks in the Blacksburg vicinity.").

In the following subsection, why geographic information on the Web matters is discussed, and a GIR architecture is presented. This will serve as a baseline to discuss the main concepts related to GIR—geoparsing and geocoding—as well as research challenges.

Geographic Information on the Web

As was introduced earlier, traditional search services are based on keyword matching and do not consider that keywords might represent geographical entities which are spatially related to each other. Yet, even though these relationships have not been explicitly used in a query, they are potentially relevant to users [126].

For example, typing "cities which are neighbors of Campinas" in Brazil into Google search will return webpages with the typed in terms (Figure 5.6). However, that query encompasses a geographic query (neighbors) meaning that all (ten) cities that share boundaries with Campinas (Figure 5.7), although not mentioned, should be returned in the result set too.

The difficulty in processing this kind of query comes from the need to combine traditional queries executed on Web search mechanisms with spatial operators usually implemented in spatial databases.

From 2002–2005, a project led by Cardiff University (UK) called SPIRIT—Spatially-Aware Information Retrieval on the Internet—aimed to develop a spatially-aware Web search engine. They tacked problems of assigning a footprint to webpages, indexing, searching, ranking, and also user interfaces for geographic queries and results [126, 210].

In [152], users were invited to use Web tools for performing tasks related to the search of geographic entities. All proposed tasks included at least one kind of spatial relationship. Obtained

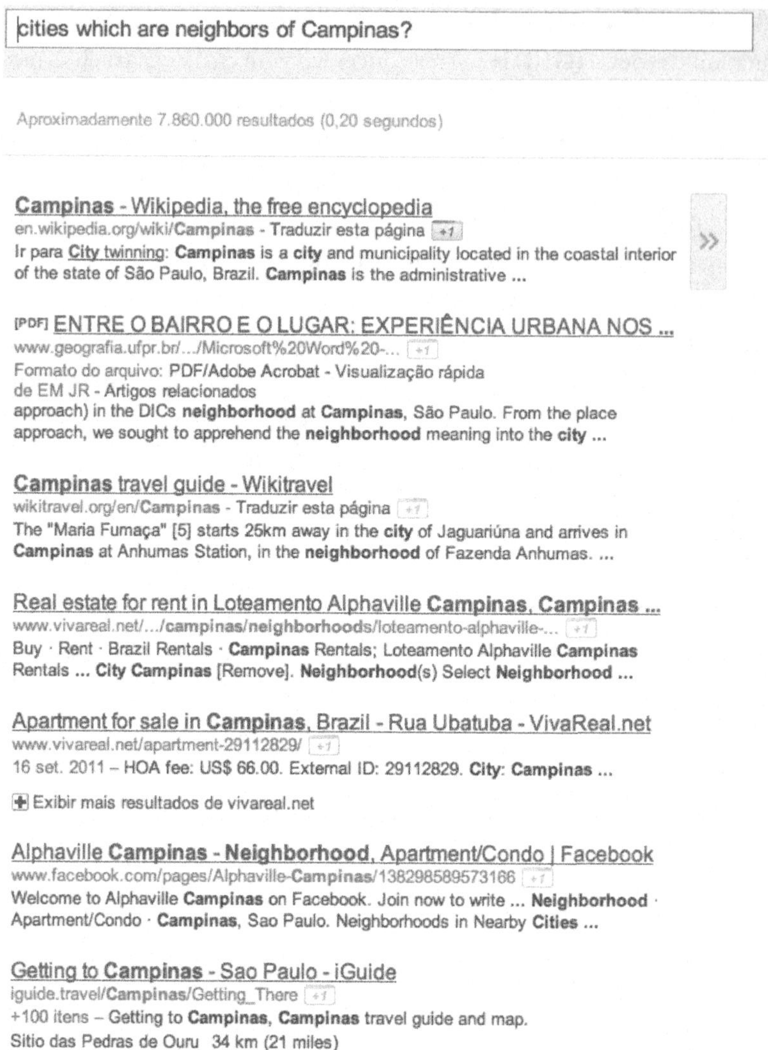

FIGURE 5.6: Google Search results for neighbors of Campinas, Brazil.

results indicate that: (a) there is a tendency of users to break down the geographic searches into two or more steps when using the current multi-purpose search tools; (b) the geographic relationship aspect of a spatial query on the Web is solved by users either inspecting visually the location on a Web map or by taking advantage of Web tools such as Wikipedia; and (c) geographic queries involving well-known or popular objects such as hotel locations in a city are solved easily by a single text-based search.

Vectorial map provided IBGE and loaded in QGIS.

FIGURE 5.7: Campinas neighborhood and cities within 50 km.

Let us take as an example one query used in that experiment: "Search for webpages of cities in the neighborhood of Curitiba, Brazil". To perform that task, users switched between keyword-based search, Web mapping, and encyclopedia tools.

It is not enough to send the city's name (e.g., Curitiba) and a term referring to a geographical relationship to a search tool, because it will just match the keywords with pages' textual contents. For those who are used to geographic queries, it is common to rewrite the query into a form which the search tools can use to retrieve relevant results.

To sum up, as a rule, addressing a complex geographical query was broken down into two main steps. Keeping in mind the example we mentioned earlier, in the first step, the user processes the geographical part of the query by using a keyword search Web tool or Web mapping tool. This step consists of, for example:

- using prior knowledge to associate a city with a region;
- visiting previously known websites (e.g., Wikipedia). From these webpages, users could find the cities nearby, or the distance between cities. In this case, users go first to Wikipedia to find the city of interest and then create a list of candidate cities;

- submitting other words to the search tool in order to return the list of cities. This is the case in which the user first searches using the phrase "Curitiba metropolitan cities" to get the list of cities in the Curitiba metropolitan area, thus resolving the part of the query that refers to Curitiba's neighborhood;
- using a map service to localize a city used as reference, visually inspecting a map, and manually creating a list of cities that satisfy the target geographical relationship. An example involves going first to a mapping tool like Google Earth or Google Maps, finding the city of interest (e.g., Curitiba), and then visually picking the neighboring cities.

Finally, the second step involves searching for each city listed in the first step by:

- submitting the city name as keyword to the search tool to find the webpage of that specific city;
- reaching the city page by using a previously known URL naming pattern (e.g., the URL of a city's home page in Brazil is formed by www.⟨*city name*⟩.⟨*acronym*⟩.gov.br, where ⟨*city name*⟩ is the city name and ⟨acronym⟩ is the acronym of its state. So for Curitiba, a city in the state of Paraná (PR), its URL is http://www.curitiba.pr.gov.br).

There were some cases where a user just relied on map tools, like Google Earth, that show the cities and their facilities locations (e.g., hotels and subway stations) on a map to answer the question posed by the task (e.g., "Barcelona's hotels which are near subway stations"). In fact, using these tools, the geographic relationship is resolved by the user, who infers and inspects it visually on the map. Therefore there is no automatic list; in this case the user is in charge of building the list manually.

Incorporating geographic relationships in Web searches is not supported yet; as seen in this study, they are mostly processed by the user first. This could be explained by their inherent complexity, which is worsened by their imprecision and subjectivity. Thus, some geo-related concepts like near or south might depend on the user's search context [128, 272].

For some specific objects (e.g., hotels and city names) and relationships, when geographic terms (e.g., near) can be found on some webpages, the use of current search tools is quite straightforward, as is illustrated by queries like: "webpages of Barcelona's hotels which are near to subway stations." Such success is explained by those objects' search popularity [113, 128, 221]; webpages that contain those keywords thus can be retrieved by popular keyword-based search tools.

The ideal Web search tool for geographic queries should be able to process the geographical relationships and retrieve all the relevant results on the Web that match the users' intention expressed by their query. This kind of query is common in a GIS (geographical information system) which works with structured data. Hence, there is need for investigation of strategies to integrate these technologies, so that Web queries that include this kind of feature can be easily processed, without

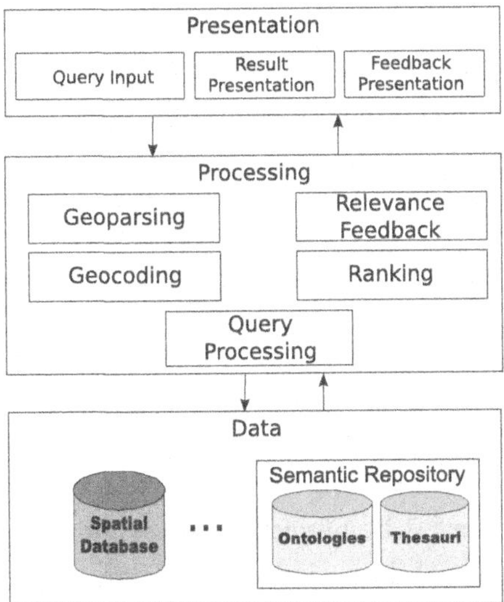

FIGURE 5.8: Architecture of a GIR system.

undue user frustration or effort. One perspective is that geocoding webpages can help, but the challenge is how to do that in light of the volume of data on the Web and the high level of ambiguity common in such queries.

GIR Architecture

As is shown in Figure 5.8, a GIR system can be divided into three layers: presentation, processing, and data. The main modules are as follows.

Presentation Layer

Query Input, Result Presentation, and Feedback Presentation. These modules are in charge of dealing with HCI: query input by the user, presentation of results returned by the system, and user feedback about the results. They forward data to lower-level modules aiming at improving obtained results.

Processing Layer

Geoparsing is a module responsible for recognizing references to geographic entities in a digital object and for disambiguating them based on their content, geo-ontologies [223], and semantic databases.

Geocoding is a module that takes care of associating appropriate geographic coordinates with a digital object, which can be one or more geographic points or even a geographic region.

Query processing is responsible for interpreting and processing the input query; besides, it handles subsequent interactions aiming to refine results.

Relevance feedback aims at making improvements in retrieval and/or ranking algorithms by taking into account user assessment of results previously returned. The objective is to return better results through one or a series of interactions.

Ranking is a module in charge of ordering the results according to an estimation of their relevance to the user query.

Data Layer

Semantic repositories. These store place names and define how they are organized and related to each other. The objective is to support geoparsing and geocoding tasks. The geographic knowledge can be represented by ontologies; these are called geo-ontologies [126, 223] or geographic ontologies [34]. More information about places can be found in gazetteers and/or thesauri, and even from previously geocoded webpages. A gazetteer is a dictionary of geographic names consisting of a name and its variants, that place's location, and its category (populated place, school, farm, hotel, lake, etc.). An example of a gazetteer is Geonames.[3] A thesaurus is a list of structured and defined terms formally organized and with concept relations clearly drawn [40], which is what distinguishes thesauri from gazetteers. For example, the *Getty Thesaurus of Geographic Names*[4] organizes places/location based on their spatial relation and administrative area, gives their geographic coordinates and all other names a place has, and supports places with similar names assisted by ontologies [256].

Spatial Database. In addition to what a regular database management system (DBMS) offers, a spatial database also stores and provides spatial operations and queries over stored geographic objects. These objects can be stored using points, lines, or polygons in a given coordinate system. Spatial indexes are built to later speed up spatial/geographic queries (Section 5.2.2). Examples of geographic objects that can be stored are: shapes representing boundaries of a state, city, or country; other shapes representing a specific area on Earth.

Geoparsing & Geocoding

Items in a collection can be associated with one or more regions on Earth, i.e., we can determine their *footprint* [91]. Jones [125, 126] defines **geocoding** as the act of associating a *footprint* with a geographic reference. Recognizing geographic references inside a document is called **geoparsing**, as we introduced previously.

---

3. http://www.geonames.org/.

4. http://www.getty.edu/research/tools/vocabularies/tgn/.

In GIR, a collection of documents that refer directly or indirectly to a place needs to have their footprint identified and thus be indexed spatially. That is, documents should be geoparsed and then geocoded.

Geoparsing should be able to identify and disambiguate a place name appearing in a document and rule out false references to it. It can be seen as a particular case of name entity recognition (NER), which identifies expressions in text and classifies them as person, event, organization, etc. [21].

However, there are challenges involved in recognizing place references and associating them with their coordinates [143, 256]. Examples include the following.

- Homonyms for places and persons. For example, New York is a city name in Brazil and the U.S.A., as well as a state in the U.S.A. Additionally, Luis Eduardo Magalhães is a Brazilian politician who also has an airport, square, and city named after him.
- Descriptive place names change according to the historical context, culture, and customs that are in place, when a textual form is produced. For example, locating "North of the Russian capital" on a map would be difficult because the location of the capital of Russia has changed several times.
- Names of places change over time. For example, St. Petersburg, once Russia's capital, was called Petrograd (1914–1924) and Leningrad (1924–1991).
- Geographic boundaries change over time. For example, Germany had different boundary over its history.
- Boundaries cannot always be clearly defined, for example in a conflict zone (e.g., Syrian-Turkish territory dispute).
- Names assigned to regions can refer to an area, rather than a well-defined place, e.g., Southern California, or the Andes (in South America).
- Different names may refer to the same geographic entity, whether by error, language variations, or the legal existence of more than one valid way of writing it. For example, both Peking and Beijing refer to the capital of China, and Deutchland is commonly used to refer to Germany.
- Ambiguities arise due to different ways to describe a place, e.g., pseudonyms or expressions used in a specific context. For example, St. Petersburg is called Piter by locals, while New York City is also referred to as the Big Apple. In Brazil the city of São Jose do Rio Preto, in São Paulo state, sometimes is called Rio Preto by locals, but, in another Brazilian state (Minas Gerais), Rio Preto is the official name of a different city.
- Names of famous buildings can lend their names to states; thus, New York is sometimes called the Empire State, after that tall building in New York City.

Campinas (Portuguese pronunciation: [kẽ'pines], *Plains*) is a city and municipality located in the coastal interior of the state of São Paulo, Brazil. Campinas is the administrative center of the meso-region of the same name, with 3,783,597 inhabitants as of the 2010 Census, consisting of 49 cities.

The municipal area of Campinas covers 795.667 square kilometres (307.209 sq mi). Campinas' population is 1,080,999 as of the 2010 IBGE Census;[1] while over 98.3% live in the urban region. The city's metropolitan area, as of 2000, contains nineteen cities and has a total population of 2.8 million people.

It is the third largest city in the state, after São Paulo and Guarulhos.The Viracopos International Airport connects Campinas with many Brazilian cities and also operates some international flights. The city is home to the State University of Campinas.

Contents [show]

Etymology [edit]

Campinas means *grass fields* in Portuguese and refers to its characteristic landscape, which originally comprised large stretches of dense subtropical forests (*mato grosso* or thick woods in Portuguese), mainly along the many rivers, interspersed with gently rolling hills covered by low-lying vegetation.

Campinas was also known as "Cidade das Andorinhas" (City of Swallows), because it was a favorite spot for these migratory birds, which flocked annually in enormous numbers to downtown Campinas. However, they almost disappeared around the 1950s, probably because the church and plaza where they used to roost were torn down. Campinas' official crest and flag has a picture of the mythical bird, the phoenix, because it was practically reborn after a devastating epidemic of yellow fever in the 1800s, which killed more than 25% of the city's inhabitants.

An inhabitant of Campinas is called a *campineiro*.

FIGURE 5.9: Geoparsing example: place names recognized in this extract of Wikipedia's page about Campinas (as of 11/03/2011).

- Indirect references, such as to a road, like the Blue Ridge Parkway, may bring to mind both a region and event, e.g., due to a scenic drive in southwest Virginia and northwest North Carolina.
- Imprecise references such as "100 km from Blacksburg" can refer to some point within 95 and 110 km. In another example, "South of Campinas" might include not just south, but also southeast and southwest locations.

Figure 5.9 illustrates an accurate geoparsing. The names highlighted should be identified when geoparsing is applied to the text shown. Figure 5.10, on the other hand, illustrates geoparsing with errors, i.e., both true and false references [125]. In this case, false geographic references include personal names (Smedes Yok, Jack London), business names (Darchester Hotel, York Properties) and common words that are also places (bath, battle, derby, over, well). A

JACK HAGEL, Staff Writer
Redevelopment of the World Trade Center site in New York is getting some input from a Raleigh real-estate maven.

York Properties President Smedes York was chairman of an Urban Land Institute panel at the World Trade Center and Lower Manhattan Summit last month.

The group heard presentations on how the area surrounding the site of the Sept. 11, 2001, terrorist attacks should be redeveloped. It suggested retail be a central focus for developers. The institute will issue a report based on the recommendations before the end of the year.

York was chairman of the Urban Land Institute, a Washington nonprofit organization, from 1989 to 1991. His dad, J.W. "Willie" York, joined the Urban Land Institute in 1947. That's where he met J.C. Nichols, the developer of Country Club Plaza in Kansas City, Mo. -- the center that inspired Willie York to build Raleigh's Cameron Village, the Southeast's first shopping center.

FIGURE 5.10: True and false references in geoparsing [125].

possible strategy to distinguish between false and true references is to look for patterns and context [125].

- For personal names, such as Jack London and Mr. York, the pattern is a first name or title followed by a location name.
- Business names like Paris Hotel have a location word preceded or followed by a business type.
- Detecting a spatial preposition helps validate a possible location; examples include: in, near, south of, outside, etc., as in "I lived in Blacksburg".
- A street name can be distinguished from a city (e.g., Oxford Street) by verifying if its pattern is a location name followed by a road type.

Some of the tools used in geoparsing and geocoding, to help to detect and disambiguate place references, are geo-ontologies [126], gazetteers, and thesauri. Even Wikipedia has been used to enrich the knowledge base for geoparsing [67]. Thus, places can be referenced using an urban address, postal code, or the area code of a phone number [35].

According to the earlier discussion of modules, geocoding is a process to associate a document/digital object with some specific latitude and longitude, based on location references recognized by geoparsing. In fact, a document can be associated with one or more geographic objects, which in turn can be represented using a point, line, or polygon. Therefore, it is better to define geocoding as a process to associate a digital object with one or more footprints instead of just a point on Earth.

As we observed in Figure 5.9, a set of place names can be recognized in a document. Therefore, one geocoding challenge is to determine which footprints should be associated with a given document. This often requires the disambiguation of locations [21]. As was illustrated above, often the same name is used for different geographic locations (referent ambiguity), or the same location is described by different names (reference ambiguity).

The geographic knowledge required for this task is provided by a geo-ontology, supporting structuring, representation, and storage. It includes all suitable data types: place name, place type (city, state, country, etc.), footprint, relation (e.g., containment, adjacency) to other place names, population, historic names and dates, activities, etc. Given a set of geoparsed names, the geocoding process finds the corresponding matches in the geo-ontology. Then, based on related information, a decision can be made regarding a location to contribute, along with a document footprint: keeping, merging, creating, or discarding. Related information could specify how two extracted locations in a document are spatially associated with each other: are they close to each other? Another type of related information refers to the definition of their closest common ancestral node (e.g., state, county, or country).

Consider an example borrowed from Batista et al. [21], where a document (D) is geoparsed, yielding the result: Lisboa and Santa Catarina. Then, the first step of geocoding, checking the geo-ontology, yields the following results (also highlighted in Figure 5.11):

(i) Lisboa is a municipality;

(ii) Lisboa is somewhere in the municipality of Monção;

(iii) Santa Catarina is a civil parish in the Lisboa municipality; and

(iv) Santa Catarina is a street in the Porto municipality.

Analyzing the results of the example above, the closest spatial relation is (i) and (iii) as depicted in Figure 5.11. In fact, there is a direct relation between (iii) and (i). Hence, the geocoding process can associate the footprint of (iii) with that document, if the aim is to capture the most specific scope.

However, sometimes in a DL, one might want to associate more than one footprint, in order to represent geographic concepts, for example associating it with the footprint of (i) or even broader scope like Portugal. This would ensure that the various possible scopes of a document are captured (geographic signature) [21].

Note also that Santa Catarina refers to a state in Brazil. But that geographic entity is not suitable as there are no exact matches for both Lisboa and Santa Catarina in its branch of the hierarchy.

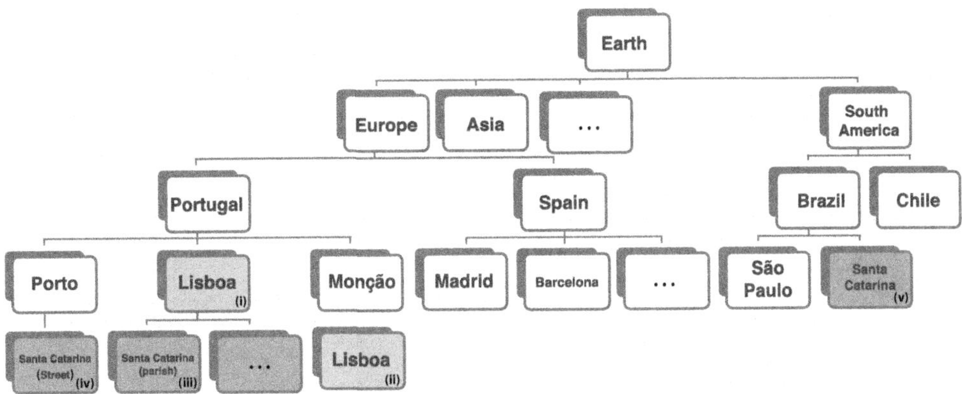

FIGURE 5.11: The hierarchical geographic concepts for Lisboa and Santa Catarina.

Research Challenges

Research opportunities are related to challenges in the presentation, processing, and data layers as shown in Figure 5.8. Regarding the presentation layer, key concerns relate to how humans can express their information needs through queries, and how they can browse through the results returned by a GIR system. In the processing layer, important challenges are related to the identification and elimination of place name ambiguity, and the design of effective (as well as efficient) algorithms: for search, result classification, and ranking. Finally, in the data layer, considering the Web as a huge data repository, inconsistent and unstructured data make it difficult to identify and geocode the documents that are found.

Presentation Layer

Early computer interfaces forced users to formulate structured queries, similar to what can be supported by a typical database query language (e.g., SQL). However, the majority of users lack knowledge and skill regarding proper use of such structured languages. As a result, they do not completely express their needs, and the retrieved information does not fulfill their expectations. Considering also that users have to express spatial notions in words, more complexity and indirection are added to this problem. Often, system results do not fulfill user expectations. All this leads to the question: Does a query need to be expressed only by words/terms?

The difficulty in designing an interface where users can express themselves informally is related to problems that natural language processing researchers have been tackling for years: ambiguity, imprecision, and human language context dependency. In addition, the imprecision and temporal dependencies attached to the spatial data can make designing a good interface an even more challenging task.

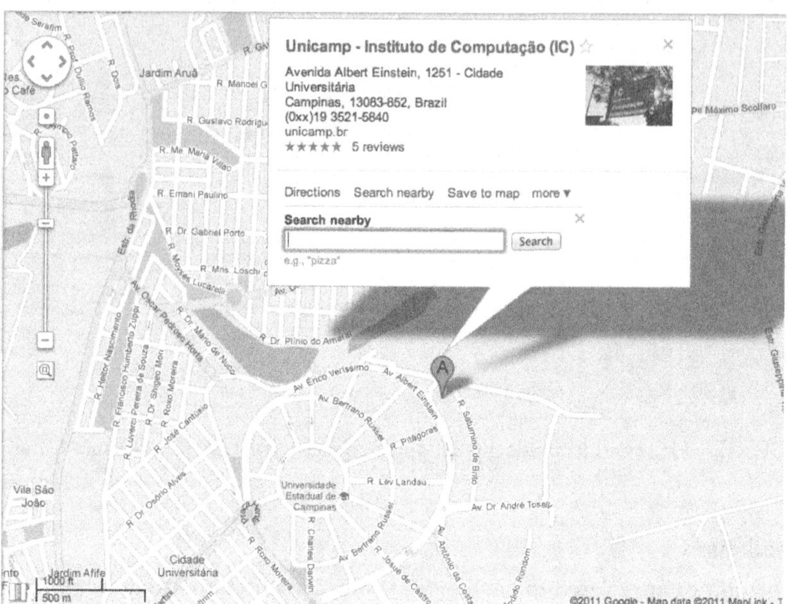

FIGURE 5.12: Example from Google Maps with a point of interest (POI) selected and search for something nearby enabled.

Consider, as an example of GIR results presentation, the execution of local searches such as those found in Google Places Search. In this case, a set of geocoded pages is retrieved by keyword-based search and they are pinpointed on Google Maps, yielding a geographic view and distribution of the results over a space (Figure 5.13). Moreover, when a point on the map is selected, users are allowed to specify what they want to "Search nearby". One strategy for a GIR query input interface could be using this kind of map-based interface, where it is easy to aggregate queries that involve spatial relationships (Figure 5.12).

There are still many challenges in the presentation layer relating to how geographical results are presented, how users can indicate which results are really relevant (so the system learns how to refine its searching), and how interactions can be improved using visual query interfaces [132, 210], such as those inspired by works developed for GIS: Spatial-Query-by-Sketch [27] and visual formulation of queries based on sets of icons representing geographic features and relationships that are combined to build a geographic query [80, 102].

Processing Layer

Challenges in the processing layer include identification and elimination of place name ambiguity (e.g., when a common name is used for a variety of places and objects). In this case, the system

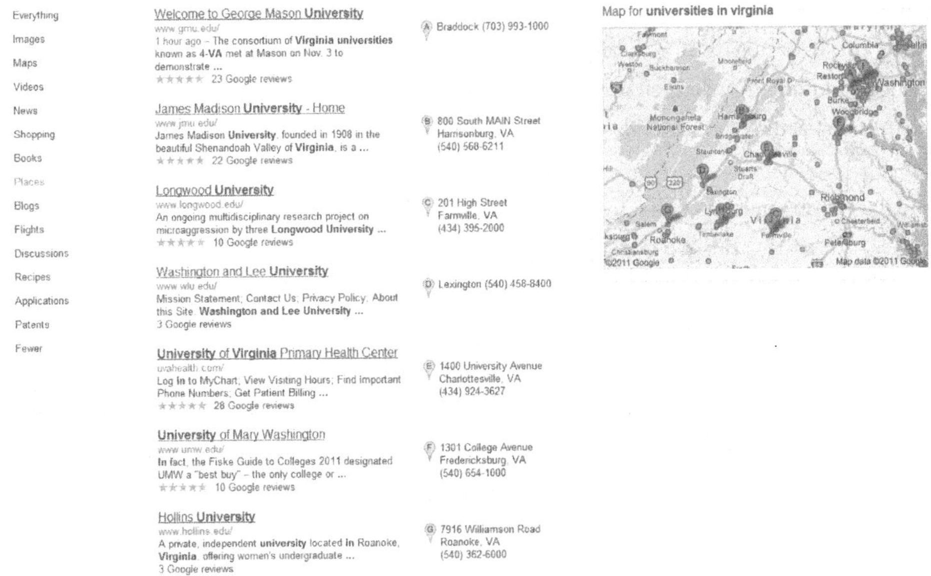

FIGURE 5.13: Example of results returned by Google Place search.

presents alternative choices (similar names) to the user. According to user feedback, a new query is sent to the system [110, 264].

Thus, supposing users are offered a interface where they can express their queries through semi-structured or natural language, it will be challenging to identify [250], extract [21], and manipulate references to places as well as intended geographical relationships between them [48, 221], and to deal with those derived imprecise and ambiguous references [43, 92, 148, 192, 195, 225].

Even if a geographic knowledge base is properly assembled and geocoded, in light of the huge amount of data spread over the Web, two challenges stand out: efficiently processing queries in a geographical Web search engine [54] and designing effective algorithms to predict if a document is relevant [79, 174, 266].

Moreover, more study is required on users' needs for geographical information, trying to understand their search behavior. For example, by analyzing search logs, Henrich and Luedecke [113] show that searches for geographic information in the USA are often about places to stay and visit, and users intend to buy or rent something from there besides learning how to reach it. In another investigation, the reason why users rewrite Web queries was studied. This aimed to identify users' preferences for physical distances between places searched, as well as the location from which a query was sent [128]. Finally, the most used geo-words and how they are reused by users was studied by Sanderson and Han [221].

Data Layer

Considering the Internet itself as a big data repository, it is challenging to create and index automatically a geographic knowledge base from what is available on the Web [126, 207]. That involves dealing with inconsistent data and also demands to identify and geocode data found in webpages [3, 5, 30, 35, 47].

The data layer includes collections of target documents, as well as supporting structures such as ontologies, thesauri, and geospatial database, to assist with spatial operations and queries (as discussed earlier). Further research is needed regarding how to build and use such structures and repositories.

5.3.2 MULTIMODAL RETRIEVAL FOR GEOGRAPHIC INFORMATION

The discussion above of GIR focused on text geocoding and geoparsing. We also argued that only after documents are geoparsed and geocoded can they be placed on a map or queried by geographic location. However, in digital libraries digital objects go beyond text documents, e.g., to include images and videos. The quantity and space involved for these are growing rapidly. Besides, there are more devices connected with GPS and camera, such as smartphones, that embed location data in picture and video metadata, along with other data such as date, time, and camera details. Therefore, it is useful to combine CBIR, multimedia, and GIR techniques in DLs.

The process of associating a geographic location with photo and video metadata is called geocoding in GIR. In the multimedia field it often is referred to as geotagging or georeferencing (also spelled geo-referencing) [163]. Further, in GIS, georeferencing is a term largely used to refer to defining a location where something exists, in a physical space, in term of a coordinate system (e.g., latitude and longitude).

Geotagging photos and videos is possible not only when you take or record them from a device with GPS, but it also is enabled by applications and services such as Flickr[5] and Panoramio.[6] In addition to supporting annotation, they allow users to organize and manually assign locations, using a map interface or geographically relevant keywords [163]. Accordingly, the amount of geotagged photos and videos is growing rapidly. For example, in Flickr, there were about 4.7 million geotagged items in 2010 [163], but this number increased to more than 165 million geotagged items by November 2, 2011.

Multimedia Retrieval for Geographic Information

According to Luo et al. [163], "geographic information has been embraced by multimedia and vision researchers within a contextual modeling framework," such as for event detection and classification,

5. http://www.flickr.com/

6. http://www.panoramio.com/

semantic scene content understanding, and annotation propagation. Their discussions are around the modalities of geographic information used and around geotagging driven applications in multimedia and vision research. They divided up the geotagging multimedia applications as follows.

Semantic multimedia understanding encompasses social and cultural semantics, as well as annotation, organization, and retrieval of events, scenes, or objects. For example, white colors associated with a photo of somewhere in the NE of the U.S.A. during winter indicates snow. Similarly, if a photo depicts people cheering and their location is related to a baseball field, then it may indicate a photo of a baseball game.

Geolocation and landmark recognition aim to determine the location of an image, video, or series of images. In this case, collections of geotagged images are used as training and matching data to help predict the location of unknown images. Landmark images recognition can be seen as detection of somewhat unique objects in unknown images, which are similar to images in a collection of geotagged images. Here, matched images' geolocation will aid in the prediction of the location of a given unknown image.

Media visualization can aid the use of collections and landmarks, camera viewing directions, travel trajectories and routes, and photos in large collections (that can be browsed for tourism in 3D fashion).

Recommendation for location-based services or products can help with planning vacations and identifying attractions based on users' locations and interests. This category of applications can be divided further into: real-time recommendation, recommendation inference via geotagged images (considering spatial and temporal patterns), travelogues, and GPS trajectories.

Social network applications. Luo et al. [163] cite works that use tweets or Flickr uploads to discover time and location information related to an event. Users are seen as social sensors; their reports can document the spread of the consequences of an event (such as a flu epidemic or the movement of a typhoon). Therefore, it is important to predict the location of Flickr users. One strategy is based on their social connections' public locations, since users tend to communicate more with closer friends.

Mapping applications can use geocoded photos to produce different kinds of maps, for example, on land use (park, green area, under/super developed area).

Geolocation and Landmark Recognition

As is explained above, landmark image recognition is based on detecting unique objects in images and matching them against a knowledge base (collection of geotagged images). This is called landmark recognition with feature point matching, as interest points from a test image are matched to interest points in one or more training set images [163]. However, interest point matching in urban areas is difficult, since some structures (e.g., windows) may repeat frequently.

In non-landmark location recognition, image exact match on a training dataset may not occur or may not be reliable. For example, Hays and Efros [109] find a probability distribution of images over the globe and base their strategy on that information, as well as on a dataset of over 6 million geotagged images (their knowledge base) from all over the world. Unknown images are described by selected image descriptors (e.g., color histograms, GIST) and compared to the big knowledge base. The top k most similar returned geotagged images are used to estimate the location of a given unknown image. Although this strategy will not be precise most of the time in finding an exact location, it will indicate roughly where an image was captured. For 16% of the time, their method correctly predicted an image location within 200 km. Extensions of this approach rely solely on the text tags associated with the images [226, 254], or apply Hays and Efros' method to the visual content of images and to their associated user tags [94]. Gallagher et al. [94], besides using a collection of over a million geotagged photographs, also built location probability maps of user tags over the globe to study the picture-taking and tagging behaviors of thousands of users. Applying the local tag probability maps and image matching of Hays and Efros [109], Gallagher et al. showed that their method yielded improvements over pure visual content-based methods.

Similar strategies have been employed for multimedia retrieval. MediaEval,[7] a benchmarking initiative to evaluate a "new algorithm for multimedia access and retrieval" which is a spin-off of VideoCLEF, launched the Placing Task in 2010, along with other tagging tasks [141]. This task requires participants to automatically assign latitude and longitude coordinates to each of the provided test videos.

Participants in the Placing Task at MedialEval 2011 were allowed to use image/video metadata, audio and visual features, as well as external resources, depending on the run submitted. The organizer [212] of this task released a set of geotagged Flickr videos as well as the metadata for geotagged Flickr images, such as title, tags, and descriptions provided by the owner of that resource, comments of her/his friends, users' contact lists, and other uploaded resources in Flickr. Data released included 10,216 geotagged videos, along with their extracted keyframes and corresponding pre-extracted low-level visual features, and metadata for 3,185,258 CC-licensed Flickr photos, uniformly sampled from all parts of the world. Test data comprised of 5,347 videos with its related metadata (without latitude and longitude information). Evaluation was based on the distance to the ground truth geographic coordinate point, in a series of widening circles: 1 km, 10 km, 100 km, 1000 km, and 10,000 km. Thus, an estimated location is counted as correct at a particular quality level if it lies within a given circle radius.

7. http://www.multimediaeval.org/

Although a minimum of one run that uses only audio/visual features was required, most of the participants focused on modeling and solving the problem based on text metadata associated with available videos.

In 2010, the Placing Task data set was divided into 5091 videos for training (with the same additional Flickr photos) and 5125 videos for testing. There were three main approaches: (a) geoparsing and geocoding texts extracted from metadata assisted by a gazetteer of geographic name such as GeoName; (b) propagation of the georeference of a similar video in the development database to the test video; and (c) dividing the training set into geographical regions determined by clustering or a fixed-size grid and later employing a model to assign items to each group. The model estimation was based on metadata text data and visual clues. The best result in 2010 for this task was accomplished by VanLaere et al. [254] by only using metadata for images and videos, combining approaches (b) and (c): first a language model identified the most likely area of the video and then the most similar resources from the training set gave the exact coordinates.

The only group in 2010 that also made use of visual features was Kelm et al. [130]; they reported that combining visual and textual results can yield better results than just relying on one of the modalities of information (just text or visual content).

5.3.3 GEOGRAPHIC INFORMATION AND DIGITAL LIBRARIES

The first large DL project interested in explicitly using geographic information was ADEPT (Alexandria Digital Earth ProtoType). It came from the Alexandria Digital Library (ADL), which is a project led by University of California (Santa Barbara, CA, USA) from 1995–2004. It is a distributed digital library comprising of a collection of geo-referenced material that could be searched [88, 124]. Its search was focused on its digital library contents. The spatial operators supported in searching this distributed digital library are: "contains item are", "overlaps", "encompasses/contained by", and 'exclude/outside".

Now let us take the CTRnet DL to exemplify the use of GIR and multimodal retrieval for geographic information. As discussed in earlier CBIR case studies, the CTRnet project collects news and online resources (webpages, public Twitter, and Facebook posts) related to natural disasters and man-made tragedies [137, 265].

One of the ways to browse through CTRnet collections is through a map interface as shown in Figure 5.14. Purple balloons represent natural disasters, and blue balloons represent man-made disasters. Clicking a balloon will open a pop-up window, where you can visit a corresponding collection in the Internet Archive or related Wikipedia articles. In that figure, a user clicked in a place marker near Blacksburg (VA, USA), which opened a pop-up with one of the CTRnet collections associated with that region: VT (Virginia Tech) April 16 Archive.

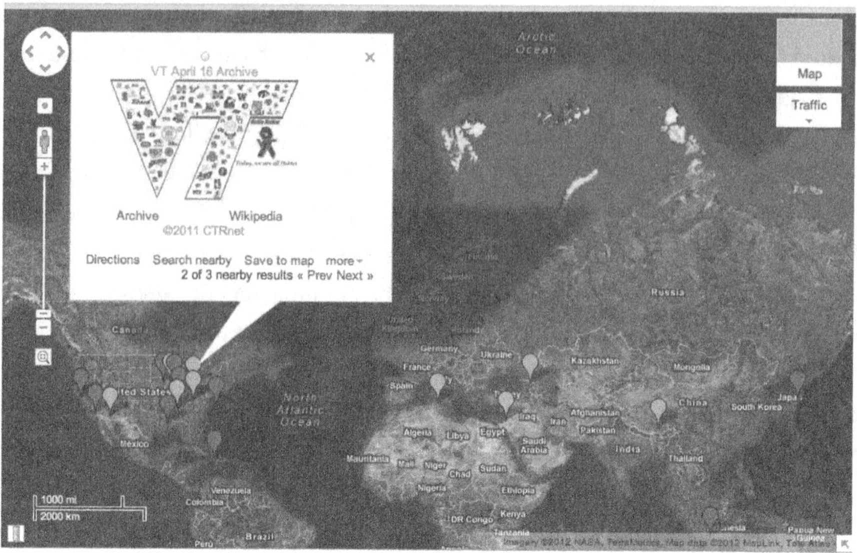

FIGURE 5.14: CTRnet collections on Google Map.

FIGURE 5.15: Emergency task force helping the injured in Norris Hall on VT's April 16, 2007 shooting tragedy. (By Alan Kim/*The Roanoke Times*)

Now let us consider the following scenario where geocoded images and collections could be helpful. A journalist has a photo, shown in Figure 5.15, as a query. He might know it is about a school shooting (event), but he would like to know if it appears in the CTRnet collection. If so, he would like to: view the document that used this image, study some facts about that photo if available, and also uncover other related photos so he can reuse them in an essay about that event, about a new similar event, or about the city where that event happened.

Therefore, meaningful results from the CTRnet DL system might be images that look like the query image from these points of view: (a) visually similar in terms of scene composition; and (b) there is some relation with Web resources like in the Internet Archive collection, blogs, Twitter and Facebook posts, and news related to the event pictured by that photo.

An event is defined by an episode that happened in a certain place and time. For example, one of the CTRnet collection is about the April 16, 2007 school shooting tragedy at Virginia Tech. It refers to the school shooting tragedy *episode* that happened *inside* the VT campus at that very *specific date*. The outcome of that sad event included 32 people murdered before the shooter killed himself.

In order to provide a map-base browsing or geographical searching services in a DL, its collections should be geocoded, which is tackled by research areas that we presented previously. In the Section 5.5, a case study discussing the process of geocoding VT building images is presented.

5.4 A MULTIMODAL GEOTAGGING FRAMEWORK

In order to begin tacking this problem we participated in Mediaeval 2011 and reported [150] our idealized architecture for multimodal geocoding as depicted in Figure 5.16. The proposed architecture for dealing with multimodal geocoding involves three modules:

1. text-based geocoding is responsible for all text processing, and GIR geocoding techniques predict locations for videos' metadata;

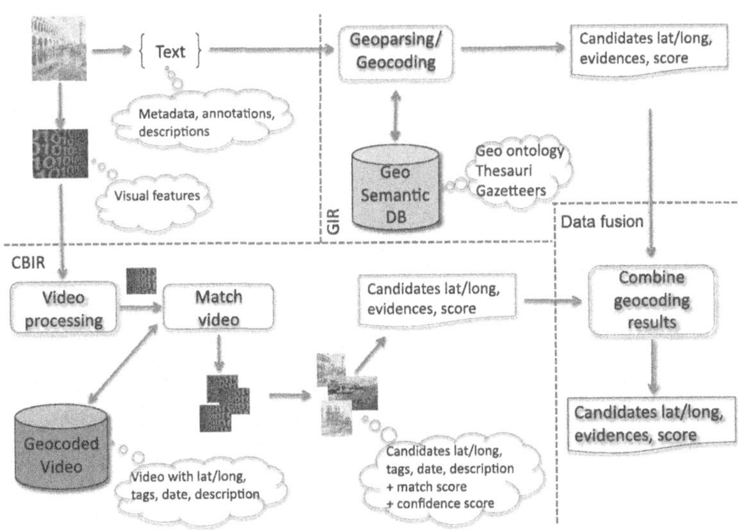

FIGURE 5.16: Multimodal geocoding architecture proposal.

2. content-based geocoding: this module will predict location based on visual similarity of the test images/videos against the knowledge database using the development dataset; and
3. data fusion/rank aggregation: the rank aggregation-based module combines the geocoding results generated by the previous modules and gives the final result of the geocoding. The idea is to rely on text and image data whenever possible.

The final result is a combination of the results from each modality, treated by a data fusion module which deals with the geocoding results of textual (metadata) and visual (frames) parts of a video. The challenge is to have good textual geocoding, good visual content-based geocoding, and an effective data fusion algorithm for geographic information.

For MediaEval 2011, we focused on the second module, exploring a method to identify similar videos whose visual content indicates where those videos were filmed. Although participants were allowed to use all the metadata associated with the given video, such as descriptions and tags provided by users, we focused on geocoding based on visual features of the videos, since many others have studied geotagging based on textual evidence. Our results [150] only using visual feature were comparable to the result of the previous work [130] for the run where only visual features were used.

APPLYING THE FRAMEWORK AT PLACING TASK AT MEDIAEVAL 2012

In the 2012 Placing Task [211], we tested our fusion implementation for combining different features [151], extending our previous year's work focused on the content-based image geocoding. For textual features, we used title, description, and keywords to calculate textual similarities between two videos. The text similarity functions used were Okapi and Dice [172]. To encode video visual properties, we used two approaches. The *bag-of-scenes* (BoS) [200] is based on static video frames and the *histogram of motion patterns* (HMP) [10] encodes motion information. The HMP was our team's approach last year [150].

The *bag-of-scenes* (BoS) approach [200] is based on the idea that video frames are like pictures from places. Therefore, by having a dictionary of pictures from places of interest, we can assign the video frames to one (or more) of the pictures in the dictionary. The video feature vector, called bag-of-scenes, works like a place activation vector. To create such a representation, we can use the same well-established strategies in the bag-of-visual-words model. In this work, we tested it based on the CEDD descriptor [52] with dictionaries made of 5000 scenes (BoS^{5000}_{CEDD}) and 500 scenes (BoS^{500}_{CEDD}).

The *histogram of motion patterns* (HMP) [10], unlike the bag-of-scenes model, identifies the video movement by the transitions between frames. For each frame of an input sequence, motion features are extracted from the video stream. After that, each feature is encoded as a unique pattern, representing its spatio-temporal configuration. Finally, those patterns are accumulated to form a normalized histogram.

Data Fusion/Rank Aggregation

We used a rank aggregation method based on a multiplication approach, initially proposed for multimodal image retrieval [198]. Let v_q be a query video that is being compared to another video v_i from the dataset. Let $sim_0(v_q, v_i)$ be a function defined in the interval [0, 1] that computes a similarity score between the videos v_q and v_i, where 1 denotes a perfect similarity. Let $\mathcal{S} = \{sim_1, sim_2, \ldots, sim_m\}$ be a set of m similarity functions defined by different features. The new aggregated score sim_a is computed by multiplying individual feature scores as follows:

$$sim_a(v_q, v_i) = \frac{\sqrt[m]{\prod_{k=1}^{m}(sim_k(v_q, v_i) + 1)}}{m}. \tag{5.1}$$

By multiplying the different similarity scores, high scores obtained by one feature are propagated to the others, leading to high aggregated values.

Geocoding Approach

Our method to predict an unseen query video is divided into three steps: text processing, visual processing, and data/information fusion. We use the videos of the development set (15,563 videos) as geo-profiles, in the sense that they are compared to each test video (4,182 videos).

The visual processing module describes the visual content of each provided video. All videos in the test set are compared to those in the development set and, for each test video, a list of videos—ranked by similarity in descending order—is produced. The textual processing module works similarly, except for the kind of information considered (textual content instead of visual).

The fusion module takes as input the different lists produced and generates a brand new list using our rank aggregation. The resulting new list is the one to be used to estimate the lat/long of a query video. In the current implementation, we consider that the lat/long of the video on the top of the list will be used to estimate the query video.

Our approach is focused on data fusion, so most of our submissions considered combined results, although the use of a single modality was evaluated for comparison purposes. The evaluation process to define the features that should be combined is summarized in another work [153].

Our evaluation results in 2012's Placing Task [151] showed that the combination of HMP and the two BoS configurations (BoS^{500}_{CEDD} and BoS^{5000}_{CEDD}) is slightly better than relying just on the best visual descriptor results.

Moreover, we also noticed that the result of combination including the use of the classical text vector space is twice as good as the use of visual cues alone. On the other hand, the combination of different textual and visual descriptors leads to statistically significant improvements over results of the method that relies only on textual clues.

In summary, our approach combined textual information found in video metadata (e.g., descriptions, title, keywords) and visual features. We used the video similarity between videos in the development set and those in the test set to estimate the location of the latter. Obtained results demonstrate that this approach is promising as it yields better results than those observed for a single modality or a single descriptor.

Although UNICAMP achieved the third place in the overall best performance, obtained results show how promising is our proposed multimodal framework to geocode videos. We have outperformed some other submissions that used extra information. Our textual and visual processing modules use straightforward information retrieval techniques (KNN searches) to query the test videos against the development set, and then to assign location. The CEALIST team (first place), for example, exploits additional information, not provided by organizers, to learn tagging patterns of users to improve its results.

In contrast to the other initiatives, usually based on *ad hoc* steps, we handle different modalities from the same perspective. Each modality is associated with different ranked lists, which are later combined to define a final ranked list, that then is used to assign appropriate locations to videos. Note that our geocoding framework is flexible enough to accommodate the evolution of each one of its module separately. The better the result obtained for each module, the better should be the final combined result. Even the fusion module can be improved independently of the others. More details can be found in [154].

5.5 CASE STUDY: IMAGE GEOCODING OF VIRGINIA TECH BUILDING PHOTOS

As presented before, the Crisis, Tragedy, and Recovery network (CTRnet) project collects news and online resources (webpages, public Twitter and Facebook posts) related to natural disasters and man-made tragedies. To support the creation of map-based browsing services building on photo content, the first step is to be able to geocode images. For this, we need to evaluate image descriptors in image geocoding tasks.

In the following, we will introduce an example related to the geocoding of VT buildings [155]. The objective is to investigate the most suitable image descriptors to be used to geocode photos belonging to the collection related to the VT April 16th shooting event. Later, geocoded photos could be used to create map-based photo browsing services.

The first insight to tackle the problem of geocoding photos about VT is to leverage research to recognize buildings. Previous initiatives, such as [205], perform matching of local descriptors to find similar regions within images of a set of buildings. Although they are not explicitly geocoding images, their approaches could be used for that purpose. They worked with buildings from the University of Oxford.[8] After describing images with a scheme based on a visual vocabulary (quantized local features), matching was done between a given query image and images from the dataset. Performance was compared for different vocabulary sizes, as well as vocabularies generated by different methods. Here we will employ a similar strategy, with the aim of evaluating the performance of local image description approaches in the task of geocoding building photos.

For this geocoding experiment, we need a data collection and the evaluation criteria which will be described below.

DATASETS

We use two datasets in our experiments. One is used as our visual knowledge base and will be referred to as training data. The other includes the test data images whose locations will be predicted by the proposed geocoding system.

Training Dataset

The training data is a subset of 4,852 photos from VT's University Relations (UniRel) Photo Library. Each photo has some metadata associated, such as keywords, caption describing the scene, date, camera model, and photographer's name. For our purpose, we filtered the photos by the content of keywords and caption fields. As we were interested in the university buildings, we searched for photos whose metadata (keywords or caption) contains building and place names (e.g., Duck Pond). The building/place names list was built up from both the VT site[9] and the campus building database maintained by GIS staff for campus facilities. The resulting training set contains photos of buildings or places with their location. Figure 5.17 shows the spatial distribution of buildings whose photos are in the training set.

Test Dataset

The test dataset[10] contains 565 photos of VT buildings. Most of them were obtained from personal collections while some others were downloaded from the VT website. The photos were obtained under different angle and light conditions. The locations of these photos are shown in Figure 5.18. Note that the test set covers a smaller area (near to the Drillfield in the campus center) when compared to the training set.

8. http://www.robots.ox.ac.uk/~vgg/data/oxbuildings/.

9. http://www.vt.edu/about/buildings/.

10. http://www.recod.ic.unicamp.br/VTBuildings/

Figures 5.17 and 5.18 are generated using a heatmap, provided by sethoscope.net[11]. We used the option that employs tiles, provided by Stamen Design, under CC BY 3.0. Data was provided by OpenStreetMap, under CC BY SA.

Ground Truth

The ground truth for the images in the training and test data sets, that is, the "correct" location for each of them, was inferred from the corresponding building/place name associated with the photo. For the training photos, we used the place/building name that appears in their metadata. For the test photos, we use the name that we manually labeled each photo. The ground truth for these photos is based on the lat/long from the VT site, as well as on names processed by Google's geocoding service. However, if no matches were found by the geocoding service or if disambiguation was needed, the place/building was manually located and confirmed in Google Map using its name. Additionally, some photos and some of the resulting geocoding locations were visually and manually inspected to determine their final location and/or coordinates.

The tool we used in this process is geopy,[12] a geocoding toolbox for Python that accesses popular Web geocoding API services. Geopy also supports the computation of geographic distance between two given lat/long points. We used this feature to evaluate our geocoding results.

EVALUATION CRITERIA

The evaluation criterion used here is inspired by the evaluation procedure adopted in the Placing Task at MediaEval [211]. The effectiveness of a method is based on the geographic distance (great-circle distance) of the estimated geo-coordinates of a digital object to its corresponding ground truth location, in a series of widening circles of radius. An estimated point is counted as correct if it is within a particular circle size, that is, a radius value or precision level.

In our case, we are interested in determining as accurately as possible the location for a photo image. Furthermore, our area of interest is restricted to the Virginia Tech campus, so our precision level should be in meters. Taking into account that the two farthest points of the town of Blacksburg (where VT is located) are about 10 km apart, we can accept that two points on the VT campus should not be further apart than 5 km. The precision levels adopted are 1, 50, 100, 150, 200, 250, 300, 350, 400, 450, 500, 550, 600, 650, 700, 750, 800, 850, 900, 950, 1000, 1100, 1200, 1300, 1400, 1500, 1600, 1700, 1800, 1900, 2000, 3000, 4000, and 5000 meters.

---

11. http://www.sethoscope.net/heatmap/

12. https://github.com/geopy/geopy#readme.

FIGURE 5.17: Spatial distribution of photos used as *training set*.

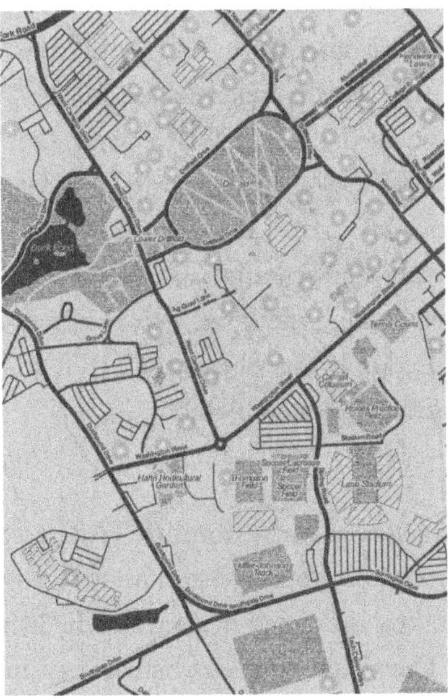

FIGURE 5.18: Spatial distribution of photos used as *test set*.

TABLE 5.1: Image representations evaluated

Acronym	Method
D.SIFT.1k	dense SIFT, 1,000 words, soft assignment (σ=60), max pooling
D.SIFT.10k	dense SIFT, 10,000 words, soft assignment (σ=60), max pooling
S.SIFT.1k	sparse SIFT, 1,000 words, soft assignment (σ=60), max pooling
S.SIFT.10k	sparse SIFT, 10,000 words, soft assignment (σ=60), max pooling
S.SURF.1k	sparse SURF, 1,000 words, soft assignment (σ=0.08), max pooling
S.SURF.10k	sparse SURF, 10,000 words, soft assignment (σ=0.08), max pooling
WSA.1k	sparse SIFT, 1,000 words, soft assignment (σ=60), WSA
WSA.10k	sparse SIFT, 10,000 words, soft assignment (σ=60), WSA

SETUP

First, the visual content properties of each provided image are encoded into feature vectors, considering all evaluated descriptors. Then, the visual distances between the photos in the test set and all photos in the training set are computed. Finally, for each test photo, a ranked list of training photos is produced.

To represent each image, we used the bag-of-visual-word model [230]. In that model, after extracting low-level features with local descriptors, we quantize the feature space in order to obtain a visual dictionary (codebook) and then we represent each local description according to the dictionary. For low-level feature extraction, we used: dense SIFT (6 pixels) [252], sparse SIFT (Harris-Laplace detector) [252], and sparse SURF (Fast-Hessian detector) [22]. We randomly quantized the feature space [257], generating two dictionary sizes: 1,000 and 10,000 visual words.

To compute the bag-of-word representation, we used soft assignment (σ=60 for SIFT and σ=0.08 for SURF) [253] and two pooling methods: max pooling [38] and Word Spatial Arrangement (WSA) [201]. WSA was used only over the sparse SIFT, while max pooling was used for all low-level features. Table 5.1 lists the evaluated methods.

Geocoding Process

The geocoding scheme adopted is based on performing K-nearest neighbor (KNN) searches. In this study, the location of a test photo is defined based on the geographic coordinates of the most similar image in the training set, i.e., is defined in terms of the location of the 1-nearest neighbor (i.e., $K = 1$) of the test photo. The visual distances between an input test image and all training images are computed. Training images are then ranked in ascending order of their visual distance to the input test image, and the latitude and longitude coordinates of the top-ranked training photo is assigned to the test image.

EXAMPLES OF GEOCODING RESULTS

Table 5.2 shows two examples of query photos of the test set and the corresponding top-similar images in the training set for each visual descriptor. Each table cell also presents the geographic distance between the top-ranked training image and the query photo's ground truth.

TABLE 5.2: The best visual match for each query image and its geocoding result. Values below the photo thumbnail refer to the geographic distance (in meters) to the ground-truth location of the query image.

Query	 P1080012	 P1080710
Building Name	Lane Hall	Torgersen Bridge
D.SIFT.1k	 424.08	 906.41
D.SIFT.10k	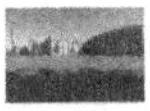 86.87	 2801.90
S.SIFT.1k	 349.62	74.33
S.SIFT.10k	 161.13	1070.43
S.SURF.1k	217.67	 0.00
S.SURF.10k	 1231.06	 0.00
WSA.1k	 238.44	 275.15
WSA.10k	 238.44	74.33

Consider, for example, the top-ranked image in the case of query P1080710 (picture of the Torgersen Bridge). The S.SURF (1k and 10k) descriptor is able to match it to a photo that only pictures a detail of that building, whereas WSA.10k and S.SIFT.1k match that to a photo from the same building but under a different light (darker) condition. However, as this photo was labeled as Torgersen Hall instead of Torgersen Bridge (part of Torgersen Hall), its geographic distance was not zero. The query P1080012 (Lane Hall) shows an example where S.SURF.10k performed very badly. D.SIFT.10k, on the other hand, matched it to a photo of a building (Shanks Hall) that is close (86.87 m) to Lane Hall, while S.SIFT.10k found the query similar to a picture of Torgersen Bridge (161.13 m away) at night.

In summary, each descriptor provides different, but potentially complementary information that could be combined to improve geocoding results. Potential future works include focusing on the use of data fusion techniques to combine non-correlated descriptors and adding available textual descriptions in geocoding tasks and new geocoding schemes. For more details regarding this study, refer to [155].

5.6 FORMALIZATION

The content and discussion of this chapter are mainly related to the 5S framework on these concepts.

Spaces. Besides the vector space-based models for digital objects, geospatial information in DLs will require the space that represents the Earth, a 2D geographic coordinate system, since geospatial information found in digital objects is associated with a 2D location.

Structures refer to the use of appropriate data models to manage geospatial information, such as geo-ontologies, geographic objects, image and video content features, and metadata.

Streams of text, images, and video (comprised of frames of images, associated sounds, and text) are mentioned in this chapter and we showed that they can be related to places on Earth.

Scenarios. A possible scenario in the context of geospatial information is a user looking for information related to a certain place on Earth. A service a DL can provide to meet this user need is a browsing service showing the world map based on which that user can locate objects of interest found in specific locations. Interaction mechanisms based on navigation (e.g., zoom and pan) and the definition of regions of interest are usually employed. At different levels of zoom, different information could be shown. For example, at a country level, people can visualize country boundaries, and a *summary* of digital objects found in that region can be shown on a map. As a user zooms in to take a closer look at the map, more detailed information or different summaries are exhibited as the user is looking at a smaller geographic region. Eventually this user will reach a map zoom level where individual digital objects are shown. By explicitly clicking on found objects, users may access detailed data related to them.

In another scenario, users might be interested in identifying what else there is in a certain place depicted by an image managed by a digital library. In this case, that user could use a DL service that can take that image, recognize what and where it refers to, and return all digital objects that are associated with that place. The computer interface could show the results pinpointed on a map, helping the user to locate other image digital objects in their spatial context (e.g., cities) and relations (e.g., are they geographically close?).

5.7 SUMMARY

In this chapter, geospatial information concepts were introduced along with the set of operations and possible queries for geographic objects.

The Geographic Information Retrieval (GIR) area also was presented in this chapter. That area comprises research aimed at recognizing, querying, retrieving, and indexing geographical information present in documents, such as those in a DL or on the Web. Existing challenges concerning the implementation of GIR systems were introduced by a quick review of existing works for presenting, processing, and storing geographic data.

Documents in both DLs and the Web include digital objects like text, images, and videos. Collections of images and videos are growing rapidly due to numerous devices that take pictures or record videos. Furthermore, devices connected with GPS and camera capabilities, such as smart phones, that embed location data in picture and video metadata, also are spreading. This leads to new challenges in different areas such as IR, multimedia, and computer vision. Some of those challenges were discussed in this chapter as well as some proposed solutions. As an example, we presented our solution to predict the location a video was shot based on its visual content.

Finally, we presented a case study in the context of the CTRnet DL to apply multimodal information retrieval for geographic information. We covered the evaluation of several image content local descriptors in the context of geocoding VT building photos. Obtained results in this study will guide us in the specification and implementation of spatially-aware DL services for the collection related to VT's April 16, 2007 school shooting tragedy. Extensions of these methods will be applied to other CTRnet collections and to those in the follow-on project, IDEAL, that also considers events related to community and governmental activities.

5.8 EXERCISES AND PROJECTS

5.1 Besides spaces, what are the other 5S concepts highly referenced in this chapter? Explain why those 5S concepts were discussed. Give examples of them, individually and in combination, and relate them to scenarios you find interesting.

5.2 In which cases does handling the geospatial information associated with digital library objects make sense? When is it not needed?

5.3 Redesign an existing digital library of your choice in order to consider novel services related to geospatial information. Regarding that:

   (a) which modules should be considered?
   (b) which DL services should be modified or added?
   (c) which types of digital objects should be handled differently?

5.4 Time and space are complementary when we are talking about events; how can one take advantage of them in DLs?

5.5 Which operators and relations are added in a DL when we explicitly handle and model the geospatial information?

5.6 How would you evaluate the effectiveness of a DL search service when a query specifies a location and uses a spatial operator? Which evaluation protocol and criteria could be used?

5.7 Describe different strategies that might be used to geocode textual, visual, and multimodal documents in DLs.

5.8 Extend the 5S framework to formalize a map-based DL browsing service.

5.9 How does metadata relate to the discussion in this chapter? What metadata standards have been utilized in similar contexts?

5.10 What formats are used to represent the types of data discussed in this chapter? What are the international and what are the common proprietary standards that apply?

5.11 What are the popular systems that have been devised to handle GIS? GIR? How could they be better linked with DL technologies? What are the pros and cons of such an approach? How does that compare with what is discussed in this chapter?

5.12 What would be different if 3D instead of 2D representations were employed when working with geographic information?

5.13 For a term project, in which GIS and GIR capabilities were to be added to some popular DL, what would be the easiest approach? What would be the key challenges to be met?

5.14 Could GIS and GIR capabilities be easily added to a popular content management system, like Drupal? How?

5.15 What novel scenarios might be enabled by an advanced DL with GIS and GIR capabilities? What benefits would accrue in each?

Bibliography

[1] S. Abbasi, F. Mokhtarian, and J. Kittler. Enhancing CSS-based Shape Retrieval for Objects with Shallow Concavities. *Image and Vision Computing*, 18(3):199–211, February 2000. DOI: 10.1016/S0262-8856(99)00019-0. 3

[2] M. Addis, M. Boniface, S. Goodall, P. Grimwood, S. Kim, P. Lewis, K. Martinez, and A. Stevenson. SCULPTEUR: Towards a new paradigm for multimedia museum information handling. In *Proc. of International Semantic Web Conference (ISWC)*, pages 582–596, 2003. DOI: 10.1007/978-3-540-39718-2_37. 22

[3] M. Adriani and M. L. Paramita. Identifying location in Indonesian documents for geographic information retrieval. In *Proceedings of the 4th ACM Workshop on Geographical Information Retrieval*, pages 19–24, Lisbon, Portugal, 2007. ACM. DOI: 10.1145/1316948.1316955. 104

[4] M. Agosti, L. Candela, D. Castelli, N. Ferro, Y. Ioannidis, G. Koutrika, C. Meghini, P. Pagano, S. Ross, H.-J. Schek, and H. Schuldt. A Reference Model for DLMSs Interim Report. In L. Candela and D. Castelli, editors, *Deliverable D1.4.2 - Reference Model for Digital Library Management Systems [Draft 1]*. DELOS, A Network of Excellence on Digital Libraries, IST-2002-2.3.1.12,Technology-enhanced Learning and Access to Cultural Heritage, http://www.delos.info/index.php?option=com_content&task=view&id=345 [visited March 23, 2007], September 2006. 65

[5] D. Ahlers and S. Boll. Retrieving address-based locations from the web. In *Proceedings of the 2nd International Workshop on Geographic Information Retrieval*, pages 27–34, Napa Valley, California, USA, 2008. ACM. DOI: 10.1145/1460007.1460015. 104

[6] S. M. Ahmed, B. Beck, C. A. Maurana, and G. Newton. Overcoming Barriers to Effective Community-based Participatory Research in US Medical Schools. *Education for Health*, 17(2):141–151, 2004. DOI: 10.1080/13576280410001710969. 45

[7] M. Akbar, W. Fan, C. A. Shaffer, Y. Chen, L. N. Cassel, L. M. L. Delcambre, D. D. Garcia, G. W. Hislop, F. M. Shipman III, R. Furuta, B. S. Carpenter II, H.-W. Hsieh, B. Siegfried, and E. A. Fox. Digital Library 2.0 for Educational Resources. In *Proc. TPDL 2011, Berlin, GE, Sept. 2011, LNCS 6966*, pages 89–100. Springer, Sept. 2011. DOI: 10.1007/978-3-642-24469-8_11. 30

[8] F. Akune, E. Valle, and R. da Silva Torres. Monorail: A disk-friendly index for huge descriptor databases. In *20th International Conference on Pattern Recognition*, pages 4145–4148, 2010. DOI: 10.1109/ICPR.2010.1008. 7

[9] AlgoViz. The AlgoViz Portal. http://www.algoviz.org/, September 2011. 27, 46

[10] J. Almeida, N. J. Leite, and R. da S. Torres. Comparison of Video Sequences with Histograms of Motion Patterns. In *Proceedings of International Conference on Image Processing*, ICIP '11, pages 3673–3676, 2011. DOI: 10.1109/ICIP.2011.6116516. 110

[11] D. C. Andrews. Audience-specific Online Community Design. *Communications of the ACM*, 45(4):64–68, 2002. DOI: 10.1145/505248.505275. 45

[12] N. Arica and F. T. Y. Vural. BAS: A Perceptual Shape Descriptor Based on the Beam Angle Statistics. *Pattern Recognition Letters*, 24(9-10):1627–1639, June 2003. DOI: 10.1016/S0167-8655(03)00002-3. 4, 12

[13] Y. A. Aslandogan and C. T. Yu. Techniques and Systems for Image and Video Retrieval. *IEEE Transactions on Knowledge and Data Engineering*, 11(1):56–63, January/February 1999. DOI: 10.1109/69.755615. 8, 9

[14] G. G. Aspiazu, S. C. Bauer, and M. Spillett. Improving the Academic Performance of Hispanic Youth: A Community Education Model. *Bilingual Research Journal*, 22(2):1–20, 1998. DOI: 10.1080/15235882.1998.10162719. 45

[15] S. Atnafu, R. Chbeir, D. Coquil, and L. Brunie. Integrating similarity-based queries in image DBMSs. In *Proceedings of the 2004 ACM Symposium on Applied Computing*, pages 735–739, 2004. DOI: 10.1145/967900.968052. 11

[16] R. Baeza-Yates and B. Ribeiro-Neto. *Modern Information Retrieval*. Addison-Wesley, Harlow, England, 1999. 8

[17] M. Balabanovi and Y. Shoham. Fab: Content-based, collaborative recommendation. *Communications of the ACM*, 40(3):66–72, 1997. DOI: 10.1145/245108.245124. 48

[18] R. G. Baraniuk, C. S. Burrus, B. M. Hendricks, G. L. Henry, A. O. Hero, D. H. Johnson, D. L. Jones, J. Kusuma, R. D. Nowak, J. E. Odegard, L. C. Potter, K. Ramchandran, R. J. Reedstrom, P. Schniter, I. W. Selesnick, D. B. Williams, and W. L. Wilson. Connexions: DSP education for a networked world. In *IEEE International Conference on Acoustics, Speech, and Signal Processing (ICASSP)*, volume 4, pages IV–4144 –IV–4147, May 2002. DOI: 10.1109/ICASSP.2002.5745570. 34, 35

[19] C. Barrett, K. Bisset, S. Eubank, X. Feng, and M. Marathe. EpiSimdemics: an Efficient and Scalable Framework for Simulating the Spread of Infectious Disease on Large Social Networks. *ACM/IEEE International Conference on Supercomputing*, 2008. 80, 83

[20] M. J. Bass and M. Branschofsky. DSpace at MIT: meeting the challenges. In *Proceedings of the 1st ACM/IEEE-CS Joint Conference on Digital Libraries*, JCDL '01, page 468, New York, NY, USA, 2001. ACM. DOI: 10.1145/379437.379803. 29

[21] D. S. Batista, M. J. Silva, F. M. Couto, and B. Behera. Geographic signatures for semantic retrieval. In *Proceedings of the 6th Workshop on Geographic Information Retrieval*, GIR '10, pages 19:1–19:8, New York, NY, USA, 2010. ACM. DOI: 10.1145/1722080.1722104. 97, 100, 103

[22] H. Bay, T. Tuytelaars, and L. Van Gool. Surf: Speeded up robust features. In *European Conference on Computer Vision*, ECCV'2006, pages 404–417, 2006. DOI: 10.1016/j.cviu.2007.09.014. 116

[23] B. B. Bederson. Photomesa: A Zoomable Image Browser Using Quantum Treemaps and Bubblemaps. In *Proceedings of the ACM Symposium on User Interface Software and Technology*, pages 71–80, Orlando, FL, USA, 2001. DOI: 10.1145/502348.502359. 9

[24] G. Beenen, K. Ling, X. Wang, K. Chang, D. Frankowski, P. Resnick, and R. E. Kraut. Using Social Psychology to Motivate Contributions to Online Communities. In *Proceedings of the 2004 ACM Conference on Computer Supported Cooperative Work*, pages 212–221, 2004. DOI: 10.1145/1031607.1031642. 47

[25] L. D. Bergman, V. Castelli, and C.-S. Li. Progressive content-based retrieval from satellite image archives. *D-Lib Magazine*, 3(10), October 1997. DOI: 10.1045/october97-li. 1, 11

[26] K. R. Bisset, J. Chen, X. Feng, V. A. Kumar, and M. V. Marathe. Epifast: a fast algorithm for large scale realistic epidemic simulations on distributed memory systems. In *Proceedings of the 23rd International Conference on Supercomputing*, ICS '09, pages 430–439, New York, NY, USA, 2009. ACM. DOI: 10.1145/1542275.1542336. 80

[27] A. D. Blaser and M. J. Egenhofer. A visual tool for querying geographic databases. In *Proceedings of the Working Conference on Advanced Visual Interfaces*, AVI '00, pages 211–216, New York, NY, USA, 2000. ACM. DOI: 10.1145/345513.345318. 102

[28] D. Blei, L. Carin, and D. Dunson. Probabilistic topic models. *Signal Processing Magazine, IEEE*, 27(6):55 – 65, 2010. DOI: 10.1109/MSP.2010.938079. 52

[29] D. M. Blei, A. Y. Ng, and M. I. Jordan. Latent Dirichlet allocation. *J. Mach. Learn. Res.*, 3:993–1022, 2003. 52

[30] A. Blessing, R. Kuntz, and H. Schütze. Towards a context model driven German geo-tagging system. In *Proceedings of the 4th ACM Workshop on Geographical Information Retrieval*, pages 25–30, Lisbon, Portugal, 2007. ACM. DOI: 10.1145/1316948.1316956. 104

[31] M. Bober. MPEG-7 Visual Shape Descriptors. *IEEE Transactions on Circuits and Systems for Video Technology*, 11(6):716–719, June 2001. DOI: 10.1109/76.927426. 3

[32] C. Bohm, S. Berchtold, and D. A. Keim. Searching in high-dimensional spaces: Index structures for improving the performance of multimedia databases. *ACM Computing Surveys (CSUR)*, 33(3):322–373, 2001. DOI: 10.1145/502807.502809. 7

[33] K. Bollacker, C. Evans, P. Paritosh, T. Sturge, and J. Taylor. Freebase: a collaboratively created graph database for structuring human knowledge. In *Proceedings of the 2008 ACM SIGMOD*

International Conference on Management of Data, SIGMOD '08, pages 1247–1250, New York, NY, USA, 2008. ACM. DOI: 10.1145/1376616.1376746. 36

[34] K. A. V. Borges. *Uso de uma ontologia de lugar urbano para reconhecimento e extração de evidências geoespaciais na Web*. Doctoral thesis, UFMG - Universidade Federal de Minas Gerais, 2006. 89, 96

[35] K. A. V. Borges, A. H. F. Laender, C. B. Medeiros, and J. Clodoveu A. Davis. Discovering geographic locations in web pages using urban addresses. In *Proceedings of the 4th ACM Workshop on Geographical Information Retrieval*, pages 31–36, Lisbon, Portugal, 2007. ACM. DOI: 10.1145/1316948.1316957. 99, 104

[36] C. L. Borgman. Social aspects of digital libraries. In *DL'96: Proceedings of the 1st ACM International Conference on Digital Libraries*, D-Lib Working Session 2A, pages 170–171, 1996. DOI: 10.1145/226931.226964. 45

[37] C. L. Borgman, J. C. Wallis, M. S. Mayernik, and A. Pepe. Drowning in data: digital library architecture to support scientific use of embedded sensor networks. In *Proceedings of the 7th ACM/IEEE-CS Joint Conference on Digital Libraries*, JCDL '07, pages 269–277, New York, NY, USA, 2007. ACM. DOI: 10.1145/1255175.1255228. 65, 83

[38] Y.-L. Boureau, F. Bach, Y. LeCun, and J. Ponce. Learning mid-level features for recognition. In *Proceedings of Conference on Computer Vision and Pattern Recognition*, CCVPR'2010, pages 2559–2566, 2010. DOI: 10.1109/CVPR.2010.5539963. 116

[39] D. M. Boyd and N. B. Ellison. Social Network Sites: Definition, History, and Scholarship. *Journal of Computer-Mediated Commu.*, 13(1):210–230, 2008. DOI: 10.1111/j.1083-6101.2007.00393.x. 48

[40] D. F. Brauner, M. A. Casanova, and R. L. Milidiü. Towards gazetteer integration through an instance-based thesauri mapping approach. In *Advances in Geoinformatics, Part 4*, pages 235–245, Campos do Jordão, SP, Brazil, 2007. Springer. S6 - Distributed GIS / GIS and the Internet. DOI: 10.1007/978-3-540-73414-7_15. 96

[41] P. Brusilovsky, J. Eklund, and E. Schwarz. Web-based education for all: A tool for development adaptive courseware. In *Proc. of the 7th International World Wide Web Conference,* 14–18 April 1988, Brisbane, Australia, published in journal *Computer Networks and ISDN Systems*, vol. 30, 1998. DOI: 10.1016/S0169-7552(98)00082-8. 34

[42] P. Brusilovsky and C. Tasso. Preface to special issue on user modeling for web information retrieval. *User Modeling and User-Adapted Interaction*, 14(2-3):147–157, 2004. DOI: 10.1023/B:USER.0000029016.80122.dd. 30

[43] D. Buscaldi and P. Rosso. A conceptual density-based approach for the disambiguation of toponyms. *International Journal of Geographical Information Science*, 22(3):301, 2008. DOI: 10.1080/13658810701626251. 103

[44] R. Z. Cabada, M. L. B. Estrada, and C. A. R. Garcia. EDUCA: A Web 2.0 authoring tool for developing adaptive and intelligent tutoring systems using a Kohonen network. *Expert Systems with Applications*, 38(8):9522 – 9529, 2011. DOI: 10.1016/j.eswa.2011.01.145. 34, 35

[45] R. Calumby, R. Silva Torres, and M. Gonçalves. Multimodal retrieval with relevance feedback based on genetic programming. *Multimedia Tools and Applications*, pages 1–29, 2012. DOI: 10.1007/s11042-012-1152-7. 10

[46] G. Câmara, M. A. Casanova, A. S. Hemerly, G. C. Magalhães, and C. M. B. Medeiros. Anatomia de sistemas de informação geográfica. In *10a. Escola de Computação*, page 197, Campinas, 1996. Instituto de Computação - UNICAMP. 90

[47] C. E. C. Campelo and C. d. S. Baptista. Geographic scope modeling for web documents. In *Proceeding of the 2nd International Workshop on Geographic Information Retrieval*, pages 11–18, Napa Valley, California, USA, 2008. ACM. DOI: 10.1145/1460007.1460010. 104

[48] N. Cardoso and M. J. Silva. Query expansion through geographical feature types. In *Proceedings of the 4th ACM Workshop on Geographical Information Retrieval*, pages 55–60, Lisbon, Portugal, 2007. DOI: 10.1145/1316948.1316963. 103

[49] F. Carmagnola, F. Cena, and C. Gena. User model interoperability: a survey. *User Modeling and User-Adapted Interaction*, 21(3):285–331, 2011. 10.1007/s11257-011-9097-5. DOI: 10.1007/s11257-011-9097-5. 36

[50] C. Carson, S. Belongie, H. Greenspan, and J. Malik. Blobworld: Image Segmentation Using Expectation-Maximization and its Application to Image Querying. *IEEE Transactions on Pattern Analysis and Machine Intelligence*, 24(8):1026–1038, August 2002. DOI: 10.1109/TPAMI.2002.1023800. 7

[51] J. Chang and D. M. Blei. Relational topic models for document networks. *Artificial Intelligence*, 9:81–88, 2009. 52

[52] S. A. Chatzichristofis and Y. S. Boutalis. Cedd: Color and edge directivity descriptor: A compact descriptor for image indexing and retrieval. In *Proceedings of the 6th International Conference on Computer Vision Systems*, ICVS'08, pages 312–322, Berlin, Heidelberg, 2008. Springer-Verlag. DOI: 10.1007/978-3-540-79547-6_30. 110

[53] D. N. Chen and Y. C. Chiang. A Document Recommendation System Based on Collaborative Filtering and Personal Ontology. In *11th International Conference on Informatics and Semiotics in Organisations*, pages 255–262, April 2009. 47

[54] Y.-Y. Chen, T. Suel, and A. Markowetz. Efficient query processing in geographic web search engines. In *Proceedings of the 2006 ACM SIGMOD International Conference on Management of Data*, pages 277–288, Chicago, IL, USA, 2006. DOI: 10.1145/1142473.1142505. 103

[55] P. Ciaccia, M. Patella, and P. Zezula. M-tree: An Efficient Access Method for Similarity Search in Metric Spaces. In *Proceedings of 23rd International Conference on Very Large Data Bases*, pages 426–435, Athens, Greece, 1997. 7, 18

[56] A. Clauset, M. E. J. Newman, and C. Moore. Finding community structure in very large networks. *Physical Review E*, 70(6):1–6, 2004. DOI: 10.1103/PhysRevE.70.066111. 51

[57] E. Clementini, P. D. Felice, and P. van Oosterom. A small set of formal topological relationships suitable for end-user interaction. In *Proceedings of the Third International Symposium on Advances in Spatial Databases*, pages 277–295. Springer-Verlag, 1993. DOI: 10.1007/3-540-56869-7_16. 89

[58] L. Costa and R. C. Jr. *Shape Analysis and Classification: Theory and Practice*. CRC Press, Boca Raton, FL, USA, 2001. 3

[59] D. Crockford. JSON: The Fat-Free Alternative to XML. Presented at XML 2006, Boston, MA, December 2006. 36

[60] S. J. Cunningham and M. Masoodian. Looking for a picture: An analysis of everyday image information searching. In *Proceedings of the 6th ACM/IEEE-CS Joint Conference on Digital Libraries*, JCDL '06, pages 198–199, New York, NY, USA, 2006. ACM. DOI: 10.1145/1141753.1141797. 1

[61] S. J. Cunningham and M. Masoodian. Identifying personal photo digital library features. In *Proceedings of the 7th ACM/IEEE-CS Joint Conference on Digital Libraries*, JCDL '07, pages 400–401, New York, NY, USA, 2007. ACM. DOI: 10.1145/1255175.1255254. 1

[62] A. T. da Silva, J. A. dos Santos, A. X. Falcão, R. da Silva Torres, and L. P. Magalhães. Incorporating multiple distance spaces in optimum-path forest classification to improve feedback-based learning. *Computer Vision and Image Understanding*, 116(4):510–523, 2012. DOI: 10.1016/j.cviu.2011.12.001. 10

[63] A. T. da Silva, A. X. Falcão, and L. P. Magalhães. Active learning paradigms for cbir systems based on optimum-path forest classification. *Pattern Recognition*, 44(12):2971–2978, 2011. DOI: 10.1016/j.patcog.2011.04.026. 10

[64] R. Datta, D. Joshi, J. Li, and J. Z. Wang. Image retrieval: Ideas, influences, and trends of the new age. *ACM Comput. Surv.*, 40(2), 2008. DOI: 10.1145/1348246.1348248. 1

[65] D. Davies and D. Bouldin. A Cluster Separation Measure. *IEEE Transactions on Pattern Analysis and Machine Intelligence*, 1(2):224–227, 1979. DOI: 10.1109/TPAMI.1979.4766909. 8

[66] M. Davis, J. Spohrer, and P. Maglio. Guest editorial: How technology is changing the design and delivery of services. *Operations Management Research*, 4(1):1–5, 2011. 10.1007/s12063-011-0046-6. DOI: 10.1007/s12063-011-0046-6. 37

[67] R. O. de Alencar, C. A. Davis,Jr., and M. A. Gonçalves. Geographical classification of documents using evidence from wikipedia. In *Proceedings of the 6th Workshop on Geographic Information Retrieval*, GIR '10, pages 12:1–12:8, New York, NY, USA, 2010. ACM. DOI: 10.1145/1722080.1722096. 99

[68] C. S. de Souza and J. Preece. A Framework for Analyzing and Understanding Online Communities. *Interacting with Computers*, 16(3):579–610, 2004. DOI: 10.1016/j.intcom.2003.12.006. 45

[69] E. Deelman, J. Blythe, Y. Gil, C. Kesselman, S. Koranda, A. Lazzarini, G. Mehta, M. A. Papa, and K. Vahi. Pegasus and the pulsar search: From metadata to execution on the grid. In *Applications Grid Workshop at the Fifth International Conference on Parallel Processing and Applied Mathematics*, pages 821–830, 2003. DOI: 10.1007/978-3-540-24669-5_107. 65, 79, 83

[70] A. del Bimbo. *Visual Information Retrieval*. Morgan Kaufmann Publishers, San Francisco, CA, USA, 1999. 5, 6

[71] S. A. Dudani, K. J. Breeding, and R. B. McGhee. Aircraft Identification by Moment Invariants. *IEEE Transactions on Computers*, 26(1):39–45, January 1977. DOI: 10.1109/TC.1977.5009272. 3

[72] R. Dunlap, L. Mark, S. Rugaber, V. Balaji, J. Chastang, L. Cinquini, C. Deluca, D. Middleton, and S. Murphy. Earth system curator: metadata infrastructure for climate modeling. *Earth Science Informatics*, 1(3):131–149, Nov. 2008. DOI: 10.1007/s12145-008-0016-1. 65, 83

[73] J. Dunn. A Fuzzy Relative of the ISODATA Process and Its Use in Detecting Compact Well-Separated Clusters. *Journal of Cybernetics*, 3(3):32–57, 1974. DOI: 10.1080/01969727308546046. 8

[74] P. Eades and M. L. Huang. Navigating Clustered Graphs using Force-Directed Methods. *Journal of Graph Algorithms and Applications*, 4:157–181, 2000. DOI: 10.7155/jgaa.00029. 54

[75] M. J. Egenhofer. Query processing in spatial-query-by-sketch. *Journal of Visual Languages & Computing*, 8:403–424, Aug. 1997. DOI: 10.1006/jvlc.1997.0054. 89

[76] Ensemble. Ensemble Computing Portal. http://www.computingportal.org/, September 2011. 27, 34

[77] I. Esslimani, A. Brun, and A. Boyer. Densifying a Behavioral Recommender System by Social Networks Link Prediction Methods. *Social Network Analysis and Mining*, 1(3):159–172, 2011. DOI: 10.1007/s13278-010-0004-6. 47, 48

[78] A. X. Falcão, J. Stolfi, and R. A. Lotufo. The Image Foresting Transform: Theory, Algorithms, and Applications. *IEEE Transactions on Pattern Analysis and Machine Intelligence*, 26(1):19–29, Jan 2004. DOI: 10.1109/TPAMI.2004.1261076. 4

[79] W. Fan, P. Pathak, and L. Wallace. Nonlinear ranking function representations in genetic programming-based ranking discovery for personalized search. *Decision Support Systems*, 42(3):1338 – 1349, 2006. DOI: 10.1016/j.dss.2005.11.002. 103

[80] D. Fernandes and A. C. Salgado. Geovisual interface - a visual query interface for geographic information systems. In *SBBD'00*, pages 7–19, 2000. 102

[81] C. D. Ferreira, J. A. dos Santos, R. da Silva Torres, M. A. Gonçalves, R. C. Rezende, and W. Fan. Relevance feedback based on genetic programming for image retrieval. *Pattern Recognition Letters*, 32(1):27–37, 2011. DOI: 10.1016/j.patrec.2010.05.015. 10

[82] M. Flickner, H. Sawhney, W. Niblack, J. Ashley, Q. Huang, B. Dom, M. Gorkani, J. Hafner, D. Lee, D. Petkovic, D. Steele, and P. Yanker. Query by Image and Video Content: The QBIC System. *IEEE Computer*, 28(9):23–32, 1995. DOI: 10.1109/2.410146. 1, 6, 7, 9

[83] S. Fortunato. Community detection in graphs. *Physics Reports*, 486(3-5):75 – 174, 2010. DOI: 10.1016/j.physrep.2009.11.002. 51

[84] S. Fortunato and C. Castellano. Community Structure in Graphs. arXiv, http://arxiv.org/abs/0712.2716. DOI: 10.1007/978-0-387-30440-3_76. 47

[85] E. A. Fox. The 5S framework for digital libraries and two case studies: NDLTD and CSTC. In *Proceedings NIT'99, The 11th International Conf. on New Information Technology*. NIT, Taipei, Taiwan, August 1999. 27

[86] E. A. Fox, Y. Chen, M. Akbar, C. A. Shaffer, S. H. Edwards, P. Brusilovsky, D. D. Garcia, L. M. Delcambre, F. Decker, D. W. Archer, R. Furuta, F. Shipman, S. Carpenter, and L. Cassel. Ensemble PDP-8: Eight Principles for Distributed Portals. In *Proc. JCDL/ICADL 2010, June 21-25, Gold Coast, Australia*, pages 341–344. ACM, 2010. DOI: 10.1145/1816123.1816174. 28

[87] E. A. Fox, S. Yang, and S. Kim. ETDs, NDLTD, and open access: a 5S perspective. *Ciencia da Informacao*, 35:75 – 90, 08 2006. DOI: 10.1590/S0100-19652006000200009. 27

[88] M. Freeston. The Alexandria digital library and the Alexandria digital earth prototype. In *Proceedings of the 4th ACM/IEEE-CS Joint Conference on Digital Libraries*, JCDL '04, pages 410–410, New York, NY, USA, 2004. ACM. DOI: 10.1109/JCDL.2004.1336214. 107

[89] R. Freitas and R. da S. Torres. OntoSAIA: Um Ambiente Baseado em Ontologias para Recuperação e Anotação Semi-Automática de Imagens. In *First Workshop in Digital Libraries, Proc. XX Brazilian Symposium on Databases - SBBD 2005*, pages 60–79, Uberlândia, Brasil, 2005. (In Portuguese). 22

[90] J. C. French, A. C. Chapin, and W. N. Martin. An application of multiple viewpoints to content-based image retrieval. In *Proceedings of the 3rd ACM/IEEE-CS Joint Conference on Digital Libraries*, pages 128–130, Washington, DC, USA, 2003. IEEE Computer Society. 1, 11

[91] J. Frew, M. Freeston, N. Freitas, L. Hill, G. Janée, K. Lovette, R. Nideffer, T. Smith, and Q. Zheng. The Alexandria digital library architecture. *International Journal on Digital Libraries*, 2:259–268, May 2000. DOI: 10.1007/s007990050004. 96

[92] G. Fu, C. B. Jones, and A. I. Abdelmoty. Ontology-based spatial query expansion in information retrieval. In *On the Move to Meaningful Internet Systems 2005: CoopIS, DOA, and ODBASE*, Lecture Notes in Computer Science, pages 1466–1482. Springer Berlin / Heidelberg, 2005. DOI: 10.1007/11575801_33. 103

[93] V. Gaede and O. Gunther. Multidimensional Access Methods. *ACM Computing Surveys*, 30(2):170–231, 1998. DOI: 10.1145/280277.280279. 7

[94] A. Gallagher, D. Joshi, J. Yu, and J. Luo. Geo-location inference from image content and user tags. In *IEEE Computer Society Conference on Computer Vision and Pattern Recognition Workshops, 2009. CVPR Workshops 2009*, pages 55–62. IEEE, June 2009. DOI: 10.1109/CVPRW.2009.5204168. 106

[95] A. Girgensohn and A. Lee. Making Web Sites be Places for Social Interaction. In *Proceedings of the 2002 ACM Conference on Computer Supported Cooperative Work*, pages 136–145, 2002. DOI: 10.1145/587078.587098. 46

[96] M. Girvan and M. E. J. Newman. Community structure in social and biological networks. *Proceedings of the National Academy of Sciences*, 99(12):7821–7826, 2002. DOI: 10.1073/pnas.122653799. 51, 52, 56

[97] D. Goldberg, D. Nichols, B. M. Oki, and D. Terry. Using Collaborative Filtering to Weave an Information Tapestry. *Communications of the ACM*, 35(12):61–70, 1992. DOI: 10.1145/138859.138867. 47

[98] M. A. Gonçalves. *Streams, Structures, Spaces, Scenarios, and Societies (5S): A Formal Digital Library Framework and Its Applications*. Ph.D. thesis, Virginia Tech, Blacksburg, VA, 2004. http://scholar.lib.vt.edu/theses/available/etd-12052004-135923/ [last visited July 4, 2012]. DOI: 10.1145/984321.984325. 73, 76

[99] M. A. Gonçalves and E. A. Fox. 5SL: a language for declarative specification and generation of digital libraries. In *JCDL '02: Proceedings of the 2nd ACM/IEEE-CS Joint Conference on Digital Libraries*, pages 263–272, New York, NY, USA, 2002. ACM Press. DOI: 10.1145/544220.544276. 23

[100] M. A. Gonçalves, E. A. Fox, L. T. Watson, and N. A. Kipp. Streams, structures, spaces, scenarios, societies (5S): A formal model for digital libraries. Technical Report TR-03-04, Computer Science, Virginia Tech, Blacksburg, VA, 2003. http://eprints.cs.vt.edu/archive/00000653/ [last visited July 4, 2012]. DOI: 10.1145/544220.544276. 2

[101] M. A. Gonçalves, E. A. Fox, L. T. Watson, and N. A. Kipp. Streams, structures, spaces, scenarios, societies (5S): A formal model for digital libraries. *ACM Transactions on Information Systems*, 22(2):270–312, 2004. DOI: 10.1145/544220.544276. 46, 65

[102] F. Guerroudji-Meddah, H. Belbachir, and R. Laurini. A visual language for GIS querying. In *Computer Science and Information Technology, 2009. ICCSIT 2009. 2nd IEEE International Conference on*, pages 518–521, aug. 2009. DOI: 10.1109/ICCSIT.2009.5234515. 102

[103] Z. Guo, L. Ma, and H. Sun. A cooperative service model for digital library alliances based on grid. In *Proceedings of the 2010 International Conference on Machine Vision and Human-machine Interface*, MVHI '10, pages 483–486, Washington, DC, USA, 2010. IEEE Computer Society. DOI: 10.1109/MVHI.2010.201. 73

[104] D. Gurzick and W. G. Lutters. Towards a Design Theory for Online Communities. In *Proceedings of the 4th International Conference on Design Science Research in Information Systems and Technology*, pages 11:1–11:20, 2009. DOI: 10.1145/1555619.1555634. 45

[105] R. Guttman. R-Tree: A Dynamic Index to Structure for Spatial Searching. In *SIGMOD Conf. Ann. Meeting*, pages 47–57, Boston, 1984. DOI: 10.1145/971697.602266. 7

[106] J. Hadidjojo and S. A. Cheong. Equal graph partitioning on estimated infection network as an effective epidemic mitigation measure. *PLoS ONE*, 6(7):e22124, 2011. DOI: 10.1371/journal.pone.0022124. 51

[107] R. M. Haralick, K. Shanmugam, and I. Dinstein. Textural Features for Image Classification. *IEEE Transactions on Systems, Man and Cybernatics*, 3(6):610–621, 1973. DOI: 10.1109/TSMC.1973.4309314. 6

[108] S. M. Hasan, K. Bisset, E. A. Fox, K. Hall, J. P. Leidig, and M. Marathe. An Extensible Digital Library Service to Support Network Science. In *Proceedings of the 13th International Conference on Computational Science*, ICCS '13, pages 409–418, 2013. DOI: 10.1016/j.procs.2013.05.205. 83

[109] J. Hays and A. A. Efros. im2gps: estimating geographic information from a single image. In *Proceedings of the IEEE Conf. on Computer Vision and Pattern Recognition (CVPR)*, pages 1–8, 2008. 86, 106

[110] D. He. A study of self-organizing map in interactive relevance feedback. In *ITNG '06: Proceedings of the Third International Conference on Information Technology: New Generations*, pages 394–401, Washington, DC, USA, 2006. IEEE Computer Society. DOI: 10.1109/ITNG.2006.18. 103

[111] D. C. Heesch, M. J. Pickering, P. Howarth, A. Yavlinsky, and S. M. Rueger. Digital library access via image similarity search. In *Proceedings of the 4th ACM/IEEE-CS Joint Conference on Digital Libraries*, JCDL '04, pages 412–412, New York, NY, USA, 2004. ACM. DOI: 10.1109/JCDL.2004.1336216. 1

[112] B. Hendrickson and R. Leland. An improved spectral graph partitioning algorithm for mapping parallel computations. *SIAM J. Sci. Comput.*, 16(2):452–469, 1995. DOI: 10.1137/0916028. 51

[113] A. Henrich and V. Luedecke. Characteristics of geographic information needs. In *Proceedings of the 4th ACM Workshop on Geographical Information Retrieval*, pages 1–6, Lisbon, Portugal, 2007. DOI: 10.1145/1316948.1316950. 94, 103

[114] J. S. Hong, H. Chen, and J. Hsiang. A Digital Museum of Taiwanese Butterflies. In *Proceedings of the Fifth ACM Conference on digital Libraries*, pages 260–261, San Antonio, Texas, United States, 2000. DOI: 10.1145/336597.336694. 1, 11

[115] K. Hoyle. Minutiae triplet-based features with extended ridge information for determining sufficiency in fingerprints. Master's thesis, Virginia Tech, Blacksburg, Virginia, 2011. 75

[116] M. K. Hu. Visual Pattern Recognition by Moment Invariants. *IRE Transactions on Information Theory*, 8(2):179–187, 1962. DOI: 10.1109/TIT.1962.1057692. 3

[117] C.-Y. Huang, L.-m. Liu, and D. D. Hung. Fingerprint analysis and singular point detection. *Pattern Recogn. Lett.*, 28(15):1937–1945, November 2007. DOI: 10.1016/j.patrec.2007.04.003. 70

[118] J. Huang, S. Kumar, M. Mitra, W. Zhu, and R. Zabih. Image Indexing Using Color Correlograms. In *IEEE International Conference on Computer Vision and Pattern Recognition*, pages 762–768, Puerto Rico, June 1997. DOI: 10.1109/CVPR.1997.609412. 5

[119] M.-x. Huang, C.-x. Xing, and J.-j. Yang. A cooperative framework of service chain for digital library. In *Proceedings of the 2009 33rd Annual IEEE International Computer Software and Applications Conference - Volume 02*, COMPSAC '09, pages 359–364, Washington, DC, USA, 2009. IEEE Computer Society. DOI: 10.1109/COMPSAC.2009.159. 73

[120] T. K. Huwe. Exploiting Synergies Among Digital Repositories, Special Collections, and Online Community. *Online*, 33(2):14–19, 2009. 45

[121] IEEE Learning Technology Standards Committee. *IEEE Standard for Learning Object Metadata*. IEEE, 2002. IEEE-SA Standard 1484.12.1. 31

[122] H. Ino, M. Kudo, and A. Nakamura. Partitioning of web graphs by community topology. In *Proceedings of the 14th international conference on World Wide Web*, WWW '05, pages 661–669. ACM, 2005. DOI: 10.1145/1060745.1060841. 51

[123] Y. Ioannidis. User working group: Towards user interoperability. In *First DL.org Workshop at European Conference on Research and Advanced Technology for Digital Libraries*, 2009. 71

[124] G. Janée and J. Frew. The ADEPT digital library architecture. In *Proceedings of the 2nd ACM/IEEE-CS Joint Conference on Digital Libraries*, pages 342–350, Portland, Oregon, USA, 2002. ACM. DOI: 10.1145/544220.544306. 107

[125] C. Jones. Geographic information retrieval, 2006. Keynote Presentation at GEOINFO 2016. Campos do Jordão, SP, Brazil. http://www.geoinfo.info/geoinfo2006/presentation/Christopher_Jones.ppt. 96, 98, 99

[126] C. B. Jones, A. I. Abdelmoty, D. Finch, G. Fu, and S. Vaid. The SPIRIT spatial search engine: Architecture, ontologies and spatial indexing. In *Geographic Information Science*, Lecture Notes in Computer Science, pages 125–139. Springer, 2004. DOI: 10.1007/978-3-540-30231-5_9. 91, 96, 99, 104

[127] C. B. Jones and R. S. Purves. Geographical information retrieval. *International Journal of Geographical Information Science*, 22(3):219, 2008. DOI: 10.1080/13658810701626343. 91

[128] R. Jones, A. Hassan, and F. Diaz. Geographic features in web search retrieval. In *Proceeding of the 2nd International Workshop on Geographic Information Retrieval*, pages 57–58, Napa Valley, California, USA, 2008. ACM. DOI: 10.1145/1460007.1460023. 94, 103

[129] T. H. Jordan. SCEC 2009 Annual Report. *Southern California Earthquake Center*, 2009. 65, 83

[130] P. Kelm, S. Schmiedeke, and T. Sikora. Multi-modal, Multi-resource Methods for Placing Flickr Videos on the Map. In *Proceedings of the 1st ACM International Conference on Multimedia Retrieval*, ICMR '11, pages 1–8, 2011. DOI: 10.1145/1991996.1992048. 86, 107, 110

[131] S. Kethers, X. Shen, A. E. Treloar, and R. G. Wilkinson. Discovering australia's research data. In *Proceedings of the 10th ACM/IEEE Joint Conference on Digital Libraries*, pages 345–348, 2010. DOI: 10.1145/1816123.1816175. 65

[132] S. A. Khirni, B. Yang, R. Purves, and M. Kopczynski. Query interface design. Project Report W4 D74101, University of Zurich, Zurich, Switzerland, 2003. 102

[133] M. Kimpton and S. Payette. Duraspace. In *Proceedings of the 4th International Conference on Open Repositories*, OR09, Atlanta, GA, USA, 2009. Georgia Institute of Technology. 29

[134] J. Koh, Y. Kim, B. Butler, and G. Bock. Encouraging Participation in Virtual Communities. *Commun. ACM*, 50(2):68–73, February 2007. DOI: 10.1145/1216016.1216023. 47

[135] J. A. Konstan, B. N. Miller, D. Maltz, J. L. Herlocker, L. R. Gordon, and J. Riedl. Grouplens: Applying collaborative filtering to usenet news. *Communications of the ACM*, 40(3):77–87, 1997. DOI: 10.1145/245108.245126. 47

[136] I. Konstas, V. Stathopoulos, and J. M. Jose. On Social Networks and Collaborative Recommendation, 2009. DOI: 10.1145/1571941.1571977. 47

[137] N. P. Kozievitch, S. Codio, J. A. Francois, E. Fox, and R. da S. Torres. Exploring CBIR concepts in the CTRnet Project. Technical Report IC-10-32, Institute of Computing, University of Campinas, November 2010. In English, 20 pages. 2, 20, 107

[138] N. P. Kozievitch, R. da S. Torres, S. H. Park, E. A. Fox, N. Short, A. L. Abbott, S. Misra, and M. Hsiao. Rethinking Fingerprint Evidence Through Integration of Very Large Digital Libraries. *VLDL Workshop at 14th European Conference on Research and Advanced Technology for Digital Libraries (ECDL2010)*, pages 23–30, 07 2010. 70, 81

[139] S. Kumar, S. K. Das, and R. Biswas. Graph partitioning for parallel applications in heterogeneous grid environments. In *Parallel and Distributed Processing Symposium - (IPDPS'02)*, pages 66–72, 2002. DOI: 10.1109/IPDPS.2002.1015564. 51

[140] B. Lagoeiro, M. A. Gonçalves, and E. A. Fox. 5SQual: A quality tool for digital libraries. In *Proceedings of the 7th ACM/IEEE Joint Conference on Digital Libraries*, page (demonstration), New York, NY, USA, 2007. ACM Press. 23

[141] M. Larson, M. Soleymani, P. Serdyukov, S. Rudinac, C. Wartena, V. Murdock, G. Friedland, R. Ordelman, and G. J. F. Jones. Automatic tagging and geotagging in video collections and communities. In *Proceedings of the 1st ACM International Conference on Multimedia Retrieval*, ICMR '11, pages 51:1–51:8, New York, NY, USA, 2011. ACM. DOI: 10.1145/1991996.1992047. 86, 106

[142] R. R. Larson. Geographic information retrieval and spatial browsing. In L. C. Smith and M. Gluck, editors, *Geographic information systems and libraries: patrons, maps, and spatial information: papers presented at the 1995 Clinic on Library Applications of Data Processing, April 10-12, 1995*, pages 81–124. Graduate School of Library and Information Science, University of Illinois at Urbana-Champaign, University of Illinois, Urbana-Champaign, Apr. 1995. 90, 91

[143] R. R. Larson. Geographic information retrieval and digital libraries. In *Proceedings of 13th European Conference, ECDL 2009*, volume 5714/2009, pages 461–464. Springer Berlin / Heidelberg, Sept 2009. DOI 10.1007/978-3-642-04346-8. DOI: 10.1007/978-3-642-04346-8_59. 97

[144] J. Leidig, E. Fox, M. Marathe, and H. Mortveit. Epidemiology experiment and simulation management through schema-based digital libraries. In *Proceedings of the 2nd DL.org Workshop at ECDL, Making Digital Libraries Interoperable: Challenges and Approaches*, pages 57–66, 2010. 66, 67, 70, 80

[145] J. Leidig, E. A. Fox, K. Hall, M. Marathe, and H. Mortveit. SimDL: a model ontology driven digital library for simulation systems. In *Proceedings of the 11th annual international ACM/IEEE Joint Conference on Digital Libraries*, JCDL '11, pages 81–84, New York, NY, USA, 2011. ACM. DOI: 10.1145/1998076.1998091. 68, 69, 74

[146] J. M. Leimeister, P. Sidiras, and H. Krcmar. Success Factors of Virtual Communities from the Perspective of Members and Operators: An Empirical Study. In *Proceedings of the 37th Annual Hawaii International Conference on System Sciences, HICSS '04*, pages 1530–1605, 2004. DOI: 10.1109/HICSS.2004.1265459. 45

[147] P. P. Leonardo Candela, Donatella Castelli. D4Science: an e-infrastructure for supporting virtual research. In *5th Italian Research Conference on Digital Libraries (IRCDL)*, pages 166–169, 2009. 65

[148] J. Leveling and S. Hartrumpf. On metonymy recognition for geographic information retrieval. *International Journal of Geographical Information Science*, 22(3):289, 2008. DOI: 10.1080/13658810701626244. 103

[149] M. Leyton. Symmetry-Curvature Duality. *Computer Vision, Graphics, and Image Processing*, 38(3):327–341, 1987. DOI: 10.1016/0734-189X(87)90117-4. 4

[150] L. T. Li, J. Almeida, and R. da S. Torres. RECOD working notes for placing task MediaEval 2011. In *Proceedings of the MediaEval 2011 Workshop, Santa Croce in Fossabanda, Pisa, Italy, September 1-2, 2011*, volume Vol-807 of *CEUR Workshop Proceedings (CEUR-WS)*, Pisa, Italy, Sept. 2011. CEUR-WS.org. 109, 110

[151] L. T. Li, J. Almeida, D. C. G. Pedronette, O. A. B. Penatti, and R. da S. Torres. A multimodal approach for video geocoding. In *Proceedings of the MediaEval 2012 Workshop*. CEUR-WS.org, 2012. 110, 111

[152] L. T. Li and R. da S. Torres. Coping with geographical relationships in web searches. Technical Report IC-10-04, Institute of Computing, University of Campinas, Jan. 2010. 91

[153] L. T. Li, D. C. G. Pedronette, J. Almeida, O. A. B. Penatti, R. T. Calumby, and R. da S. Torres. Multimedia Multimodal Geocoding. In *Proceedings of ACM SIGSPATIAL International Conference on Advances in Geographic Information Systems*, ACM SIGSPATIAL GIS 2012, pages 474–477, 2012. DOI: 10.1145/2424321.2424393. 111

[154] L. T. Li, D. C. G. Pedronette, J. Almeida, O. A. B. Penatti, R. T. Calumby, and R. da Silva Torres. A rank aggregation framework for video multimodal geocoding. *Multimedia Tools and Applications*, pages 1–37, 2013. http://dx.doi.org/10.1007/s11042-013-1588-4. DOI: 10.1007/s11042-013-1588-4. 112

[155] L. T. Li, O. A. B. Penatti, E. A. Fox, and R. da S. Torres. Domain-specific Image Geocoding: a Case Study on Virginia Tech Building Photos. In *Proc. of the 13th ACM/IEEE-CS Joint Conference on Digital Libraries*, JCDL '13, New York, NY, USA, 2013. ACM. DOI: 10.1145/2467696.2467727. 1, 112, 118

[156] N. Li, L. Zhu, P. Mitra, K. Mueller, E. Poweleit, and C. L. Giles. oreChem ChemXSeer: a semantic digital library for chemistry. In *Proceedings of the 10th ACM/IEEE Joint Conference on Digital Libraries*, pages 245–254, 2010. DOI: 10.1145/1816123.1816160. 65, 83

[157] H. Lin. Determinants of Successful Virtual Communities: Contributions from System Characteristics and Social Factors. *Information and Management*, 45(8):522–527, 2008. DOI: 10.1016/j.im.2008.08.002. 45

[158] Y. Liu, D. Zhang, G. Lu, and W.-Y. Ma. A survey of content-based image retrieval with high-level semantics. *Pattern Recognition*, 40(1):262–282, 2007. DOI: 10.1016/j.patcog.2006.04.045. 1

[159] S. Loncaric. A Survey of Shape Analysis Techniques. *Pattern Recognition*, 31(8):983–1190, Aug 1998. DOI: 10.1016/S0031-2023(97)00122-2. 3

[160] C. Lopez-Pujalte, V. P. G. Bote, and F. de Moya Anegon. Order-based fitness functions for genetic algorithms applied to relevance feedback. *Journal of the American Society for Information Science and Technology*, 54(2):152–160, 2003. DOI: 10.1002/asi.10179. 10

[161] B. Ludäscher, I. Altintas, C. Berkley, D. Higgins, E. Jaeger, M. Jones, E. A. Lee, J. Tao, and Y. Zhao. Scientific workflow management and the Kepler system. *Concurrency and Computation: Practice and Experience*, 18(10):1039–1065, 2006. DOI: 10.1002/cpe.994. 65, 79, 83

[162] P. J. Ludford, D. Cosley, D. Frankowski, and L. Terveen. Think Different: Increasing Online Community Participation using Uniqueness and Group Dissimilarity. In *Proceedings of the SIGCHI Conference on Human Factors in Computing Systems*, pages 631–638, 2004. DOI: 10.1145/985692.985772. 47

[163] J. Luo, D. Joshi, J. Yu, and A. Gallagher. Geotagging in multimedia and computer vision–a survey. *Multimedia Tools Appl.*, 51(1):187–211, January 2011. DOI: 10.1007/s11042-010-0623-y. 86, 104, 105

[164] W. Y. Ma and B. S. Manjunath. Netra: A Toolbox for Navigating Large Image Databases. In *IEEE International Conference on Image Processing*, pages 256–268, 1997. DOI: 10.1109/ICIP.1997.647976. 7

[165] S. D. MacArthur, C. E. Brodley, A. C. Kak, and L. S. Broderick. Interactive Content-Based Image Retrieval Using Relevance Feedback. *Computer Vision and Image Understanding*, 88(2):55–75, 2002. DOI: 10.1006/cviu.2002.0977. 10

[166] G. Mainar-Ruiz and J. C. Pérez-Cortes. Approximate nearest neighbor search using a single space-filling curve and multiple representations of the data points. In *18th International Conference on Pattern Recognition*, pages 502–505, 2006. DOI: 10.1109/ICPR.2006.275. 7

[167] S. Majithia, M. S. Shields, I. J. Taylor, and I. Wang. Triana: A graphical web service composition and execution toolkit. In *Proceedings of the IEEE International Conference on Web Services*, pages 514–521, 2004. DOI: 10.1109/ICWS.2004.1314777. 65, 79, 83

[168] T. Malloy and G. Hanley. Merlot: A faculty-focused web site of educational resources. *Behavior Research Methods*, 33(2):274–276, 2001. 10.3758/BF03195376. DOI: 10.3758/BF03195376. 32

[169] D. Maltoni and R. Cappelli. Advances in fingerprint modeling. *Image Vision Comput.*, 27(3):258–268, February 2009. DOI: 10.1016/j.imavis.2007.01.005. 83

[170] B. S. Manjunath and W. Y. Ma. Texture Features for Browsing and Retrieval of Image Data. *IEEE Transactions on Pattern Analysis and Machine Intelligence*, 18(8):837–842, August 1996. DOI: 10.1109/34.531803. 6

[171] B. S. Manjunath, J. R. Ohm, V. V. Vasudevan, and A. Yamada. Color and Texture Descriptors. *IEEE Transactions on Circuits and Systems for Video Technology*, 11(6):703–715, June 2001. DOI: 10.1109/76.927424. 5, 6, 8

[172] C. D. Manning, P. Raghavan, and H. Schütze. *Introduction to Information Retrieval*. Cambridge University Press, New York, NY, USA, 2008. DOI: 10.1017/CBO9780511809071. 110

[173] M. Markland. Technology and People: Some Challenges when Integrating Digital Library Systems into Online Learning Environments. *The New Review of Information and Library Research*, 9(1):85–96, 2003. DOI: 10.1080/13614550410001687936. 45

[174] B. Martins, M. J. Silva, and L. Andrade. Indexing and ranking in Geo-IR systems. In *GIR '05: Proceedings of the 2005 Workshop on Geographic Information Retrieval*, pages 31–34, New York, NY, USA, 2005. ACM. DOI: 10.1145/1096985.1096993. 103

[175] R. McGreal. A typology of learning object repositories. In H. H. Adelsberger, P. Kinshuk, J. M. Pawlowski, and D. G. Sampson, editors, *Handbook on Information Technologies for Education and Training*, International Handbooks on Information Systems, pages 5–28. Springer Berlin Heidelberg, 2008. DOI: 10.1007/978-3-540-74155-8. 34

[176] B. M. Mehtre, M. S. Kankanhalli, and W. F. Lee. Shape Measures for Content Based Image Retrieval: A Comparison. *Information Processing and Management*, 33(3):319–337, 1997. DOI: 10.1016/S0306-4573(96)00069-6. 3

[177] S. E. Middleton, D. D. Roure, and N. R. Shadbolt. Ontology-based recommender systems. In S. Staab and D. Rudi Studer, editors, *Handbook on Ontologies*, International Handbooks on Information Systems, pages 779–796. Springer Berlin Heidelberg, 2009. 10.1007/978-3-540-92673-3_35. DOI: 10.1007/978-3-540-92673-3. 30

[178] D. R. Millen and J. F. Patterson. Stimulating Social Engagement in a Community Network. In *Proceedings of the 2002 ACM Conference on Computer Supported Cooperative Work*, pages 306–313, 2002. DOI: 10.1145/587078.587121. 47

[179] P. Miranda, R. da S. Torres, and A. X. Falcão. TSD: A Shape Descriptor Based on a Distribution of Tensor Scale Local Orientation. In *XVIII Brazilian Symposium on Computer Graphics and Image Processing*, pages 139–146, Natal, RN, Brazil, October 2005. DOI: 10.1109/SIBGRAPI.2005.51. 4

[180] F. Mokhtarian and S. Abbasi. Shape Similarity Retrieval Under Affine Transforms. *Pattern Recognition*, 35(1):31–41, January 2002. DOI: 10.1016/S0031-3203(01)00040-1. 3

[181] R. W. Moore, A. Rajasekar, M. Wan, Y. Katsis, D. Zhou, A. Deutsch, and Y. Papakonstantinou. Constraint-based knowledge systems for grids, digital libraries, and persistent archives: Yearly report. Technical Report 2005-5, SDSC, University of California, San Diego, 2005. 65

[182] L. Moreau, B. Clifford, J. Freire, Y. Gil, P. Groth, J. Futrelle, N. Kwasnikowska, S. Miles, P. Missier, J. Myers, Y. Simmhan, E. Stephan, and J. V. den Bussche. The Open Provenance

Model—core specification (v1.1). In *JCDL '09: Proceedings of the 9th ACM/IEEE-CS Joint Conference on Digital Libraries, Doctoral Consortium, available* http://www.ieee-tcdl.org/Bulletin/v5n3/Kozievitch/kozievitch.html, *last accessed on 05/05/11.* Elsevier, 2009. 67

[183] H. Muller, N. Michoux, D. Bandon, and A. Geissbuhler. A Review of Content-Based Image Retrieval Systems in Medical Applications – Clinical Benefits and Future Directions. *International Journal of Medical Informatics*, 73(1):1–23, Feb 2004. DOI: 10.1016/j.ijmedinf.2003.11.024. 10

[184] M. E. J. Newman and M. Girvan. Finding and evaluating community structure in networks. *Phys. Rev. E*, 69(2):026113, Feb 2004. DOI: 10.1103/PhysRevE.69.066133. 52, 56

[185] O. Nov, M. Naaman, and C. Ye. Analysis of Participation in an Online Photo-sharing Community: A Multidimensional Perspective. *Journal of the American Society for Information Science and Technology*, 61(3):555–566, 2010. DOI: 10.1002/asi.v61:3. 47

[186] OAI. The Open Archives Initiative Protocol for Metadata Harvesting – Version 2.0. Eds. Lagoze, C., Van De Sompel, H., Nelson, M., Warner, S., http://www.openarchives.org/OAI/openarchivesprotocol.html [last visited July 4, 2012], October 2004. 12

[187] V. E. Ogle and M. Stonebraker. Chabot: Retrieval from Relational Database of Images. *IEEE Computer*, 28(9):40–48, Sep 1995. DOI: 10.1109/2.410150. 1, 6, 9

[188] T. Oinn, M. Greenwood, M. Addis, N. Alpdemir, J. Ferris, K. Glover, C. Goble, A. Goderis, D. Hull, D. Marvin, P. Li, P. Lord, M. Pocock, M. Senger, R. Stevens, A. Wipat, and C. Wroe. Taverna: lessons in creating a workflow environment for the life sciences. *Concurrency and Computation: Practice and Experience*, 18(10):1067–1100, 2006. DOI: 10.1002/cpe.993. 65, 79, 83

[189] M. A. Oliveira and N. J. Leite. A multiscale directional operator and morphological tools for reconnecting broken ridges in fingerprint images. *Pattern Recogn.*, 41(1):367–377, January 2008. DOI: 10.1016/j.patcog.2007.05.019. 70

[190] OMG. OMG-XML Metadata Interchange (XMI) Specification, v1.2. http://cgi.omg.org/docs/formal/02-01-01.pdf, 2002. 36

[191] T. O'Reilly. What Is Web 2.0. Design Patterns and Business Models for the Next Generation of Software. http://www.oreillynet.com/pub/a/oreilly/tim/news/2005/09/30/what-is-web-20.html, September 2005. 45

[192] S. Overell and S. Rüger. Using co-occurrence models for placename disambiguation. *International Journal of Geographical Information Science*, 22(3):265, 2008. DOI: 10.1080/13658810701626236. 103

[193] G. Palla, I. Derényi, I. Farkas, and T. Vicsek. Uncovering the overlapping community structure of complex networks in nature and society. *Nature*, 435(7043):814–818, 2005. DOI: 10.1038/nature03607. 51

[194] S. Park, J. Leidig, L. Li, E. Fox, N. Short, K. Hoyle, A. Abbott, and M. Hsiao. Experiment and analysis services in a fingerprint digital library for collaborative research. In S. Gradmann, F. Borri, C. Meghini, and H. Schuldt, editors, *Research and Advanced Technology for Digital Libraries*, volume 6966 of *Lecture Notes in Computer Science*, pages 179–191. Springer Berlin / Heidelberg, 2011. DOI: 10.1007/978-3-642-24469-8. 69, 79, 81, 82

[195] R. C. Pasley, P. D. Clough, and M. Sanderson. Geo-tagging for imprecise regions of different sizes. In *Proceedings of the 4th ACM Workshop on Geographical Information Retrieval*, pages 77–82, Lisbon, Portugal, 2007. DOI: 10.1145/1316948.1316969. 103

[196] G. Pass, R. Zabih, and J. Miller. Comparing Images Using Color Coherence Vectors. In *Proceedings of the fourth ACM international conference on Multimedia*, pages 65–73, 1996. DOI: 10.1145/244130.244148. 5, 23

[197] PBS. PBS teachers. http://www.pbs.org/teachers/. Accessed March 2011. 46

[198] D. C. G. Pedronette, R. da S. Torres, and R. T. Calumby. Using contextual spaces for image re-ranking and rank aggregation. *Multimedia Tools and Applications*, pages 1–28, 2012. http://dx.doi.org/10.1007/s11042-012-1115-z. DOI: 10.1007/s11042-012-1115-z. 111

[199] O. A. B. Penatti and R. da S. Torres. Eva: an evaluation tool for comparing descriptors in content-based image retrieval tasks. In *Proceedings of the International Conference on Multimedia Information Retrieval*, MIR '10, pages 413–416, New York, NY, USA, 2010. ACM. DOI: 10.1145/1743384.1743455. 20

[200] O. A. B. Penatti, L. T. Li, J. Almeida, and R. da S. Torres. A Visual Approach for Video Geocoding Using Bag-of-scenes. In *Proceedings of the 2nd ACM International Conference on Multimedia Retrieval*, ICMR '12, pages 53:1–53:8, New York, NY, USA, 2012. ACM. DOI: 10.1145/2324796.2324857. 110

[201] O. A. B. Penatti, E. Valle, and R. da Silva Torres. Encoding spatial arrangement of visual words. In *Proceedings of Iberoamerican Congress on Pattern Recognition*, volume 7042 of *CIARP'2011*, pages 240–247, 2011. DOI: 10.1007/978-3-642-25085-9_28. 116

[202] O. A. B. Penatti, E. Valle, and R. da Silva Torres. Comparative study of global color and texture descriptors for web image retrieval. *J. Visual Communication and Image Representation*, 23(2):359–380, 2012. DOI: 10.1016/j.jvcir.2011.11.002. 6

[203] A. Pentland, R. Picard, and S. Sclaroff. Photobook: Content-based Manipulation of Image Databases. In *SPIE Storage and Retrieval for Image and Video Databases II*, pages 34–47, San Jose, CA, 1994. DOI: 10.1117/12.171786. 6

[204] E. Persoon and K. Fu. Shape Discrimination Using Fourier Descriptors. *IEEE Transanctions on Systems, Man, and Cybernetics*, 7(3):170– 178, 1977. DOI: 10.1109/TSMC.1977.4309681. 12

[205] J. Philbin, O. Chum, M. Isard, J. Sivic, and A. Zisserman. Object retrieval with large vocabularies and fast spatial matching. In *Proceedings of Conference on Computer Vision and Pattern Recognition*, CVPR'2007, pages 1–8, 2007. DOI: 10.1109/CVPR.2007.383172. 112

[206] I. J. PicHunter, M. L. Miller, T. P. Minka, T. V. Papathomas, and P. N. Yianilos. The Bayesian Image Retrieval System, PicHunter: Theory, Implementation, and Psychophysical Experiments. *IEEE Transactions on Image Processing*, 9(1):20–37, January 2000. DOI: 10.1109/83.817596. 7, 10

[207] A. Popescu, G. Grefenstette, and P. A. Moëllic. Gazetiki: automatic creation of a geographical gazetteer. In *Proceedings of the 8th ACM/IEEE-CS Joint Conference on Digital Libraries*, pages 85–93, Pittsburgh PA, PA, USA, 2008. ACM. DOI: 10.1145/1378889.1378906. 104

[208] J. Preece, B. Nonnecke, and D. Andrews. The Top Five Reasons for Lurking: Improving Community Experiences for Everyone. *Computers in Human Behavior*, 20(2):201–223, 2004. DOI: 10.1016/j.chb.2003.10.015. 47

[209] Project_ARROW. ARROW: Australian Research Repositories Online to the World. http://www.arrow.edu.au/, October 2011. 28

[210] R. S. Purves, P. Clough, C. B. Jones, A. Arampatzis, B. Bucher, D. Finch, G. Fu, H. Joho, A. K. Syed, S. Vaid, and B. Yang. The design and implementation of SPIRIT: a spatially aware search engine for information retrieval on the internet. *International Journal of Geographical Information Science*, 21(7):717–745, 2007. DOI: 10.1080/13658810601169840. 91, 102

[211] A. Rae and P. Kelm. Working notes for the placing task at MediaEval 2012. In *Proceedings of the MediaEval 2012 Workshop*, 2012. 110, 114

[212] A. Rae, V. Murdock, P. Serdyukov, and P. Kelm. Working notes for the placing task at MediaEval 2011. In *Proceedings of the MediaEval 2011 Workshop, Santa Croce in Fossabanda, Pisa, Italy, September 1-2, 2011*, volume Vol-807 of *CEUR Workshop Proceedings (CEUR-WS)*, Pisa, Italy, Sept. 2011. CEUR-WS.org. 106

[213] D. Ramage, S. Dumais, and D. Liebling. Characterizing Microblogs with Topic Models. In *In Proceedings of the Fourth International AAAI Conference on Weblogs and Social Media*, 2010. 52

[214] Refugee Studies Centre, U. of Oxford. Forced Migration Online. http://www.forcedmigration.org/, October 2011. 28

[215] K. Rodden, W. Basalaj, D. Sinclair, and K. Wood. Does Organization by Similarity Assist Image Browsing? In *ACM Conference on Human Factors in Computing Systems*, volume 3, pages 190–197, 2001. DOI: 10.1145/365024.365097. 9

[216] S. Roy, Y. Wan, and A. Saberi. A flexible algorithm for sensor network partitioning and self-partitioning problems. In *Algorithmic Aspects of Wireless Sensor Networks*, volume 4240 of *Lecture Notes in Computer Science*, pages 152–163. Springer Berlin / Heidelberg, 2006. DOI: 10.1007/11963271_14. 51

[217] Y. Rui, T. S. Huang, M. Ortega, and S. Mehrotra. A Power Tool in Interactive Content-Based Image Retrieval. *IEEE Transactions on Circuits and Systems for Video Technology*, 8(5):644–655, 1998. 10

[218] T. S. S. Chang and A. Puri. Overview of the MPEG-7 standard. *IEEE Transactions on Circuits and Systems for Video Technology*, 11(6):688–695, 2001. DOI: 10.1109/76.927421. 6

[219] M. Safar, C. Shahabi, and X. Sun. Image Retrieval by Shape: A Comparative Study. In *IEEE International Conference on Multimedia and Expo (I)*, pages 141–144, 2000. DOI: 10.1109/ICME.2000.869564. 3

[220] P. Saha. Tensor Scale: A Local Morphometric Parameter With Applications to Computer Vision and Image Processing. Technical Report 306, Medical Image Processing Group, Department of Radiology, University of Pennsylvania, September 2003. DOI: 10.1016/j.cviu.2005.03.003. 4

[221] M. Sanderson and Y. Han. Search words and geography. In *Proceedings of the 4th ACM Joint Conference on Digital Libraries*, pages 13–14, Lisbon, Portugal, 2007. DOI: 10.1145/1316948.1316952. 94, 103

[222] S. Santini, A. Gupta, and R. Jain. Emergent Semantics through Interaction in Image Databases. *IEEE Transactions on Knowledge and Data Engineering*, 13(3):337–351, May/June 2001. DOI: 10.1109/69.929893. 9, 10

[223] D. Santos and M. S. Chaves. The place of place in geographical IR. In *Proceedings of the 3rd ACM Workshop On Geographic Information*, pages 5–8, Seattle, Aug. 2006. Department of Geography, University of Zurich. 95, 96

[224] S. Sarkar and A. Dong. Community detection in graphs using singular value decomposition. *Phys. Rev. E*, 83(4):046114, Apr 2011. DOI: 10.1103/PhysRevE.83.046114. 51

[225] S. Schockaert, M. De Cock, and E. E. Kerre. Location approximation for local search services using natural language hints. *International Journal of Geographical Information Science*, 22(3):315, 2008. DOI: 10.1080/13658810701626277. 103

[226] P. Serdyukov, V. Murdock, and R. van Zwol. Placing Flickr photos on a map. In *Proceedings of the 32nd international ACM SIGIR conference on Research and development in information retrieval*, SIGIR '09, pages 484–491, New York, NY, USA, 2009. ACM. DOI: 10.1145/1571941.1572025. 106

[227] D. Shah and T. Zaman. Community detection in networks: The leader-follower algorithm. *CoRR*, 2010. 52

[228] R. Shen. *Applying the 5S Framework to Integrating Digital Libraries*. Ph.D. dissertation, Virginia Tech CS Department, Blacksburg, Virginia, 2006. http://scholar.lib.vt.edu/theses/available/etd-04212006-135018/ [last visited July 4, 2012]. 18

[229] R. Shen, N. S. Vemuri, W. Fan, R. da S. Torres, and E. A. Fox. Exploring digital libraries: integrating browsing, searching, and visualization. In *JCDL '06: Proceedings of the 6th ACM/IEEE-CS Joint Conference on Digital Libraries*, pages 1–10, New York, NY, USA, 2006. ACM. DOI: 10.1145/1141753.1141755. 46

[230] J. Sivic and A. Zisserman. Video Google: a text retrieval approach to object matching in videos. In *Proceedings of International Conference on Computer Vision*, volume 2 of *ICCV'2003*, pages 1470–1477, 2003. DOI: 10.1109/ICCV.2003.1238663. 116

[231] J. R. Smith and S. F. Chang. VisualSEEk: A fully automated content-based image query system. In *Proceedings of ACM Multimedia*, pages 87–98, Boston, MA, November 1996. DOI: 10.1145/244130.244151. 6

[232] T. Smith, G. F. Killeen, N. Maire, A. Ross, L. Molineaux, F. Tediosi, G. Hutton, J. Utzinger, K. Dietz, and M. Tanner. Mathematical modeling of the impact of malaria vaccines on the clinical epidemiology and natural history of plasmodium falciparum malaria: Overview. In *Am. J. Trop. Med. Hyg.*, volume 75, pages 1–10, 2006. 80

[233] D. Stan and I. K. Sethi. eID: a System for Exploration of Image Databases. *Information Processing and Management*, 39(3):335–365, 2003. DOI: 10.1016/S0306-4573(02)00131-0. 9

[234] R. Stehling, M. Nascimento, and A. Falcão. A Compact and Efficient Image Retrieval Approach Based on Border/Interior Pixel Classification. In *Proceedings of the 11th ACM International Conference on Information and Knowledge Management*, pages 102–109, McLean, Virginia, USA, November 2002. DOI: 10.1145/584792.584812. 5, 8, 20, 21

[235] M. A. Stricker and M. Orengo. Similarity of Color Images. In *Storage and Retrieval for Image and Video Databases (SPIE)*, pages 381–392, 1995. DOI: 10.1117/12.205308. 5

[236] T. Sumner and M. Marlino. Digital libraries and educational practice: a case for new models. In *Proceedings of the 2004 Joint ACM/IEEE Conference on Digital Libraries*, pages 170 – 178, June 2004. DOI: 10.1145/996350.996389. 29

[237] M. Swain and D. Ballard. Color Indexing. *International Journal of Computer Vision*, 7(1):11–32, 1991. DOI: 10.1007/BF00130487. 5, 12

[238] H. Tamura, S. Mori, and T. Yamawaki. Textural Features Corresponding to Visual Perception. *IEEE Transactions on Systems, Man and Cybernatics*, 8(6):460–473, 1978. DOI: 10.1109/TSMC.1978.4309999. 6

[239] G. Teodoro, E. Valle, N. Mariano, R. da Silva Torres, and W. M. Jr. Adaptive parallel approximate similarity search for responsive multimedia retrieval. In *20th ACM Conference on Information and Knowledge Management*, pages 495–504, 2011. DOI: 10.1145/2063576.2063651. 7

[240] Q. Tian, B. Moghaddam, and T. S. Huang. Display Optimization for Image Browsing. In *Proceedings of the 2nd International Workshop on Multimedia Databases and Image Communications*, Amalfi, Italy, Sep 2001. DOI: 10.1007/3-540-44819-5_14. 10

[241] S. Tong and E. Y. Chang. Support vector machine active learning for image retrieval. In *Proceedings of 9th ACM international conference on multimedia*, pages 107–118, NYC, 2001. ACM. DOI: 10.1145/500141.500159. 10

[242] S. Toral, M. Martinez-Torres, F. Barrero, and F. Cortes. An Empirical Study of the Driving Forces behind Online Communities. *Internet Research*, 19(4):378–392, 2009. DOI: 10.1108/10662240910981353. 45

[243] R. S. Torres and A. X. Falcão. Content-Based Image Retrieval: Theory and Applications. *Revista de Informática Teórica e Aplicada*, 13(2):161–185, 2006. 12

[244] R. S. Torres and A. X. Falcão. Contour Salience Descriptors for Effective Image Retrieval and Analysis. *Image and Vision Computing*, 25(1):313, 13, Jan. 2007. DOI: 10.1016/j.imavis.2005.12.010. 4, 8

[245] R. S. Torres, A. X. Falcão, and L. d. F. Costa. A Graph-based Approach for Multiscale Shape Analysis. *Pattern Recognition*, 37(6):1163–1174, June 2004. DOI: 10.1016/j.patcog.2003.10.007. 4, 8, 12

[246] R. S. Torres, C. Medeiros, M. Gonçalves, and E. Fox. A digital library framework for biodiversity information systems. *International Journal on Digital Libraries*, 6(1):3–17, 2006. DOI: 10.1007/s00799-005-0124-1. 11, 12

[247] R. S. Torres, C. G. Silva, C. B. Medeiros, and H. V. Rocha. Visual Structures for Image Browsing. In *Proceedings of the Twelfth International Conference on Information and Knowledge Management*, pages 167–174, New Orleans, LA, USA, November 2003. DOI: 10.1145/956863.956874. 10, 19

[248] C. Traina, J. M. Figueiredo, and A. J. M. Traina. Image domain formalization for content-based image retrieval. In *Proceedings of the 2005 ACM symposium on applied computing*, pages 604–609, 2005. DOI: 10.1145/1066677.1066818. 11

[249] C. Traina, B. Seeger, C. Faloutsos, and A. Traina. Fast Indexing and Visualization of Metric Datasets Using Slim-Trees. *IEEE Transactions on Knowledge and Data Engineering*, 14(2):244–60, March/April 2002. DOI: 10.1109/69.991715. 7

[250] F. A. Twaroch, P. D. Smart, and C. B. Jones. Mining the web to detect place names. In *Proceeding of the 2nd International Workshop on Geographic Information Retrieval*, pages 43–44, Napa Valley, California, USA, 2008. ACM. DOI: 10.1145/1460007.1460017. 103

[251] UNESCO Institute for Information Technologies in Education. Digital Libraries in Education, Science and Culture: Analytical survey. http://iite.unesco.org/pics/publications/en/files/3214660.pdf, Moscow, 2007. 41

[252] K. E. A. van de Sande, T. Gevers, and C. G. M. Snoek. Evaluating color descriptors for object and scene recognition. *Transactions on Pattern Analysis and Machine Intelligence*, 32(9):1582–1596, 2010. DOI: 10.1109/TPAMI.2009.154. 116

[253] J. C. van Gemert, C. J. Veenman, A. W. M. Smeulders, and J.-M. Geusebroek. Visual word ambiguity. *Transactions on Pattern Analysis and Machine Intelligence*, 32(7):1271–1283, 2010. DOI: 10.1109/TPAMI.2009.132. 116

[254] O. Van Laere, S. Schockaert, and B. Dhoedt. Finding locations of Flickr resources using language models and similarity search. In *Proceedings of the 1st ACM International Conference on Multimedia Retrieval*, ICMR '11, pages 48:1–48:8, New York, NY, USA, 2011. ACM. DOI: 10.1145/1991996.1992044. 86, 106, 107

[255] R. C. Veltkamp and M. Tanase. Content-based image retrieval systems: A survey. Technical Report TR UU-CS-2000-34, Department of Computing Science, Utrecht University, October 2002. 7

[256] Ø. Vestavik. Geographic information retrieval: An overview. online, 2003. IDI, NTNU, Norway. http://www.idi.ntnu.no/~oyvindve/article.pdf. 96, 97

[257] V. Viitaniemi and J. Laaksonen. Experiments on selection of codebooks for local image feature histograms. In *Proceedings of International Conference on Visual Information Systems: Web-Based Visual Information Search and Management*, ICVIS'2008, pages 126–137, 2008. DOI: 10.1007/978-3-540-85891-1_16. 116

[258] U. von Luxburg. A tutorial on spectral clustering. *Statistics and Computing*, 17(4):395–416, 2007. DOI: 10.1007/s11222-007-9033-z. 51

[259] K. Vu, K. A. Hua, and W. Tavanapong. Image Retrieval Based on Regions of Interest. *IEEE Transactions on Knowledge and Data Engineering*, 15(4):1045–1049, July/August 2003. DOI: 10.1109/TKDE.2003.1209021. 7

[260] F. Wang, C. Rabsch, P. Kling, P. Liu, and J. Pearson. Web-based collaborative information integration for scientific research. In *IEEE 23rd International Conference on Data Engineering*, pages 1232–1241, 2007. DOI: 10.1109/ICDE.2007.368982. 69

[261] J. Z. Wang and Y. Du. Scalable integrated region-based image retrieval using IRM and statistical clustering. In *Proceedings of the 1st ACM/IEEE-CS Joint Conference on Digital Libraries*, pages 268–277, 2001. DOI: 10.1145/379437.379679. 1, 11

[262] Y. Wang, F. Makedon, J. Ford, L. Shen, and D. Goldin. Generating fuzzy semantic metadata describing spatial relations from images using the r-histogram. In *Proceedings of the 4th ACM/IEEE-CS Joint Conference on Digital Libraries*, pages 202–211, 2004. DOI: 10.1109/JCDL.2004.1336121. 1, 11

[263] D. A. Wiley. Connecting learning objects to instructional design theory: A definition, a metaphor, and a taxonomy. In D.A. Wiley, ed., *The Instructional Use of Learning Objects*, 2000. http://reusability.org/read/chapters/wiley.doc. 37, 38

[264] Z. Xu, X. Xu, and V. Tresp. A hybrid relevance feedback approach to text retrieval. In *In Proceedings of the 25th European Conference on Information Retrieval Research, Lecture Notes in Computer Science*, pages 281–293. Springer-Verlag, 2003. DOI: 10.1007/3-540-36618-0_20. 103

[265] S. Yang, A. L. Kavanaugh, N. P. Kozievitch, L. T. Li, V. Srinivasan, S. D. Sheetz, T. Whalen, D. Shoemaker, R. da S. Torres, and E. A. Fox. CTRnet DL for disaster information services. In *JCDL*, pages 437–438, 2011. DOI: 10.1145/1998076.1998173. 2, 20, 107

[266] B. Yu and G. Cai. A query-aware document ranking method for geographic information retrieval. In *Proceedings of the 4th ACM Workshop on Geographical Information Retrieval*, pages 49–54, Lisbon, Portugal, 2007. ACM. DOI: 10.1145/1316948.1316962. 103

[267] D. Zhang and G. Lu. Review of Shape Representation and Description. *Pattern Recognition*, 37(1):1–19, Jan 2004. DOI: 10.1016/j.patcog.2003.07.008. 3

[268] J. Zhao, M.-Y. Kan, and Y. L. Theng. Math information retrieval: user requirements and prototype implementation. In *Proceedings of the 8th ACM/IEEE-CS Joint Conference on Digital Libraries*, pages 187–196. ACM, 2008. DOI: 10.1145/1378889.1378921. 65, 83

[269] X. S. Zhou and T. S. Huang. Relevance feedback in image retrieval: A comprehensive review. *Multimedia Systems*, 8:536–544, 2003. DOI: 10.1007/s00530-002-0070-3. 9, 10

[270] B. Zhu, M. Ramsey, and H. Chen. Creating a Large-Scale Content-Based Airphoto Image Digital Library. *IEEE Transactions on Image Processing*, 9(1):163–167, January 2000. DOI: 10.1109/83.817609. 1, 11

[271] Q. Zhu. 5SGraph: A Modeling Tool for Digital Libraries. Masters thesis, Virginia Tech Dept. of Computer Science, 2002. http://scholar.lib.vt.edu/theses/available/etd-11272002-210531/ [last visited July 4, 2012]. 23

[272] A. Zubizarreta, P. de la Fuente, J. M. Cantera, M. Arias, J. Cabrero, G. García, C. Llamas, and J. Vegas. Extracting geographic context from the web: GeoReferencing in MyMoSe. In *ECIR '09: Proceedings of the 31th European Conference on IR Research on Advances in Information Retrieval*, volume 5478 of *LNCS*, pages 554–561, Toulouse, France, Apr. 2009. DOI: 10.1007/978-3-642-00958-7_50. 94

Editors' Biographies

EDWARD A. FOX

Edward A. Fox grew up on Long Island, New York. He attended the Massachusetts Institute of Technology (MIT), receiving a B.S. in 1972 in Electrical Engineering, through the Computer Science option. His undergraduate adviser was J.C.R. Licklider and his thesis adviser was Michael Kessler. At MIT he founded the ACM Student Chapter and the Student Information Processing Board, receiving the William Stewart Award.

From 1971–1972 he worked as Data Processing Instructor at the Florence Darlington Technical College. From 1972–1978 he was Data Processing Manager at Vulcraft, a Division of NUCOR Corporation, also in Florence, SC. In the fall of 1978 he began his graduate studies at Cornell University in Ithaca, NY, where his adviser was Gerard Salton. He received an M.S. in Computer Science in 1981 and a Ph.D. in 1983. From the summer of 1982 through the spring of 1983 he served as Manager of Information Systems at the International Institute of Tropical Agriculture, Ibadan, Nigeria. From the fall of 1983 through the present he has been on the faculty of the Department of Computer Science at Virginia Tech (also called VPI&SU or Virginia Polytechnic Institute and State University). In 1988 he was given tenure and promoted to the rank of Associate Professor. In 1995 he was promoted to Professor.

Dr. Fox has been an IEEE Senior Member since 2004, an IEEE Member since 2002, an IEEE-CS Member since 2001, and a member of ACM since 1967. He was vice chairman of ACM SIGIR 1987–1991 and then chair 1991–1995. During that period, he helped launch the new ACM SIG on Multimedia. He served as a member of the ACM Publications Board 1988-1992 and as Editor-in-Chief of ACM Press Database and Electronic Products 1988–1991, during which time he helped conceive and launch the ACM Digital Library. He served 2000–2006 as a founder and Co-Editor-in-Chief of the ACM Journal of Education Resources In Computing (JERIC), which led to the ACM Transactions on Education. Since 2013 he has been editor for Information Retrieval and Digital Libraries for the ACM Book Series. Over the period 2004–2008 he served as Chairman of the IEEE-CS Technical Committee on Digital Libraries, and continues to serve on its Executive Committee. Dr. Fox served 1995–2008 as Editor of the Morgan Kaufmann Publishers, Inc. Series on Multimedia Information and Systems. Dr. Fox has been a member of Sigma Xi since the 1970s and a member of Upsilon Pi Epsilon since 1998.

In 1987 Dr. Fox began to explore the idea of all students shifting to electronic theses and dissertations (ETDs), and has worked in this area ever since. He led the establishment of the Networked Digital Library of Theses and Dissertations (operating informally starting in 1995, incorporated in May 2003). He serves as founder and Executive Director of NDLTD. He won its 1st Annual NDLTD Leadership Award in May 2004.

Dr. Fox has been involved in a wide variety of professional service activities. He has chaired scores of conferences or workshops, and served on hundreds of program or conference committees. At present he serves on ten editorial boards. From 2010–2013 he was a member of the board of directors of the Computing Research Association (CRA; he was co-chair of its membership committee, as well as a member of CRA-E, its education committee). He chairs the steering committee of the ACM/IEEE-CS Joint Conference on Digital Libraries.

Dr. Fox has been (co)PI on over 115 research and development projects. In addition to his courses at Virginia Tech, Dr. Fox has taught over 78 tutorials in more than 28 countries. His publications and presentations include: 17 books, 107 journal/magazine articles, 49 book chapters, 184 refereed (+40 other) conference/workshop papers, 61 posters, 66 keynote/banquet/international invited/distinguished speaker presentations, 38 demonstrations, and over 300 additional presentations. His research and teaching has been on digital libraries, information storage and retrieval, hypertext/hypermedia/multimedia, computing education, computational linguistics, and sub-areas of artificial intelligence.

JONATHAN P. LEIDIG

Jonathan P. Leidig is an Assistant Professor at the School of Computing and Information systems of Grand Valley State University in Allendale, MI. He holds a Ph.D. in Computer Science from Virginia Tech (2012), a M.S. in Computer Science from Virginia Tech (2011), and a B.S. in Information Systems from Grand Valley State University (2007). He has worked on digital library research and development projects in a variety of domains, including epidemiology, network science, fingerprinting, natural resources, geosciences, and athletics. His research interests include information retrieval, digital libraries, modeling and simulation, public health, infectious diseases, high performance computing, population modeling, health informatics, bioinformatics, data mining, and data visualization. He currently has affiliate memberships with Argonne National Laboratory (Department of Energy) and the Virginia Bioinformatics Institute.

Printed in the United States
by Baker & Taylor Publisher Services